MISFORTUNES OF WAR

Press and Public Reactions to Civilian Deaths in Wartime

Eric V. Larson • Bogdan Savych

Prepared for the United States Air Force

Approved for public release; distribution unlimited

PROJECT AIR FORCE

The research reported here was sponsored by the United States Air Force under Contract F49642-01-C-0003. Further information may be obtained from the Strategic Planning Division, Directorate of Plans, Hq USAF.

Library of Congress Cataloging-in-Publication Data

Larson, Eric V. (Eric Victor), 1957–
    Misfortunes of war : press and public reactions to civilian deaths in wartime /
Eric V. Larson, Bogdan Savych.
        p. cm.
    "Aerospace Force Development Program of RAND Project AIR FORCE."
    Includes bibliographical references.
    ISBN-13: 978-0-8330-3897-5 (pbk.)
    1. Civilian war casualties. 2. Mass media and war. 3. War in mass media. 4.
United States. Air Force—History—20th century. 5. United States. Air Force—
History—21st century. 6. United States. Air Force—Public relations. 7. Combatants
and noncombatants (International law) 8. Military history, Modern—20th century.
9. Military history, Modern—21st century. 10. War—Moral and ethical aspects.
    I. Savych, Bogdan. II. Project Air Force (U.S.) III. Rand Corporation. IV. Title.

U21.2.L375 2006
363.34'98—dc22
                                                                    2006030856

The RAND Corporation is a nonprofit research organization providing objective analysis and effective solutions that address the challenges facing the public and private sectors around the world. RAND's publications do not necessarily reflect the opinions of its research clients and sponsors.

RAND® is a registered trademark.

Published 2007 by the RAND Corporation
1776 Main Street, P.O. Box 2138, Santa Monica, CA 90407-2138
1200 South Hayes Street, Arlington, VA 22202-5050
4570 Fifth Avenue, Suite 600, Pittsburgh, PA 15213-2665
RAND URL: http://www.rand.org/
To order RAND documents or to obtain additional information, contact
Distribution Services: Telephone: (310) 451-7002;
Fax: (310) 451-6915; Email: order@rand.org

Preface

Concern in U.S. military and policymaking circles about civilian casualties and collateral damage in U.S. military operations appears to have
increased since the end of the Cold War. In part, this concern appears
to be based upon beliefs about the reactions of U.S. and foreign press
and publics in response to these incidents, especially the belief that
incidents of civilian deaths reduce public support for military operations. There has not, however, been any sort of empirical analysis of
press and public reactions to these incidents or of the effect of these
incidents on public support.

To improve policymakers' and senior military leaders' understanding of this topic, this monograph provides the results of a mixed quantitative and qualitative analysis of U.S. and foreign media and public
opinion reactions to incidents of collateral damage involving civilian
deaths in recent U.S. wars and military operations. It is part of a larger
RAND Project AIR FORCE fiscal year 2004 study titled "Controlling
Collateral Damage in Air Operations." The research reported here was
sponsored by Maj Gen Teresa M. Peterson (AF/XOO) and conducted
within the Aerospace Force Development Program of RAND Project
AIR FORCE.

RAND Project AIR FORCE

RAND Project AIR FORCE (PAF), a division of the RAND Corporation, is the U.S. Air Force's federally funded research and development center for studies and analyses. PAF provides the Air Force with

independent analyses of policy alternatives affecting the development, employment, combat readiness, and support of current and future aerospace forces. Research is conducted in four programs: Aerospace Force Development; Manpower, Personnel, and Training; Resource Management; and Strategy and Doctrine.

Additional information about PAF is available on our Web site at http://www.rand.org/paf.

Contents

Figures

Tables

Summary

Although the number of armed conflicts worldwide has declined since the spasm of violence that followed the breakup of the Soviet Union and the Balkans, war has continued to wreak havoc, albeit in a diminishing number of locations. Western nations, such as the United States, have, through the development of international law, military strategy, doctrine, tactics, technologies, and procedures, sought to alleviate some of the burdens that war imposes on innocents.

Nevertheless, U.S. adversaries have just as creatively found ways to place innocents at risk and thereby increase the human and moral costs of the nation's wars, evidently in the hope of deterring the United States from taking military action in the first place or of imposing political costs and constraints on the conduct of military operations if their deterrent efforts fail.

Judging both by their statements and the evident energy they expend on the matter, national political and military leaders appear to attach a great deal of importance to avoiding collateral damage and civilian casualties during U.S. military operations.[1] In part, this simply reflects a desire to reduce the inhumanity of warfare for innocent civilians. But it also seems to be attributable to beliefs they have about how the media and public react to incidents of civilian casualties. Indeed,

---

[1] *Collateral damage* is defined in Joint Publication 1-02 (JP 1-02) as

> [u]nintentional or incidental injury or damage to persons or objects that would not be lawful military targets in the circumstances ruling at the time. Such damage is not unlawful so long as it is not excessive in light of the overall military advantage anticipated from the attack. (DoD, 2005, p. 93)

there is some reason to believe that concern about casualties shapes the constraints that are imposed on military operations.[2] To date, however, there has been no systematic analysis of media and public reactions to civilian casualty incidents, whether these incidents affect media reporting or public support for military operations, and if so, how.

This monograph, part of a larger study of collateral damage undertaken for the United States Air Force, aims to fill this gap. It accomplishes this through an analysis of case studies of incidents of civilian deaths in recent U.S. wars and military operations that describe and explain how the U.S. and foreign media and publics have responded to these incidents:

- the February 1991 bombing of the Al Firdos bunker, which was also being used as a shelter by noncombatants, in the Gulf War
- the April and May 1999 attacks on the Djakovica convoy and Chinese embassy during the war in Kosovo
- the late June 2002 attack involving an Afghan wedding party during operations in Afghanistan
- the late March 2003 incident involving a large explosion in a crowded Baghdad marketplace.

For each case study, the study team examined press, public, and leadership responses to these incidents:

- To understand press reactions, we first performed quantitative content analyses of media reporting. Specifically, we counted the frequency that a common set of phrases (e.g., "Iraq" and "civilian casualties" or "collateral damage" or "civilian deaths") occurred in a fixed set of elite U.S. and foreign newspapers or television news sources.[3] We also qualitatively reviewed selected reports from

---

[2]   For a discussion of the interaction between public opinion and the media and constraints imposed on military operations, see "Domestic Constraints on Coercion," in Byman, Waxman, and Larson (1999, pp. 59–85).

[3]   "Elite papers" are those that generally regarded as having national (as opposed to local) influence. For the elite U.S. newspapers, we performed keyword searches on the full text of *The New York Times, The Washington Post, The Wall Street Journal, Los Angeles Times*, and

these sources to get a better sense of how the collateral damage incidents were being reported.

- To understand public reactions to civilian casualty incidents, we examined the top-line (marginal) results of public opinion polling conducted over the course of the operation and before and after the incidents of interest. We also analyzed respondent-level public opinion data to understand the relationship between various attitudes about civilian casualties and individuals' decisions to support or oppose U.S. military operations. To assess the association between public support for each military operation and various civilian casualty–related attitudes, we conducted analyses both at a bivariate level (using the Chi-square test of association), and using multivariate statistical regression techniques (using ordered probit regression techniques). We also examined media reporting on antiwar demonstration activities to try to understand the extent to which civilian casualty incidents might have increased the frequency or scale of social protest activity against the war.
- To understand leadership responses to civilian casualty incidents, we reviewed the transcripts of public statements, press conferences, testimony, and other official sources.

Findings

Our analysis of these cases leads to seven main findings:

- **First, while avoiding civilian casualties is important to the American public, they have much more realistic expectations about the actual possibilities for avoiding casualties than most understand.** Large majorities of the American public consistently say that efforts to avoid civilian casualties should be given a high

---

The Christian Science Monitor, as represented in the ProQuest Newspapers database. For U.S. television, we searched the full text of the Lexis-Nexis service's television abstracts for ABC News, CBS News, CNN, and NBC News. For foreign press reporting, we searched the full text of the Lexis-Nexis service's files for Agence France Presse (AFP) (France), *The Guardian* (London), Xinhua (People's Republic of China [PRC]), and TASS (Russia).

priority and have indicated that their prospective support for U.S. military operations is at least in part contingent on minimizing civilian deaths. Very large majorities, however, consistently stated their belief that civilian casualties in these wars were unavoidable accidents of war. *This finding suggests that most Americans have few illusions about the U.S. military's ability to prevent all civilian deaths in wartime. The argument that the American public has unreasonably high expectations for zero-casualty warfare is not supported; in fact, most Americans appear to have a fairly realistic view of the possibilities for eliminating civilian casualties entirely from modern warfare.* (See pp. 50, 82–84, 103–104, 121–122, and 136.)

- **Second, the press report heavily on civilian casualty incidents.** Civilian casualty incidents are highly "mediagenic" events that tend to receive high levels of reporting by the press, and making the issue of civilian casualties more salient can lead the public to weigh the morality of wars against the importance of their aims. (See pp. 27, 76–78, 129–131, and 163–167.)

- **Third, adversaries understand the public's sensitivities to civilian deaths and have sought to exploit civilian casualty incidents to erode the support of domestic publics; drive wedges in coalitions; and affect campaign strategy, targeting, and rules of engagement.** The cases of Iraq (1991) and Kosovo (1999) in particular suggested how adversaries have sought to use human shields, provide press access to sites of alleged civilian deaths, and otherwise trumpet these incidents in the press to affect warfighting strategy, not without some success. (See pp. 43–46, 71–76, 125–128, and 161–162.)

- **Fourth, while the prospect of civilian casualties can affect support prior to the onset of a military operation, during armed conflict it is not so much beliefs about the *numbers* of civilian casualties that affect support for U.S. military operations as the belief that the United States and its allies are making enough effort to avoid casualties. Substantial majorities of Americans typically subscribe to this view.** Our multivariate statistical models, which have a good record of predicting individual-level support and opposition in past military operations, showed that beliefs about the *number* of civilian casualties typically did not attain statistical significance. Importantly, however, when variables for beliefs about the adequacy of the U.S. military's efforts to avoid civilian deaths were included in our models, the variables for civilian casualties frequently attained statistical significance. An analysis of aggregate data on foreign attitudes and a cross-tabulation of Iraqi attitudes suggested a similar relationship in foreign publics as well. (See pp. 29–33, 81–84, 131–139, and 167–185.)

- **Fifth, while strong majorities of Americans typically give U.S. military and political leaders the benefit of the doubt when civilian casualty incidents occur, this does not necessarily extend to foreign audiences.** In the U.S. case, this derives in large measure from the credibility of military leaders and the high levels of trust in the military as an institution in U.S. society. It generally does not appear to extend to foreign audiences, however, which are far less inclined to believe that the United States makes enough of an effort to avoid civilian casualties and are far more likely to view incidents involving civilian deaths as resulting from careless or callous disregard for human life, or even something far more malign. (See pp. 36–41, 85–99, 140–150, and 188–202.)

- **Sixth, when civilian casualty incidents occur, it is at least as important to get the story right as to get the story out.** Notwithstanding the view that is sometimes heard that it is critical to get one's story out first, to operate within the media's news cycle, and to dominate an adversary's own efforts to influence U.S. and foreign audiences, it is at least as important—and possibly more important—that the information that is put out is in fact correct. While it would be best to provide *timely, complete, and accurate* information about the specific circumstances of civilian casualty incidents—providing *inaccurate* information that later needs to be amended can erode the credibility of the United States and its coalition. As observed in Kosovo after the Djakovica convoy incident, a constant stream of partial and errant information and subsequent corrections issued by the North Atlantic Treaty Organization (NATO) about the incident—many of which also soon proved to be in error themselves—seem to have hurt NATO's credibility with the press and also may have eroded its credibility in some NATO publics. (See pp. 92–106.)

• **Seventh and finally, attention to and concern about civilian casualties both at home and abroad have increased in recent years and may continue to do so, suggesting that they are likely to be a recurring—and perhaps even more salient— concern in the conduct of future military operations.** Our content analyses suggest that the issue of civilian casualties has become increasingly prominent in media reporting, as have humanitarian organizations' commentary on wars and military operations. It thus seems likely not only that U.S. military action will continue to be judged by domestic and foreign audiences on the basis of its conduct but that the focus on civilian casualties may increase in the future. If, as we suspect, the belief that the U.S. military is doing everything it can to minimize civilian casualties is the key to public support for U.S. military operations, this suggests that a serious public commitment to further reducing civilian casualties by the U.S. military will be necessary to preserve Americans' faith that their military is seeking to reduce harm to innocents during its wars and military operations. (See pp. 2–4 and 205–208.)

Implications and Recommendations

Incidents of civilian deaths are, by definition, tragedies, and there are no "silver bullets" that can diminish the media attention and emotion—ranging from hopelessness and sorrow to anger—they can generate. There are, however, some things that the USAF and the U.S. Department of Defense (DoD) profitably can do in this area:

• As in the 1991 Gulf War and the 1999 war in Kosovo, there is a good chance that future U.S. adversaries also will seek to use human shields. Enhancing capabilities to screen mobile targets such as the Djakovica convoy for a civilian presence prior to strike could help to avoid such incidents in the future. This may be a good role for unmanned aerial vehicles (UAVs). (See pp. 43–46, 71–74, 125–128, and 161–162.)

- Until timely and accurate combat assessment capabilities are available, the ability to counter an adversary's claims of civilian damage incidents promptly will be quite limited. More timely and accurate combat assessment capabilities could improve commanders' ability to reconstruct more quickly and reliably the facts surrounding civilian casualty incidents and to communicate more timely and accurate explanations of these incidents to the media and public. Such improvements also would have the benefit of reducing the likelihood of issuing constantly changing (or contradictory) explanations that can erode credibility. It also could open the possibility of putting these incidents to rest much more quickly, rather than drawing out speculation over days—or even weeks—while the necessary facts are being collected and assessed. (See pp. 92–99.)

- Public affairs personnel can and should prepare for possible incidents even before they actually happen. For example, public affairs officers can brief the press and public on measures that are being taken to minimize casualties to better sensitize these audiences to the importance the military attaches to avoiding civilian casualties, and the sophisticated—if by no means foolproof—processes and procedures that have been developed to minimize their likelihood. They also can develop in advance overall guidance and procedures for dealing with civilian casualty incidents. In a similar vein, even before missions are flown, Judge Advocate General (JAG) personnel can document their judgments about the legal justifications for the highest-risk missions, thereby better positioning commanders to respond in an informed and timely manner should an incident occur. Some of these efforts already are under way within the combatant commands and DoD. (See pp. 92–99.)

- Public affairs guidance used to explain specific incidents should touch upon all the issues likely to be of concern to key audiences. The provisions of Article 57 (2) of Protocol I to the Geneva

Conventions offer a very useful framework for discussing incidents in such terms as military value, military necessity, discrimination, and other constructs that are likely to be of greatest concern to, and resonate with, various audiences ("Additional to the Geneva Conventions of 12 August 1949," 1977). (See pp. 92–99.)

- Finally, over the longer term, by emphasizing the efforts that are being made to reduce civilian casualties (e.g., improved target verification, increased precision, focused weapon effects, and so on), the USAF and DoD can help ensure that the U.S. Congress and public have continued reason to trust that the U.S. military is seeking new ways to reduce the prospects for civilian deaths in future military operations. A demonstrated commitment to a philosophy of continuous improvement may be what is needed to ensure this trust in the future and, in the case of foreign audiences, to build trust in the first place. (See pp. 2–4 and 205–208.)

While efforts to further reduce the likelihood of these incidents and their impacts are laudable, policymakers and military leaders should, however, be very careful to avoid giving the impression that civilian deaths ultimately can be eliminated from warfare; such a belief is unwarranted. Indeed, there is good reason to believe that future U.S. adversaries may increasingly rely on human shields and other techniques to increase the possibility of innocent deaths at U.S. hands.

Acknowledgments

The authors would like to thank Eric Nielsen of The Gallup Organization for cross-tabulations from the March–April 2004 Gallup Poll of Iraq, RAND colleague William Stanley for comments on an earlier version of this monograph, and careful reviews by Professor Richard C. Eichenberg of Tufts University and RAND colleague Audra Grant.

Abbreviations

AAA	anti-aircraft artillery
AAAS	American Association for the Advancement of Science
ABCCC	Airborne Battlefield Command and Control Center
AFP	Agence France Presse
AWACS	airborne warning and control system
BVA	Brulé Ville et Associé
CCFR	Chicago Council on Foreign Relations
CEELI	Central and East European Law Initiative
CENTCOM	U.S. Central Command
CIA	Central Intelligence Agency
CMPA	Center for Media and Public Affairs
CNN	Cable News Network
DoD	U.S. Department of Defense
EC	European Community
FBIS	Foreign Broadcast Information Service
FNN	Financial News Network

FRY	Federal Republic of Yugoslavia
GMT	Greenwich Mean Time
HRW	Human Rights Watch
ICTY	International Criminal Tribunal for the Former Republic of Yugoslavia
IDP	internally displaced persons
JAG	Judge Advocate General
JDAM	Joint Direct Attack Munition
KLA	Kosovo Liberation Army
LSE	least squares estimation
MLE	maximum likelihood estimation
MUP	Ministarstvo Unutrasnih Poslova
NATO	North Atlantic Treaty Organization
NGO	nongovernmental organization
NHK	Nippon Hoso Kyokai
OLS	ordinary least square
OMPF	Office of Missing Persons and Forensics
OSCE	Organization for Security and Cooperation in Europe
PAF	Project AIR FORCE
PIPA	Program on International Policy Attitudes
PPO	principal policy objective
PRC	People's Republic of China
PSRA	Princeton Survey Research Associates

RAF	Royal Air Force
ROE	rules of engagement
SAM	surface-to-air missile
SAT RTS	Radio-Televizija Srbije
UAV	unmanned aerial vehicle
UNHCR	United Nations High Commissioner for Refugees
UNMIK	United Nations Mission in Kosovo
UNSC	United Nations Security Council
USAFE	U.S. Air Forces in Europe
VIF	variance inflation factors

CHAPTER ONE

Introduction

Although the number of armed conflicts worldwide has declined since the spasm of violence that followed the breakup of the Soviet Union and the Balkans, war, one of civilization's most reviled and durable institutions, has continued to wreak havoc against innocent civilians.[1]

Western nations, such as the United States, have, through international law, military strategy, doctrine, tactics, and technology sought to alleviate some of the burdens that war imposes on innocents. Nevertheless, U.S. adversaries—apparently in the hope of deterring the United States from taking military action in the first place or of imposing political costs if their deterrent efforts fail—have just as creatively found ways to place innocents at risk and thereby increase the human and moral costs of the nation's wars. The result has been that noncombatants have continued to become caught in the crossfire of U.S. military operations, even as civilian casualties and collateral damage have become a more prominent topic of media reporting.

Like imagery of starving children or displaced refugees, civilian casualty incidents tend to draw the attention of the United States and international media, especially during U.S. military operations (Figures 1.1 and 1.2).[2]

---

[1] According to Dwan and Gustavsson (2004), "In 2003 there were 19 major armed conflicts in 18 locations worldwide, the lowest number for the post–Cold War period with the exception of 1997, when 18 such conflicts were registered."

[2] Throughout this study, we refer to "civilian casualties," which we define primarily to mean deaths, but also injuries, to civilian noncombatants in wars and military operations.

Figure 1.1
U.S. Major Television and Newspaper Reporting on Civilian Casualties,
1990–2003

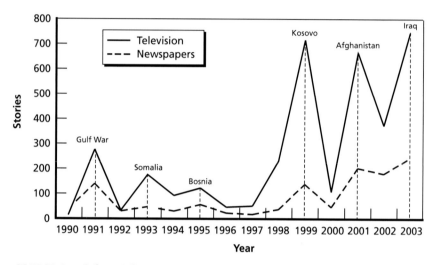

SOURCE: Search for "civilian casualties," "civilian deaths," or "collateral damage" in *The Christian Science Monitor, Los Angeles Times, The New York Times, The Wall Street Journal, The Washington Post,* ABC, CBS, CNN, and NBC.
RAND *MG441-1.1*

Not terribly surprisingly given the interplay between media report-ing and public interest, Americans have said that they attach great importance to avoiding civilian casualties in U.S. military operations. Table 1.1, which presents data from a 1998 survey, shows that avoid-ing civilian casualties was the second most prominent consideration in Americans' prospective support for a military operation, second only to the number of American lives that might be lost.[3]

Because of the mediagenic quality of incidents and the high level of public interest, our analysis focuses on incidents involving civilian casualties rather than damage to civilian infrastructure.

---

[3] For detailed analysis of the factors that are associated with support and opposition to U.S. military operations, with an emphasis on U.S. casualties, see Larson (1996a).

Figure 1.2
Selected Foreign Media Reporting on Civilian Casualties, 1990–2003

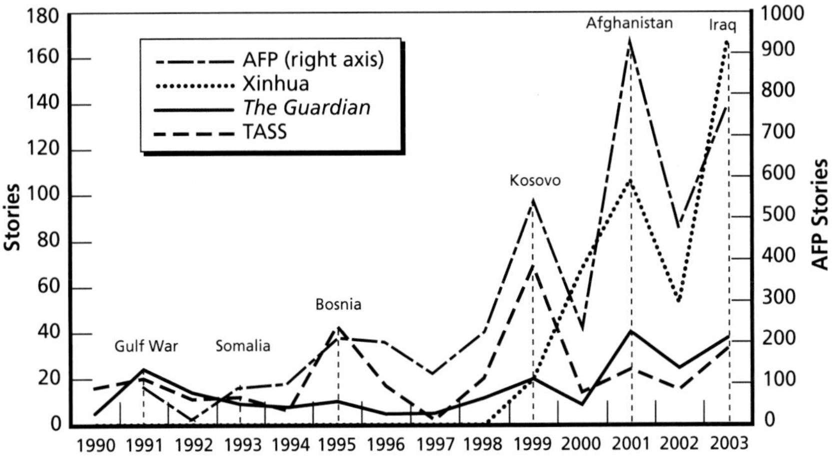

SOURCE: Search for "civilian casualties," "civilian deaths," or "civilian damage"
in Agence France Presse (AFP), *The Guardian* (London), TASS (Russia), and Xinhua
(People's Republic of China [PRC]).
RAND *MG441-1.2*

Although it is sometimes argued that large numbers of civilian
casualties could reverse public support for U.S. military operations,[4] this
monograph will show that Americans generally have not responded to
high-profile incidents of civilian casualties during U.S. military operations by withdrawing their support for the operation. In most cases, it
is difficult to find much evidence of any change in basic attitudes at all
as a result of these incidents. In fact, when variables for civilian casualties are added to our multivariate regression models (which include
other variables that have been shown to be important predictors of
support for military operations), they generally fail to attain statistical
significance.

The reason for this paradox is not indifference or callousness
on the part of the American public. Rather, it is the resilience of the
belief—notwithstanding any civilian casualty incidents that may

---

[4] See the comments of James Burk in Stein (2003).

Table 1.1
Importance to Americans of Civilian Deaths in Using the U.S. Military

"No one wants our nation to get into any conflicts in the future, but as in the past, our leaders might someday decide to use our armed forces in hostilities because our interests are jeopardized. I know that this is a tough question, but if you had to make a decision about using the American military, how important would each of the following factors be to you?"	Affirmative Responses (%)
Number of American lives that might be lost	86
Number of civilians who might be killed	79
Whether American people will support	71
Involvement by major power (e.g., USSR, PRC)	69
Length of time of fighting	61
Possibility of failure	56
Whether allies/other nations will support	56
Fact that we might break international laws or treaties	55
Cost in dollars	45

SOURCE: Americans Talk Security #9 poll conducted September 7–18, 1999, N = 1,005.

have taken place—that the U.S. military is making its best effort to avoid civilian casualties. When variables for beliefs about the sufficiency of U.S. military efforts to avoid civilian casualties were included in our multivariate respondent-level models alongside other known predictors of support and opposition, they routinely attained statistical significance. An analysis of foreign public opinion data suggests that this belief also is an important predictor of support and opposition in foreign publics.

Literature Review

As will be described in this section, much of the scholarly literature on American public opinion and war seeks to explain how U.S. military casualties affect support for wars and military operations.[5] Although there are some exceptions, scant attention generally has been devoted to the role of civilian casualties in support and opposition to U.S. military operations. It typically has been a subject of only passing interest to most scholars.

Moreover, the academic literature on public opinion toward U.S. military operations is somewhat ad hoc, contradictory, and noncumulative in nature. This work has focused primarily on the analysis of marginals (aggregate data) to the exclusion of respondent-level data, and has not demonstrated much robustness in predicting support in new cases. A brief review of some of this literature follows.

John E. Mueller

John E. Mueller uses a case study–based approach in which he relates differences in polling results to cues in the wording of public opinion questions, and seeks to interpret public opinion trend data through the lens of a larger chronological narrative (Mueller, 1971, 1973, 1994). Mueller's main contribution to the understanding of public opinion on military operations was his identification and analysis of the two key phenomena of principal interest to policymakers and military leaders: (1) approval and disapproval for military operations, and (2) escalation and withdrawal preferences.[6] In many respects, Mueller's work on American public opinion of military operations is a model of good practice, and one that provides useful insights into the sorts of factors that can move public opinion. Other than making the case that American casualties are a (or rather, *the*) key predictor of support for U.S. military operations, however, most of this work has not benefited from statistical analyses that would foster an empirical understanding of the relative importance of various predictors of support or opposition for U.S. military operations, and a general model of support and opposi-

---

[5] For a review of this literature, see Eichenberg (2005).

[6] Mueller analyzed support and escalation and withdrawal preferences during the Korean and Vietnam Wars.

tion.[7] Mueller has nonetheless identified several factors that he believes drive public support for military operations, and he has addressed reactions to civilian casualties in wartime during the first Gulf War.[8]

The Principal Policy Objective (PPO) Approach

The approach that appears to have generated the most interest, at least among international-relations scholars, focuses on the PPO of military operations. In the view of practitioners who use this approach, Americans have consistent preferences regarding how the military should be used: For example, they prefer the use of the military in restraining threatening adversaries and conducting humanitarian operations over employment to effect internal political change or in support of peace-keeping operations. A review of the work of two authors who promote the use of the PPO approach follows.

Bruce W. Jentleson. Bruce W. Jentleson's work on American public opinion has sought to develop a general model of support for military operations, and his general approach has been widely embraced by international-relations scholars. He has not, however, addressed the impact of civilian casualties in wartime. Jentleson compiled marginal (aggregate-level) data on Americans' approval of past U.S. military operations, and concluded that support for U.S. military operations was best explained in terms of the PPOs of the operation. In Jentleson's view, operations that had the objective of restraining a threatening adversary realized a higher level of support than operations that aimed at internal political change (Jentleson, 1992). Because the two PPOs in his 1992 study did not explain the high level of support for

---

[7] Larson (1996a, 1996b) confirmed the importance of U.S. military casualties in declining support for Vietnam, but also suggested that erosion in the belief that Vietnam was strategically important and the war was in fact winnable; increasing divisions among national political leaders also contributed to declining support. Mueller's analysis also has been criticized on statistical grounds because, in relating cumulative casualties, which do tend to grow over time, to support, which does tend to decline over time, the observed relationship might be a statistical artifact. See Kostroski (1977) and Gartner and Segura (1998).

[8] Mueller's 1994 book on public opinion during the Gulf War examines the impact of the bombing of the Al Firdos bunker, one of the case studies examined in this monograph. Mueller's argument will be described in greater detail later in this monograph.

the humanitarian operation in Somalia, in his 1996 analysis, Jentleson added a third PPO for humanitarian operations and tested this theory by regressing support on variables for PPOs and other factors. He was able to account for slightly less than 60 percent of the variance in support; aversion to casualties was not among the variables that attained statistical significance.[9]

Richard Eichenberg. Richard Eichenberg has also examined American public opinion on U.S. military operations and has considered the role of civilian casualties in public support.[10] Like Jentleson, Eichenberg analyzes marginal data from public opinion questions that asked about approval for a wide number of past military operations, and relies on a modified version of the PPO-based approach.[11]

Because Jentleson's theory did not account for the low level of support for the 1990s peacekeeping operations, Eichenberg added a fourth category of PPO (peacekeeping), and introduced control variables for type of military operation, the nature of multilateral participation, the effect of mentioning military or civilian casualties in questions, and other factors. Using ordinary least squares, he concluded that the PPOs, casualty cues, type of military operation, and many other factors affect support. According to his regression analysis, mentioning military casualties in a question typically reduces support by about 8 percent, whereas mentioning civilian casualties reduces support by 9.75 percent. Thus, Eichenberg's result on the importance of casualties in public support for military operations refutes Jentleson's conclusions.

Using marginal data from 1,685 questions asked in 81 countries from August 1990 to October 2004, Eichenberg also has explored

---

[9] The variables Jentleson explored were PPO; presidential cues and congressional opposition; risk, as operationalized by questions that explicitly mentioned the use of ground troops; multilateralism; and vital interests. Only the first three categories of variables made statistically significant contributions to the overall prediction. See Jentleson and Britton (1998).

[10] On American public opinion, see Eichenberg (2005). Eichenberg's analysis of foreign public opinion on the U.S. war in Iraq is "Global Public Opinion from the First Gulf War to the Invasion and Occupation of Iraq," in Eichenberg (forthcoming).

[11] Eichenberg used a total of 1,092 questions asked about 22 military operations conducted from 1980 to 2005.

"universal logics" in cross-national support for using force and found that the PPO, perceived legitimacy of the action, and the risk aversion and sensitivity to military and civilian casualties all made a statistically significant contribution: According to this work, the mention of either military or civilian casualties resulted in a drop of 17 percentage points in support for military action. Despite the more comprehensive approach, Eichenberg has not provided cross-validation of his model using respondent-level data.

As should be clear from the preceding discussion, the failure of the PPO-based theory to account for new cases satisfactorily has led to a number of essentially ad hoc exceptions and adjustments to the theory.[12] First, Jentleson included a "halo effect" in his 1992 piece to account for the high level of support for the U.S. intervention to effect internal political change in Panama, attributing the high support to the fact that the operation, essentially a coup d'état, was successfully concluded fairly rapidly. Next, humanitarian, peacekeeping, and counterterrorism operations were added to the taxonomy of PPOs to better account for these "new" cases.[13] Finally, Eichenberg added two ad hoc variables ("Removing Saddam Hussein from power" and "Retaliating for attack on the United States") to account for the exceedingly high levels of support given the operations to effect internal political change in Afghanistan and Iraq, operations that the PPO approach would have predicted to receive much lower support.[14]

The principal attraction of the PPO approach seems to be its evident flexibility and utility as a simple framework for ad hoc theorizing. However, the approach is neither derived from nor builds upon deduc-

---

[12] And when his 1992 taxonomy of PPOs was challenged by the initial high level of support for the intervention in Somalia (about 75 percent typically supported), he added a third category of PPO to his taxonomy: "humanitarian intervention." More recently, the high levels of support for internal political change in Afghanistan (more than eight in ten typically supported) and Iraq (support began in the 70–75-percent range) would seem to pose additional challenges to the robustness of his theory.

[13] Gelpi, Feaver, and Reifler (2005) added counterterrorism as a PPO.

[14] These variables, moreover, had larger coefficients than did any of the PPO variables, suggesting the greater importance of factors other than PPO—such as the perceived importance of the stakes and outcome.

tive theory so much as ad hoc efforts to detect and try to account for observed statistical regularities; it does not lend itself to operationalization in terms of ordinal or continuous variables; and as it has grown to accommodate new cases, the theory has lost any claim to parsimony it might once have had.[15] Moreover, it does not account very well for change over time in core beliefs about the operation and their effect on support, and as witnessed by the need to revise the taxonomy continuously, it seems to have little or no demonstrated predictive power. The strong likelihood that the taxonomy of objectives is masking or conflating the effects of other variables,[16] its implausible predictions in easily imagined cases,[17] the ready availability of conflicting results using the same basic data and approach,[18] and the absence of cross-validation of the theory at the respondent level raise additional questions about the robustness of the PPO theory.

Eric Larson

Earlier work by one of the authors of the present monograph laid out a model grounded in microeconomic theory that identified the factors that influence support for military operations and preferences regarding escalation and withdrawal, and embedded that model in a social process model that considered the role of leadership and the diffusion of mass attitudes (Larson, 1996a, 1996b).[19]

---

[15] For example, Eichenberg lists 18 variables that make a statistically significant contribution to support (Eichenberg, 2005, p. 173, Table 8).

[16] For example, the high level of support Jentleson finds for humanitarian operations may in part be be due to the fact that nearly all these operations are conducted in a relatively benign environment, posing little risk to U.S. forces. Thus, the objective of humanitarian aims could well be masking Americans' risk aversion.

[17] For example, the PPO approach would seem to predict that higher percentages of Americans would support a U.S. effort to restrain Burundi from attacking Rwanda than continuing a peacekeeping operation in the Sinai.

[18] For example, using an analytic approach and data similar to Jentleson's, Klarevas concluded that casualties (risk aversion) were the most important variable in determining support. (See Klarevas, 1999.)

[19] The theoretical work drew heavily on Milstein (1974) and George and Smoke (1974).

The deductive model suggested that Americans' support or opposition to U.S. military operations—and their preferences regarding escalation and withdrawal—were tied to beliefs about the nature and importance of the stakes (both moral positions such as the "goodness" or "rightness" of the war and traditionally conceived national security interests such as protection of vital interests and self-defense from attack); the perceived prospects for success; the expected and actual costs incurred (especially in terms of U.S. military deaths); and agreement or disagreement about the merits of a military operation among national political leaders, primarily the President and Congress. Casualty tolerance, in turn, was related to beliefs about the stakes, prospects, and leadership.

Using trend data and bivariate analyses of respondent-level data, Larson assessed this model through a review of American public opinion on a wide range of past U.S. wars and military operations, including the Second World War, the Korean and Vietnam Wars, U.S. operations in Panama, the 1991 Gulf War, and operations in Somalia. This work suggested significant resonance with the deductive theory at both the aggregate and individual levels of analysis, suggesting a high degree of robustness (Larson, 1996a, 1996b). It also demonstrated that support was quite context-sensitive and that changes in any of the independent variables could, in some circumstances, affect public support.[20]

In a recent reanalysis of American public opinion toward U.S. military operations in Somalia, as well as subsequent U.S. operations in Haiti, Bosnia, Kosovo, Afghanistan, and Iraq, the present authors tested the multivariate model developed in the earlier work using respondent-level data from polling conducted contemporane-

---

[20] For example, support for World War II was largely unaffected by declining optimism about the progress being made, and seems generally to have been buoyed by beliefs about the importance of the United States' stakes in the war. And most of the decline in support for Somalia was not accountable to U.S. casualties, but seems to have occurred as a result of a change in objective from humanitarian to peace-enforcement operations and the deterioration of the situation (and declining beliefs about the prospects for success) over the summer of 1993 (Larson, 1996a, 1996b).

ously during each operation.[21] The authors again found resonance for the model in aggregate trend data and at the respondent level, and found that their individual-level models correctly predicted support or opposition for 60–85 percent of the respondents in the new cases analyzed. The accurate prediction of support in cases that were not used to develop the original model provided additional empirical evidence of the robustness of the model across cases and levels of analysis. The authors also tracked a wide range of public opinion questions related to the key predictors of support and opposition in each case, to provide a coherent explanation of the factors affecting support and opposition for these operations and the likely sources of changes over time.

Peter D. Feaver and Christopher Gelpi

As part of a larger study, Peter D. Feaver and Christopher Gelpi of the Triangle Institute for Security Studies conducted a unique, special-purpose survey about civil-military issues that asked a number of questions about respondents' willingness to support the use of force in a number of hypothetical U.S. military operations. They first released their findings in an op-ed piece in which they concluded that Americans are willing to accept much higher casualties than the conventional wisdom would allow, and that the perceived prospects for success in military operations were the key variables in predicting casualty tolerance.[22] They also asserted that most Americans would have supported continued military action to pacify Somalia following the October 1993 firefight in Mogadishu. None of these findings have proved to be particularly robust:

- On casualties, the authors predicted that the average American would accept nearly 30,000 U.S. military deaths in a future war to prevent Iraq from developing weapons of mass destruction, and nearly 7,000 deaths to promote democracy in the Congo, num-

---

[21] Larson and Savych (2005a, 2005b). These models also included variables for gender and race, which also have been shown to be related to support for military operations.

[22] Specifically, they claimed that Americans were more "defeat-phobic" than "casualty-phobic" (Feaver and Gelpi, 1999, 2004; Gelpi, Feaver, and Reifler, 2005; Hyde, 2000).

bers that appear, even on a prima facie basis, absurd.[23] As nearly
all measures of support for the war in Iraq fell below 50 percent at
some point between 1,000 and 1,500 war dead, it is now known
that the authors overestimated casualty tolerance for a war in Iraq
by a factor of 20 to 30; the estimate for the Congo is probably
inflated by an even greater amount.[24]

- Nor is their conclusion that beliefs about the prospects for success or victory are the preeminent factor in support particularly
  robust. Rather, it seems to be an artifact of the artificiality of their
  one-off survey. Other work that has analyzed polling conducted
  contemporaneously during several recent military operations suggests that beliefs about the nature and importance of the stakes
  or benefits of a military operation typically have been far more
  important predictors of support than beliefs about the prospects
  for success (Larson and Savych, 2005a, 2005b).

- Finally, their assertion that Americans would have followed President Clinton's lead if he had simply taken a more forceful position
  on Iraq lacks plausibility—and hinges upon a *deux ex machina*–
  like expectation of a rally larger than that typically associated with
  presidents whose policies are under attack by members of both

---

[23] The authors asked,

> When American troops are sent overseas, there are almost always casualties. For
> instance, 43 Americans were killed in Somalia, 383 in the Gulf War, roughly 54,000 in
> Korea, roughly 58,000 in Vietnam and roughly 400,000 in World War II. Imagine for
> a moment that a president decided to send military troops on one of the following mis-
> sions. In your opinion, what would be the highest number of American military deaths
> that would be acceptable to achieve this goal?

They reported that their survey indicated that the average American would accept 6,861
deaths "to stabilize a democratic government in Congo," 29,853 deaths "to prevent Iraq from
obtaining weapons of mass destruction," and 20,172 deaths "to defend Taiwan against invasion by China." (See Feaver and Gelpi, 1999.)

[24] In estimating the number of casualties that the average respondent would tolerate in
each of their scenarios, Feaver and Gelpi used the mean rather than the median, an entirely
inappropriate measure. Even after correcting for this error, the result for Iraq was orders of
magnitude too high, suggesting a more fundamental problem with their survey instrument
and data.

parties.[25] Moreover, newly discovered data show that most Americans actually preferred withdrawal from Somalia even *before* the firefight in Mogadishu.

More recently, Gelpi, Feaver, and Reifler (2005) addressed the question of sensitivity to casualties in the war in Iraq. They argued that "beliefs about the rightness or wrongness of the war in the first place, and beliefs about the war's likely success," determined the public's tolerance for casualties (i.e., continued support in the face of casualties). More specifically, they argued that the interaction of beliefs about the importance of the stakes and the prospects for success determined the willingness to accept casualties, a view that is much closer to Larson's original (1996b) position.[26]

Notably, in the present authors' own respondent-level modeling of support for war in Iraq, the prospects for success failed to attain statistical significance. Thus, Feaver and Gelpi's finding may not be all that robust even for the case of Iraq; needless to say, without a much greater number of cases to validate the finding, one should not, as Feaver and Gelpi do, treat it as a general law that perforce applies to other cases.[27]

Scott S. Gartner and Gary M. Segura

Scott S. Gartner and Gary M. Segura have largely focused their attention on the role of casualties in public support for the war in Vietnam (Gartner and Segura, 1998, 2000; Gartner, Segura, and Wilkening,

---

[25] Brody (1991), for example, has shown that the size of a rally seems to be associated with the degree of bipartisan support for a president's policy as conveyed by the media. In the Somalia case, President Clinton was under attack both by Republicans and Democrats. For a critical analysis of Feaver and Gelpi's counterfactual assertion, see Larson and Savych (2005a, especially pp. 39–41).

[26] Gelpi, Feaver, and Reifler (2005). Larson suggested a general algebraic form in which support was a function of $(p*b)/c$ (i.e., the probability of success times the benefits, divided by the costs), and that casualty tolerance (i.e., support given any level of casualties) was a function of $p*b$. See Larson (1996b, 2000) and Larson and Savych (2005a).

[27] Partisanship (or leadership) also was quite important. Nevertheless, given that the prospects for success dropped out of our model of support for Iraq due to their lack of statistical (and substantive) significance, the importance of the prospects for success may not have been as important as Feaver and Gelpi's work suggests.

1997). These authors appear to agree with Mueller that casualties are an important—if not the most important—determinant of support, and agree with Mueller's conclusion that Americans were more sensitive to casualties early in the war than later in the war. Thus, from a policy standpoint, their conclusions about the relationship between casualties and support are somewhat indistinguishable from Mueller's.

Based largely upon polling of Californians during the Vietnam War, these authors argue that it is not cumulative casualties that affected support for the Vietnam War as Mueller argued, but rather the marginal casualties that were accumulated in each period, especially during the period when casualties were accumulating at an increasing rate (Gartner and Segura, 1998). According to these authors, moreover, we should anticipate that a point will be reached in *any* conflict that initially is popular and has an S-shaped cumulative casualty curve, when casualties cease to play a role in explaining opinion and other factors become more important (Gartner, Segura, and Wilkening, 1997). At that point, other individual-level variables that had minimal explanatory power at the beginning of the conflict can be expected to grow in importance over time. In the end, however, given that the only dynamic variable in their model seems to be the number of marginal casualties incurred in each period, it should be of little surprise that this variable was found to be associated with changes in support during Vietnam.

Moreover, it is not clear how useful their main finding—that the principal driver of support is the proximate marginal casualties that have been incurred—actually is in predicting support in cases other than Vietnam. In the case of Somalia, for example, their theory would seem to predict that the greatest decline in support should have come *after* the firefight in Mogadishu, when the most casualties were taken. But support for Somalia tumbled from about 75 percent to about 50 percent in the spring of 1993 during a time when there were rather few U.S. casualties but an important change in the nature of the mission had taken place. Moreover, support had pretty much bottomed out (at about four in ten) even before the firefight in Mogadishu, at a time when fewer than a dozen casualties had been accumulated but hope for a successful outcome had eroded (see Larson, 1996b). Thus, from the very beginning, the decline in support for Somalia seems to have had more to do with factors other than casualties, something that would not be predicted from these authors' work on Vietnam.

Although they include some demographic factors in their modeling, these authors do not appear to make any assumptions about the process by which Americans actually weigh ends, ways, and means in wars and military operations, which is presumably one of the issues of greatest concern to policymakers.

Approach

To assess the role of civilian deaths—or any other individual variable—in support and opposition for military operations, one first needs a general model that has demonstrated its robustness: an ability to predict support based upon known predictors across cases. One can use such a model as an anvil on which to hammer (i.e., assess the importance of) other variables while controlling for the main factors that are already included.[28] The confidence one has in any given model should grow with demonstrations of its robustness, both across cases and in terms of cross-level validation from aggregate and individual levels of analysis.

The present effort builds upon the authors' own long-term program of research into the factors that drive public opinion on military operations. As described previously, this earlier work provides an empirically supported framework for assessing the role of civilian casualties while controlling for other factors that have been shown to be reliable predictors of support and opposition to U.S. military operations. The present monograph extends the authors' earlier work in this area to assess the role of civilian casualties in support or opposition for U.S. wars and military operations while controlling for other important influences.

To understand how civilian casualty incidents affect media reporting and public attitudes, we used a comparative case study approach.

---

[28] Such an approach also can be helpful in ascertaining whether previously identified factors wash out (lose their statistical significance) when new variables are included.

We selected as case studies incidents that appeared to be prominently reported in the media and, we believed, would be relatively salient to members of the public:

- the February 1991 bombing of the Al Firdos bunker, which also was being used as a shelter by noncombatants, in the Gulf War
- the April and May 1999 attacks on the Djakovica convoy and Chinese embassy during the war in Kosovo
- the early July 2002 attack involving an Afghan wedding party during operations in Afghanistan
- the late March 2003 incident involving a large explosion in a crowded Baghdad marketplace.[29]

It is important to note that these incidents were selected solely because of their high profile as judged by the relatively high level of media attention and commentary they received. We do not mean to imply that U.S. forces failed in some way to take prudent measures to prevent them; indeed, in one case (the 2003 Baghdad marketplace incident), the best evidence suggests that the incident probably was the result of Iraqi air defense munitions falling back to earth.

The logic of focusing on media reporting, public opinion, and antiwar demonstration activity was simply as follows: Media reporting on military operations connects most individuals to events "on the ground," and individuals' reactions to media reports on a military operation—including reports of civilian casualties—may be either attitudinal (in which case they might be assessed using public opinion data) or behavioral (in which case we need some measure of relevant behaviors). As data on antiwar letter-writing, fax, email, telephone, and other private protest activity generally are not available, we decided to focus on a crude measure of public protest activity: the reported fre-

---

[29] In retrospect, the case of Fallujah in April 2004 also would have been an ideal case for study, since it appears that high levels of negative press reporting led to political pressures that resulted in a decision to halt the Marines' operation before the operation was completed.

quency and size of antiwar demonstrations both before and after major civilian casualty incidents.[30]

Media reporting on civilian casualties and other related topics were assessed both qualitatively and quantitatively: The qualitative analysis of media involved reviewing news reports related to the incidents. The quantitative analysis involved a consistent set of content analyses that tabulated the frequency with which various themes (e.g., "civilian casualties," "civilian deaths") appeared in a consistent set of U.S. and foreign media sources in fixed time periods (e.g., year, month, or day).

For U.S. media reporting, we focused on the five major U.S. national newspapers (*The New York Times, The Washington Post, Los Angeles Times, The Christian Science Monitor,* and *The Wall Street Journal*), and four of the major television news networks (ABC News, CBS News, NBC News, and CNN). To assess foreign reporting, we focused on reporting by a set of foreign media organizations that we believed would be prone to reporting civilian casualty incidents in U.S. wars: AFP, *The Guardian* (London), TASS, and Xinhua.

To understand leadership responses to the incidents, we examined the transcripts of public statements, press conferences, and congressional testimony, as well as statements quoted in the press.

To assess public reactions to civilian casualty incidents, we examined U.S. and foreign public opinion data, as well as media reporting on antiwar demonstrations. For the U.S. public opinion data, we also adapted respondent-level multivariate statistical models that predict support or opposition for U.S. military operations based upon a small set of beliefs and demographic characteristics. These models have a good track record in predicting individuals' support or opposition for past military operations based upon respondents' beliefs about the nature and importance of the stakes involved; the operation's prospects for success; the costs in casualties; membership in the President's party; and race and gender (Larson and Savych, 2005a, 2005b). To assess

---

[30] We also sought to ascertain whether civilian casualties as an antiwar protest theme became more prevalent, but reporting on the content of protest activity generally was far too spotty to accomplish this.

the importance of civilian casualties to support and opposition, we simply added variables for beliefs about civilian casualties to our existing models and assessed whether the civilian casualty variables were statistically significant, and yielded any additional explanatory power in the presence of these other variables.

This monograph will show that public opinion data typically suggest that only a small percentage of Americans participate in antiwar demonstrations. Concerned that the available public opinion data might not adequately capture the *intensity* of reactions to civilian casualty incidents in terms of the prevalence of social protest activity, therefore, we also sought evidence that civilian casualty incidents might have led to an increase in the frequency or size of antiwar demonstrations.[31]

As might be expected, relevant public opinion data on foreign attitudes toward past U.S. military operations and specific incidents of civilian casualties turned out to be far more difficult to obtain than U.S. data, which made assessments of foreign publics' reactions somewhat more sketchy and impressionistic than reactions of the U.S. public. As a result, a multivariate understanding of how foreign publics' concerns about civilian casualties relate to support for or opposition to U.S. military operations remains somewhat opaque.

Organization of This Monograph

This monograph is organized around brief case studies of media and public responses to civilian casualty incidents in four U.S. military operations:

- Chapter Two: the Al Firdos bunker incident during the 1991 Gulf War
- Chapter Three: the Djakovica convoy and Chinese embassy incidents during the 1999 war in Kosovo

---

[31] Among the classic scholarly works on the mobilization of social protest movements, see Olson (1965), Gamson (1989, 1990), and Gurr (1970).

- Chapter Four: the Afghan wedding party incident during Operation Enduring Freedom in Afghanistan in late June 2002
- Chapter Five: the Baghdad marketplace incident during Operation Iraqi Freedom in late March 2003.

Chapter Six details the implications of this research for the Air Force and the U.S. Department of Defense (DoD).

CHAPTER TWO

Operation Desert Storm (Iraq, 1991)

The first case we examined was the 1991 Gulf War to eject Iraqi forces from Kuwait. Because the war presented the prospect of extremely high numbers of U.S. combat casualties,[1] the war was conducted in two phases: an air war against strategic targets and fielded forces, followed by a ground offensive once Iraqi ground capabilities had been sufficiently reduced. As the air war involved targeting Iraqi strategic and other targets in Baghdad and other populated areas, it was in the first phase of the war that civilian casualties figured most prominently. This monograph will show, however, that most Americans believed that the U.S. coalition was making every possible effort to avoid civilian casualties, the result of which was that the preternaturally high support for the war among Americans appears to have been essentially unaffected by civilian casualty incidents.

Civilian Casualty Estimates

The U.S. Department of Defense never publicly estimated the number of Iraqi civilians killed in the air war. Taken together, however, the range of estimates of civilian deaths that resulted directly from the air war suggests that Iraqi civilian deaths were somewhere between fewer

---

[1] For example, prior to the Gulf War, General Edward Meyer, a former Chief of Staff of the U.S. Army, estimated that up to 30,000 U.S. casualties could be sustained in evicting Iraq from Kuwait. (See Fialka and Pasztor, 1990.)

than 1,000 and approximately 3,500.[2] This range also suggests that it is unlikely that the precise number of deaths that were directly accountable to the air war will ever be known with any greater precision:

- Although Iraq's estimates of civilian deaths fluctuated during the war (as described later), Baghdad ultimately took the position that 2,248 Iraqi civilians had been killed as a direct result of the war.
- At the low end of the spectrum of independent estimates, former Defense Intelligence Agency analyst John Heidenrich and political science professor John Mueller separately estimated that fewer than 1,000 Iraqi civilians were killed during the war (Kelly, 2003).
- The consensus view among military experts in early 2003 was said to be that the number of Iraqi civilians killed as a result of the air war lay somewhere between 1,000 and 2,000 (Kelly, 2003).
- Using interviews and other sources, Middle East Watch conducted an analysis of civilian deaths in the Gulf War and reported that the likely number of civilians directly killed by air attacks had an "upper limit" in the 2,500–3,000 range, suggesting that the most likely number was something lower.[3]
- A 1993 study funded by Greenpeace claimed that 3,500 civilians had been killed during the war.[4]

Although not the focus of the present work, it also bears mentioning that it was deliberate Iraqi policy to engage in a variety of activities that constituted war crimes. Prior to the war, for example, the Iraqis

---

[2] The estimates reported here do not include those who died in the uprisings following the Gulf War or as a result of postwar health effects.

[3] It reported,

> Middle East Watch concludes that the number of Iraqi civilians killed as a direct result of injury from allied bombs and missiles will ultimately be calculated in the thousands, not the hundreds. At the same time, we are reasonably confident that the total number of civilians killed directly by allied attacks did not exceed several thousand, with an upper limit of perhaps between 2,500 and 3,000 Iraqi dead. (Human Rights Watch, 1991, p. 19)

[4] Estimate cited in Kelly (2003). See also "Gulf War Casualties Continue" (undated).

positioned military assets in or near densely populated civilian neighborhoods so as to forestall attack or manipulate public opinion, and took more than 4,900 hostages, 106 of whom were used by the Iraqis as human shields prior to the war.[5] During the war, the Iraqi regime also threatened to use U.S. prisoners of war as human shields (Central Intelligence Agency, 2003).

Moreover, all the U.S. prisoners of war taken by the Iraqis were said to have been the victims of war crimes, including physical beatings and sexual assaults (Maier, 2003). And during their occupation of Kuwait, the Iraqis reportedly committed a vast number of war crimes against Kuwaiti civilians—including rape, torture, and murder. A November 1992 report to the Army's Judge Advocate General documented the magnitude and severity of Iraq's war crimes:

> [F]or the period of the Iraqi occupation of Kuwait (2 August 1990 to 3 March 1991), a total of 1,082 Kuwaiti civilian deaths could be directly attributed to Iraqi criminal conduct. The deaths include 120 babies left to die after being removed from incubators that were taken to Iraq; 153 children between the ages of one and thirteen killed for various reasons; and fifty-seven mentally ill individuals killed simply because of their handicap. All of these deaths constitute grave breaches of the Fourth Geneva Convention.[6]

Put another way, whereas the loss of life among civilian Iraqis as a result of the air war was an unintended consequence of the war, it was evidence of deliberate Iraqi policy to engage in war crimes.

---

[5] For these statistics and a detailed review of Iraq's use of human shields in the 1991 Gulf War, see Central Intelligence Agency (2003). All foreigners held hostage were released in early December 1990, more than a month before the beginning of the war.

[6] McNeill (1992, p. 9). See also Scheffer (2000). Scheffer is former Ambassador-at-Large for War Crimes Issues.

Handling of the Civilian Casualties Issue

Baghdad's public treatment of the civilian casualties issue went through a fairly dramatic change just prior to the February 14, 1991, Al Firdos incident.

In the first days of the war, the Iraqi regime generally had sought to downplay the issue of civilian casualties and collateral damage, evidently in the hope of encouraging Iraqis to support the regime and, possibly, to reduce the prospects that the civilian population would revolt against the regime at a time when it was facing its most severe challenge. By February 5, in a letter to Iraqi newspapers, Iraqi foreign minister Tariq Aziz wrote that Iraq's civilian casualties totaled more than 1,000, including 428 killed and more than 650 wounded (AP, 1991d). On February 6, Iraq claimed 150 civilian deaths in the city of Nassariyah alone (Boustany, 1991), and on February 10, Iraq maintained that about 650 civilians had been killed and another 750 had been wounded (Simmons, 1991). At the same time, Masoud Barzani, the commander of Iraqi Kurdish guerrillas opposed to the Iraqi regime, estimated that allied bombing had killed or wounded "about 3,000 civilians" in the Kurdish districts of northern Iraq alone (Randal, 1991).

On February 11, Iraqi leaders stepped up their denunciations of the killing of innocent civilians and alleged war crimes when Iraqi Religious Affairs Minister Abdullah Fadel claimed there had been thousands of civilian casualties in the allied bombardment, and that bombs had destroyed several mosques and churches and 80 homes in the holy Shiite Muslim cities of Karbala, Samarra, and Najaf.[7] And on February 12, Iraq's Deputy Prime Minister Sa'dun Hammadi claimed that civilian casualties from the air war were running into the thousands (Apple, 1991; BBC, 1991).

Following the attack on the Al Firdos bunker on February 13, Iraq's ambassador to Japan estimated that 7,000 Iraqi civilians had been killed in the allies' bombing raids to date, and Iraq's first deputy minister of health claimed that there were "thousands of thousands" of

---

[7] One source reported that on February 11, Iraqi officials claimed 5,000–7,000 civilian deaths. (See Hiltermann, 1991; see also Nasrawi, 1991.)

civilian casualties (Human Rights Watch, 1991, p. 18). A short time later, five weeks into the six-week air war, Baghdad Radio claimed only 1,100 civilian deaths ("Calculating Casualties," 2003). Following the war, the Iraqi government again revised its official estimate of civilian deaths due to the war, essentially doubling the earlier estimate reported on Baghdad Radio to 2,248 ("Calculating Casualties," 2003).

Speculation regarding the specific reasons for the Iraqis' increased emphasis on civilian casualties centered on the desirability from an Iraqi perspective of driving a wedge between the U.S. and Arab and European publics, encouraging nascent peace movements in the United States and elsewhere in an effort to bring pressure on governments participating in the coalition, and possibly even to gain some relief from the coalition's air attacks.[8]

The Iraqi leadership also may have been encouraged by others' efforts to draw attention to the issue of Iraqi civilian casualties in the war: On February 9, Soviet President Gorbachev—an ally of Baghdad—warned that civilian casualties were growing and added that "whole countries—first Kuwait, now Iraq, then perhaps other countries—are facing the threat of catastrophic destruction" (Diebel, 1991). And United Nations Secretary-General Javier Perez de Cuellar warned on February 10 that "the lives of millions of civilians are endangered by a confrontation that, for the moment, shows no sign of abating," that civilian casualties were mounting, and that "damage to residential areas throughout Iraq has been widespread" (Ward, 1991a). By February 19, nearly a week after the Al Firdos incident, Soviet envoy Yevgeni Primakov declared that "the slaughter must be stopped" (Atkinson and Devroy, 1991).

For its part, the United States frequently stressed its commitment to minimizing civilian casualties and collateral damage, its position that

---

[8]   As early as February 10, increasingly frequent and noisy demonstrations in Morocco and other north African countries were taking place. (See Bulloch, 1991.) An example of Iraqi efforts to use the civilian casualties issue to their advantage is the February 13 letter from Iraqi Foreign Minister Tariq Aziz to UN Secretary-General Javier Perez de Cuellar decrying coalition "war crimes" against innocent civilians.

the war was not being waged against the Iraqi people, and that military—and not civilian—targets were being targeted and attacked.[9]

The Arc of Media and Public Concern

U.S. Media and Public Opinion Responses

U.S. Media. Because public knowledge about casualties would be expected to be a function of the level of media reporting on the subject and the public's attention to the war, we now turn to some measures of media reporting and public interest in the war.

In a pattern that will soon become familiar to the reader, media and public interest in the war peaked early in the war and then declined. Figure 2.1 presents data on the monthly number of stories dealing with Iraq in major U.S. television and newspaper reporting from July 1990 to June 1991. Figure 2.2 presents data on the number of newspaper and television news stories dealing with Iraq from just before the war in early January through the last week of the war, ending on March 4.

Figure 2.1 reports that there was a dramatic increase in major U.S. television news and newspaper reporting on Iraq following the invasion of Kuwait in August 1990; a drop-off in reporting until November 1990, when the President announced the deployment of additional U.S. troops to create an offensive option; and then a peak in January 1991 when the war actually began. Following the peak in January 1991, there was a steady decline in reporting levels.

The figure shows that both major newspaper and television reporting grew steadily over the first two weeks of January 1991 as the war approached (the war began on January 16), peaked the week the conflict began, then tapered off. There was then another surge in reporting as the ground war—which began on February 24 and concluded on February 28—approached.

---

[9] For example, on January 18, General Norman Schwarzkopf stated, "[W]e are doing absolutely everything we possibly can in this campaign to avoid injuring or hurting or destroying innocent people. We have said all along that this is not a war against the Iraqi people." For a compilation of U.S. public statements on civilian deaths and collateral damage during the air war, see Human Rights Watch (1991, pp. 75–85).

Figure 2.1
Monthly Major Television and Newspaper Reporting on Iraq,
August 1990–June 1991

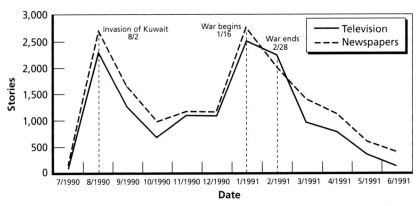

SOURCE: Search for "Iraq" in *The Christian Science Monitor, Los Angeles Times, The New York Times, The Wall Street Journal, The Washington Post*, ABC News, CBS News, CNN, and NBC News.

RAND *MG441-2.1*

Figure 2.2
Major U.S. Television and Newspaper Weekly Reporting on Iraq During the
Gulf War

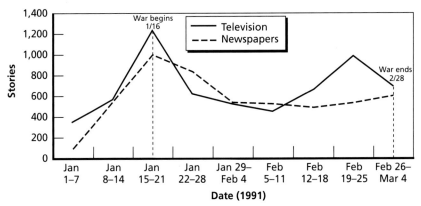

SOURCE: Search for "Iraq" in *The Christian Science Monitor, Los Angeles Times, The New York Times, The Wall Street Journal, The Washington Post*, ABC News, CBS News, CNN, and NBC News.

RAND *MG441-2.2*

U.S. Public Opinion. The public opinion data in Table 2.1 suggest that, like the media coverage, public attention to the war peaked in the first week of the war and then fell off somewhat, but it still remained fairly high by historical standards.[10]

Statistical Results. Past research has shown that support and opposition for U.S. military operations are related to beliefs about the importance of the national security and moral stakes that are involved in a situation involving the use of force, progress in the campaign and its perceived prospects for success, and the actual and potential costs in U.S. military combat casualties. Support and opposition also are influenced by political party (members of the President's political party are typically more supportive than are nonmembers), race (blacks are typically less supportive than others), and gender (men are more likely to support military operations than women).[11] Finally, support is likely to be higher when there is bipartisan support for the military operation from political leaders, and lower when leaders are divided over its wisdom (Larson, 1996a, 2000; Larson and Savych, 2005a).

To better understand the importance of concerns about collateral damage relative to other considerations that affected support for the Gulf War, we conducted bivariate and multivariate analyses of respondent-level data from polling by the *Los Angeles Times* from February 15–17, 1991. We first present the results of our bivariate analyses, and then the results of the multivariate analyses.

Bivariate Analyses. Table 2.2 presents the percentages approving of the war given respondents' beliefs about the number of U.S. military and civilian casualties. The table shows that support declined as the prospective number of casualties—whether military or civilian—

---

[10] Past work has suggested that major wars frequently occasion majorities of Americans to report that they are watching developments very closely.

[11] Eichenberg (2003a) suggests that women are less supportive of military operations than men because they are more sensitive to humanitarian concerns and the loss of human life, while Nincic and Nincic (2002) argue that a combination of political alienation and other factors were at play for both women and blacks during the Korean, Vietnam, and Gulf Wars.

Table 2.1
How Closely Did Americans Follow Developments in the Gulf?

"How closely have you followed news about the situation in the Persian Gulf region? Would you say you have followed it very closely, fairly closely, not too closely, or not at all closely?" (N = 1,013)	January 17–20, 1991 (%)	January 23–26, 1991 (%)	February 7–10, 1991 (%)
Very closely	70	59	55
Somewhat closely	27	34	38
Not too closely	3	6	6
Not at all	0	1	1
No opinion	*	0	*

SOURCE: Gallup poll conducted January 17–20, 1991; January 23–26, 1991; and February 7–10, 1991.

NOTE: * indicates less than 0.5 percent.

increased, and the result in both cases was statistically significant.[12] An inverse relationship between beliefs about U.S. military casualties and support has been observed in a number of past U.S. operations.[13]

It is important to note that these data indicate that respondents were not highly sensitive to casualties of any kind: Support was high even among those who expected high U.S. military or civilian casualties. The table also suggests that respondents were slightly more sensitive to military than civilian deaths.

For example, 86 percent of those who expected hundreds of U.S. deaths and 83 percent of those who believed there had been hundreds of civilian deaths supported the war; 80 percent of those who expected thousands of U.S. deaths or believed thousands of civilians had died supported the war; and a little over six in ten of those who expected 10,000 U.S. deaths or believed tens of thousands of civilians had died supported the war. This is very robust support, especially when

---

[12] Chi-square tests of independence returned a p-value of less than 0.001 in both cases, suggesting that support and beliefs about casualties were related on a bivariate basis.

[13] See Larson (1996a, 1996b).

Table 2.2

Approval of the Campaign by Expected Military and Civilian Casualties, February 15–17, 1991

Approval: "Overall, you approve or disapprove of the United States carrying on the war against Iraq?" Military Deaths: "Overall, how many U.S. soldiers do you expect will be killed in the war against Iraq: close to 100, close to 500, close to 1,000, close to 2,500, close to 5,000, close to 20,000 or more than 20,000?" Civilian Deaths: "To the best of your knowledge, do you think Iraqi civilian deaths as a result of the war so far are in the dozens, in the hundreds, in the thousands or in the tens of thousands?"	Affirmative Responses (%)
Civilian casualties (percent)	
Dozens (5)	93
Hundreds (44)	83
Thousands (37)	80
Tens of thousands (4)	63
Not sure (10)	76
Total (100)	81
Statistical significance in Chi-square test of association	$p < 0.001$
Military casualties (percent)	
Close to 100 (7)	85
Close to 500 (14)	86
Close to 1,000 (19)	83
Close to 2,500 (13)	90
Close to 5,000 (12)	80
Close to 10,000 (7)	62
Close to 20,000 (2)	69
More than 20,000 (4)	52
Not sure (19)	80

Table 2.2—Continued

Approval: "Overall, you approve or disapprove of the United States carrying on the war against Iraq?" Military Deaths: "Overall, how many U.S. soldiers do you expect will be killed in the war against Iraq: close to 100, close to 500, close to 1,000, close to 2,500, close to 5,000, close to 20,000 or more than 20,000?" Civilian Deaths: "To the best of your knowledge, do you think Iraqi civilian deaths as a result of the war so far are in the dozens, in the hundreds, in the thousands or in the tens of thousands?"	Affirmative Responses (%)
Military casualties (percent)	**% Approving**
Refused (3)	94
Total (100)	81
Statistical significance in Chi-square test of association	p<0.001

SOURCE: *Los Angeles Times* poll conducted 1991, N = 1,822.

compared to casualty sensitivity in support for the peace operations of the 1990s (e.g., Somalia, Haiti, Bosnia, and Kosovo).[14]

Multivariate Statistical Modeling. Because these analyses do not take into account possible simultaneous effects of other variables that might be important to support for the campaign, we also performed a number of multivariate statistical analyses. Detailed results are provided in the Appendix and the Technical Appendixes, published separately (Larson and Savych, 2005b).

To ascertain the importance of civilian casualties in judgments about approval and disapproval of the war, we estimated a number of multivariate probit regression models that included variables for civilian casualties along with variables that past work has suggested are the key predictors of support or opposition for military operations.[15]

The civilian casualties variables were from questions that asked respondents whether they thought that the United States was doing all it could to keep down the number of civilian casualties and also asked respondents to estimate the number of civilian deaths. The other vari-

---

[14] See Larson and Savych (2005a, 2005b).

[15] Multivariate probit models are appropriate when one is predicting a binary outcome (e.g., support or oppose); ordinal probit models are appropriate when one is predicting an ordinal outcome (e.g., support strongly, support somewhat, oppose somewhat, oppose strongly).

ables that were included in our multivariate model were variables for respondents' beliefs about whether vital national interests were at stake, whether U.S. actions were morally justified, how well the war was proceeding, how many U.S. casualties had been sustained, membership in the president's party, and race and gender.[16]

The first model correctly predicted support or opposition for 86 percent of the respondents, but neither of the civilian casualties variables were statistically or substantively significant. The most important predictors of support follow, in order of importance; note that a "(+)" means that the coefficient on the variable was positive and increased approval, whereas a "(–)" means that the coefficient was negative and reduced approval:

- race (–): Blacks were less likely to approve than others.
- the belief in a moral justification (+): Those who believed that the operation was morally justified were more likely to approve than those who did not.
- self-identification as a Democrat (–) or Independent (–): Non-Republicans were less likely to support the operation than Republicans, probably because the President was the natural partisan leader for Republicans but not for the others.[17]

We also estimated two other models. The first predicted the belief that what the United States had accomplished in the war to date had been worth the number of U.S. military deaths and injuries. This model correctly predicted the responses of 78 percent of the responses. The second asked whether it had been worth the civilian deaths and injuries; this second model correctly predicted 71 percent of the responses.

---

[16] Very briefly, the probability of approval would be expected to be higher for those with beliefs that vital interests were involved, that U.S. actions were morally justified, that the war was proceeding well, and that only a small number of U.S. casualties had been sustained, as well as those who were members of the president's party, not black, or male (see Larson and Savych, 2005a).

[17] Detailed coefficients and diagnostics for all regressions are found in Appendix A in this monograph.

The most important predictors of the belief that the war had been worth the civilian casualties were, in declining order of importance (valence of coefficients in parentheses),

- the belief that the war was morally justified (+)
- self-identification as a woman (–): Women were less likely to support than men.
- self-identification as a Democrat (–)
- beliefs as to whether the argument that "the United States did not have a vital interest" was a good (–) or bad (+) reason for opposing the war: Those who believed that it was a bad reason to oppose the war were more likely to support than those who felt otherwise.

Importantly, the belief that the United States was doing all it could to minimize civilian casualties was a statistically significant predictor of beliefs about whether the war was worth the civilian deaths that had been incurred in *both* models (Table A.1 in the Appendix), roughly as important as beliefs regarding U.S. vital interests in Iraq and status as a self-identified political Independent, but not so important as beliefs that the war was morally justified, or gender or Democratic party identification.

The modeling results suggest that beliefs about the *number* of civilian casualties were not an important factor in support for the war, at least in comparison to other factors that have been shown to be important in predicting support or opposition. The results also suggest that beliefs about whether the U.S. military was doing all it could to avoid civilian casualties were a substantively and statistically significant predictor of the belief that the war had been worth these casualties, which suggests that they also may be an important predictor of support and opposition. As the reader will learn from our analysis of the other cases, there is substantial evidence in support of this interpretation.

Antiwar Demonstrations. As was described in Chapter One, another measure of public attitudes toward wars and military operations is involvement in antiwar demonstration activity. The U.S. antiwar movement began forming as early as August 1990,[18] well before the war began, and was comprised of a confederation of religious organizations and secular antiwar groups.[19] Reporting suggests that these groups organized mass antiwar demonstrations and vigils that began in the fall of 1990 and picked up soon after the air war began, peaking perhaps on January 16 or January 26 and then tapering off.

Despite the rather high levels of media attention antiwar demonstrations received, demonstrators, whether antiwar or prowar, constituted only a tiny fraction of the overall public: Ninety-eight percent of those polled by ABC News/*The Washington Post* on January 20 said that they had not attended any demonstrations, while those saying that they had were evenly split with 1 percent in each camp.[20] By mid-February, a total of 5 percent of those polled said they had attended some sort of demonstration related to the war.[21] In other words, press

---

[18] An organization called the Coalition to Stop U.S. Intervention in the Middle East was formed in early August, for example, and another, called the National Campaign for Peace in the Middle East, was formed in September. Other antiwar organizations included the National African American Network Against U.S. Intervention in the Gulf, and four Latino organizations: the League of United Latin American Citizens, the Mexican American Political Association, the Latino Issues Forum, and the American G.I. Forum. (See Elbaum, 1991.)

[19] For example, the National Council of Churches, which represented 42 million Christians of 32 denominations, and the National Conference of Catholic Bishops, representing 54 million Roman Catholics, condemned the threat of invasion. Of two of the major antiwar groups, the National Campaign for Peace condemned the Iraqi invasion, whereas the Coalition to Stop U.S. Intervention did not (Landsberg, 1991). Eleven protesters from an organization called Pledge of Resistance, part of the Coalition to Stop U.S. Intervention in the Middle East, were arrested after disrupting Senate debate over Iraq on January 11 (Lawrence, 1991). One source suggested that the antiwar movement included student activists, lesbian and gay activists, and members of the women's movement (Elbaum, 1991, p. 147).

[20] ABC News/*The Washington Post* poll conducted January 20, 1991, N = 532. The *Los Angeles Times'* polling in February found that only 1 percent of those polled supported neither the troops nor the administration's policy. (See *Los Angeles Times*, 1991, N = 1,822.)

[21] ABC News/*The Washington Post* polling on January 20 found that only 1 percent had attended antiwar demonstrations and another 1 percent had attended prowar demonstrations. Gallup's polling found that 5 percent said that they had participated in a demonstration for or against the war (Gallup poll conducted February 14–17, 1991, N = 1,009).

reporting on demonstrators appears to have been out of proportion to their actual numbers.

Foreign Media and Public Opinion

Foreign Media. Judged by the reporting levels in *The Guardian* (London) and TASS (Figure 2.3), foreign media reporting followed the same general pattern as that in the United States: a burst of coverage following the invasion of Kuwait in August 1990, followed by a decline in reporting, another peak once the war was under way in January 1991, and a drop-off in reporting following the war.

The rapid increase in foreign media reporting on the war is even more apparent in Figure 2.4, which shows the weekly number of stories in *The Guardian* and TASS before and during the war.

Figure 2.4 shows that media reporting increased dramatically in the week of January 15–21, trailed off, and then climbed again during the week of February 26–March 4, when the ground war occurred.

Figure 2.3
Selected Foreign Media Reporting on Iraq, August 1990–June 1991

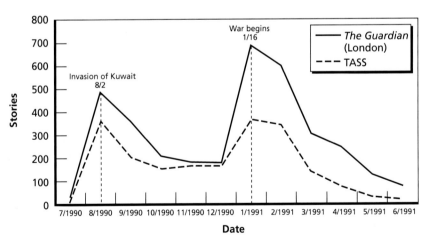

SOURCE: Search for "Iraq" in full text of *The Guardian* (London) and TASS.
RAND *MG441-2.3*

Figure 2.4
Selected Foreign Media Weekly Reporting on Iraq, January–February 1991

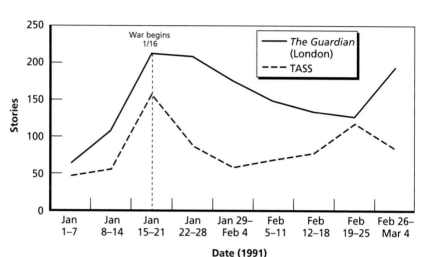

SOURCE: Search for "Iraq" in full text of *The Guardian* (London) and TASS.
RAND *MG441-2.4*

Foreign Public Opinion. The Gulf War enjoyed the authorization of the United Nations Security Council and an international coalition that included 36 countries. Other nations such as Japan made financial contributions or provided other assistance. Given the broad international support that the Gulf War received, it should be little surprise that, with some exceptions, the war received substantial public support abroad.[22]

---

[22] According to one study of German media during the Gulf War,

> virtually unanimous agreement existed in the characterization of Iraq . . . in a negative light—Saddam Hussein was a dictator, Iraq had committed clear aggression against Kuwait, Iraq had used chemical weapons against Iraq and the Kurds, etc. During the actual fighting in January 1991, there was also a flurry of mentions in *der Spiegel* and *die Tageszeitung* of the threat posed by Iraqi Scuds to Israel. On the other hand, the peace movement received more support than the government from Taz and Spiegel framing of the other components of the Gulf War debate. (Cooper, 2002, pp. 53–54)

It was much more difficult to find data and analyses of foreign public opinion during the Gulf War than American public opinion.[23] We summarize here results from the small amount of relevant polling and other analyses that we were able to find on European and Arab attitudes toward the war.

European Public Opinion. Although it is not entirely clear that antiwar sentiment predominated in Europe,[24] according to one account of European public opinion just prior to the onset of the war,

> All the polls showed that the predominate [sic] feeling was against the war; the central motto of demonstrations was "No to the war" with a demand for the withdrawal of Western troops. In France the proportion of people opposed remained high. . . . People [in France] saw things in a highly contradictory way. In the same public opinion polls a majority would express its support for U.S. policy, and for the intervention of French troops, while simultaneously supporting the proposal for renewed negotiations with Iraq, or expressing a favorable appreciation of the actions of the peace movement. (Cirera, 1991, pp. 283–284)

Rather than being outright antiwar, this suggests that some European publics seem to have hoped that a negotiated settlement was possible, even while supporting the tough U.S. and coalition policy. Although the writing had been on the wall since the United Nations Security Council (UNSC) set the January 16, 1991, deadline in November 1990, it is not clear at what point majorities of Europeans (or others) accepted the inevitability of the war.

Although they did not ask any direct questions about the matter of civilian casualties or collateral damage, the EU's Eurobarometer surveys conducted in fall 1990 and March 1991 asked questions about the

---

[23] The Foreign Broadcast Information Service (FBIS) online archive does not go back to 1990–1991, for example, and whereas it typically is fairly easy to locate, on the Internet, surveys and survey analyses that have been conducted in recent years on the Internet, it is much more difficult to find surveys conducted before the Web became a primary means of disseminating information.

[24] It is important to note that the author of the following quote participated in the European antiwar movement during the Gulf War, and his argument is a somewhat tendentious one.

Gulf Crisis and other matters that provide some perspective on Europeans' overall attitudes toward the war.

In October 1990, the month before the United States announced its decision to increase force levels in the Persian Gulf to provide an offensive capability, most Europeans appear to have been somewhat optimistic that the situation in the gulf might be resolved without European military involvement. On the one hand, a bare majority of Europeans EC-wide (52 percent) thought that a war involving European forces was *unlikely* in the next year (Commission of the European Communities, 1990). Sentiment that war was likely was strongest among the British (62 percent), Danish (59 percent), and Dutch (55 percent), whereas the French, Luxembourgers, and Portuguese were undecided, and a majority of those in other EC member states were convinced that war would not happen (Commission of the European Communities, 1990, p. 43). Support for a European rapid-deployment force was highest among the British (69 percent), French (65 percent), and Belgians (58 percent), and from the political right in Europe; the Germans (35 percent) and Spanish (33 percent) least favored one.[25]

Europeans also ventured retrospective assessments on the decision to go to war in the Eurobarometer poll of March 1991, fielded almost immediately after the conclusion of the war (Reif and Melich, 1994). Although some reading between the lines is necessarily involved, according to this poll, most Europeans seem to have approved of the decision to go to war (Figure 2.5).

Figure 2.5 shows that at least 70 percent of those polled in nine of the 10 nations or regions polled (Germany was polled separately in the west and east), retroactively approved of the decision to use force against Iraq. Nevertheless, only a slight majority in the eastern part of Germany approved, and a majority of Greeks opposed the decision.

---

[25] One explanation offered by the Eurobarometer study was that the Germans were constitutionally forbidden to deploy military forces outside NATO territory, and the Spanish already were quite critical of Spain's naval involvement in the Persian Gulf (Commission of the European Communities, 1990, p. 41).

Figure 2.5
Europeans' Approval of the Decision to Use Military Force Against Iraq,
March 1991

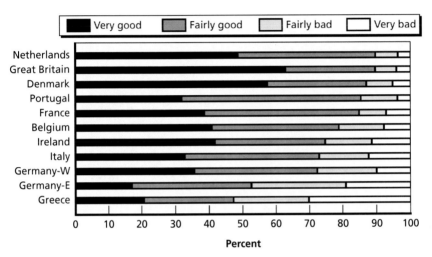

SOURCE: European Commission (1991).
NOTE: Question read, "Q12. Now a question on the Gulf War. All things considered, do you think the decision to use military force against Iraq in order to liberate Kuwait was a very good idea, a fairly good idea, a fairly bad or a very bad idea?"
RAND *MG441-2.5*

Given that this sort of net assessment would require respondents to weigh a wide range of considerations—including the ultimate success of the war in ejecting Iraq from Kuwait, beliefs about the extent of civilian casualties and collateral damage, and coalition efforts to avoid them, and other factors—these data would seem to suggest something of an endorsement of both the outcome of the war and the way in which the war was conducted. Beyond the data cited thus far, we did not find any other readily available foreign public opinion data on the Gulf War.[26]

Finally, the belief that NATO was essential to their nations' security—a crude indicator of the extent to which European publics

---

[26] Eichenberg (2003b) suggested to us that his compilation of foreign public opinion data shows no change in the average level of support in 23 countries polled before and after Al Firdos.

shared important security interests with the United States—declined from March to May 1991 by three points in France, rose seven points in Germany and eight points in Italy, and fell six points in the United Kingdom (Eichenberg, 2003b, pp. 651–654).

Arab Opinion. An analysis of Arab opinion on the Gulf War suggested that Arab attitudes were filtered through their more general assessment of their own nation's situation at the time:

> Whatever the sources of Saddam Hussein's ambitions toward Kuwait, his calculation of risk and his chances for success were linked to the prevailing mood in the region that afflicted the populace and the elites alike—a mood related to the end of the Cold War and its perceived implications for the Arab-Israeli conflict. Most Arab leaders and elites did not see at the end of the Cold War a victory of democracy over dictatorship, or the victory of consensus politics over power politics. Instead, to Arabs, the end of the Cold War, which signaled the decline of the Soviet Union as a major superpower, ushered in an era of American hegemony that also entailed Israeli's regional hegemony.[27]

According to this analysis, Palestinians and Jordanians (more than half of whom are Palestinian) cared most about the crisis and generally supported Iraq, whereas among Syrians and Egyptians,

> the popular soul was more divided, although opinion tipped toward confronting Iraq only by strong government decisions. First, both Syria and Egypt feared Iraq's regional dominance; second, neither thought that Iraq could stand up to the United States, and both thought that they would be on the losing side if they did not confront Iraq. Third, extensive U.S. lobbying played an important role in shaping opinion.[28]

---

[27] Telhami (1993, p. 442). As public opinion polling is virtually unknown in Arab regions, Telhami based his analysis on interviews.

[28] Telhami (1993, pp. 448–449). For a somewhat impressionistic analysis of Palestinian public opinion during the Gulf War, see Finkelstein (1992).

Israeli public sentiment, meanwhile, was characterized largely by a basic tendency to carry on in the face of the Iraqi Scud attacks:

> While many, perhaps most, Israelis were afraid and anxious during the Gulf War, they nevertheless carried on with their lives and did not become preoccupied with death. In fact, one could almost say that, overall, pathology was down in the country. Mental health clinics and private therapists reported a dramatic decline in the number of people who sought help. Psychologists were on duty at hospitals twenty-four hours a day—but almost no one came in. Israelis were busy coping.[29]

Unfortunately, the absence of public opinion data militates against a deeper and more far-reaching analysis of Middle Eastern attitudes toward the war.

Antiwar Demonstrations. It was somewhat easier to find reporting on demonstrations against the war than public opinion. Whatever their size and frequency, however, it is not at all clear what fraction of European and Arab populations might have participated in such activities.

The antiwar movement in Europe seems to have included many who had been involved in the nuclear disarmament campaign in the 1980s, but it also evidenced diversity, both within and between countries.[30] According to one account, from September 1990 to January 1991, the movement grew stronger, culminating around January 12, just before the deadline set by the UNSC (Cirera, 1991, p. 283):

> Demonstrations were organized as early as August in Spain, and they followed in most European countries, often coinciding with the departure of troops. Great surprise was expressed at the scale and scope of these demonstrations: 30,000 in Paris on October

---

[29] Arian and Gordon (1993) suggested that positive opinions of the United States and the beliefs that U.S.-Israeli relations were very good or good and that U.S. security commitments were reliable grew from 1990 (before the war) to 1991 (after the war). They did not document changing opinion during the war.

[30] According to Cirera (1991, p. 281), "in every country in Western Europe, even in Turkey, there were anti-war actions and mobilizations."

20, on the same day as large demonstrations took place in New York and Tokyo. The movement kept developing from then on, until it included all European countries by mid-November. On January 12, 200,000 people marched in Paris; similar numbers were seen in capitals and major cities across Europe.[31]

Additional to the demonstrations cited above were the following:

- Antiwar demonstrations took place in London, Ottawa, and Prague in early January (AP, 1991a; and "Demonstrator Arrested Outside U.S. Consulate," 1991).
- Antiwar protests took place worldwide in the days leading up to the January 16 deadline, involving protests in the United Kingdom, Germany, Japan, Canada, France, Spain, Italy, Austria, Belgium, Sweden, Turkey, South Africa, and Mauritania (Beelman, 1991a, 1999b; Cameron and Quinn, 1991).
- On January 16, a worldwide rally of peace protesters occurred in Europe, Canada, and Asia, attracting tens of thousands of protesters to such varied locales as London, Bonn, Berlin, Munich, Copenhagen, Oslo, Milan, Madrid, Barcelona, Ottawa, Tokyo, and New Delhi (Cormier, 1991; AP, 1991b).
- Antiwar protests continued worldwide on January 17, with large anti-American marches in Pakistan and Algeria.
- On January 20, large antiwar crowds marched in Germany and Libya.
- On February 3, a large march in Morocco supported Iraq in the war.

In the Arab world,[32] demonstrations in Jordan appear primarily to have been related to the Arab-Israeli conflict, whereas in Algeria, the Gulf crisis appears merely to have strengthened the ability of opposition groups to mobilize the masses and challenge the status quo.

---

[31] Cirera (1991, p. 284). In France, Italy, and Spain, workers also engaged in work stoppages.

[32] The following characterization of demonstrations in the Arab world is from Telhami (1993, p. 449).

No demonstrations were reported in the Gulf states, and only one was reported in Egypt. In Sudan and Yemen, by contrast, 14 demonstrations reportedly took place in August, the primary grievance apparently being opposition to foreign intervention. A few popular demonstrations occurred in several Arab states, but those that occurred in states that had joined the U.S.-led coalition evidently posed little threat to the Arab governments there. The Iraqi regime also "stage-managed" demonstrations supporting Saddam Hussein that reportedly were attended by hundreds of thousands of Iraqis (Beeston, 1991).

The Al Firdos Bunker Incident

Perhaps the most prominently reported collateral damage incident in the Gulf War, and the subject of our first case study, was the Al Firdos bunker incident on February 13, 1991.

At approximately 4:30 am on Monday, February 13, 1991, local Baghdad time, during some of the heaviest bombardment of Baghdad since the war began on January 16, two 2,000-pound bombs from an F-117A attack aircraft struck the Al Firdos bunker, a civil defense shelter that had been upgraded to, and was being used as, an Iraqi command-and-control facility in the Al Ameriyyah section of Baghdad. The incident resulted in the deaths of 200–300 civilians, including over 100 children who were taking shelter there.[33]

The left side of Table 2.3 shows that news of the incident reached Cable News Network (CNN) a little more than six hours later, and was subsequently heavily reported by the other major television networks the next day.

The official reactions listed on the right side of the table show that the incident figured prominently in White House, DoD, and British press statements on February 13. Also shown, in the immediate aftermath of the attack, Iraqi Foreign Minister Tariq Aziz sent a letter to

---

[33] Human Rights Watch (1991). According to this source, several days before the bombing, local residents of the Ameriyah district of Baghdad had complained to local officials about their lack of access to what had, during the Iran-Iraq war, been a civilian air defense shelter. Iraqi officials reportedly relented and opened the upper level to civilians.

Table 2.3
Postincident Timeline for Al Firdos Incident

Media Reporting Highlights	Official Handling Highlights
2/12	
1730: Incident occurs	
(2/13 0430 local time)	
2/13	**2/13**
0000: CNN	1147: White House spokesperson
0630: *CBS Morning News*	Marlin Fitzwater statement
Iraqi Ambassador to U.S. on	—White House/Fitzwater regular press
Larry King Live	briefing
1258: *CBS News Special Report*	—DoD regular briefing
1543: *CBS News Special Report*	—Cheney statement
Evening news programs	—UK Foreign Secretary Douglas Hurd
ABC World News Tonight	questioned in Parliament
CBS Evening News	—Iraqi Foreign Minister Tariq Aziz
The MacNeil/Lehrer NewsHour	sends letter to UN Secretary-General
2230: *Nightline* (ABC)	
2330: *America Tonight* (CBS)	

NOTE: All times are Eastern unless otherwise noted.

UN Secretary-General Javier Perez de Cuellar accusing the coalition of "war crimes," and demanded that the Secretary-General and the Security Council condemn the bombing (Victoria Graham, 1991). The Security Council demurred.

Initial Iraqi estimates of civilian deaths in the Al Firdos incident were in the 400–500 range, but by February 15, the Iraqis had revised their estimate downward to the 288 bodies that had been brought out of the shelter by that time (Riddell, 1991). The final estimates of the civilian toll in the incident were in the 200–300 range.[34]

As described in the following section, this incident resulted in a spike in media reporting on Iraqi civilian casualties, but does not appear to have affected public attitudes toward the war.

---

[34] Iraq's June 1991 report to the United Nations Human Rights Committee stated that 204 citizens were killed in the attack, whereas Middle East Watch's final estimate of civilian deaths in the shelter, based upon a source from the Baghdad Forensic Institute, was 310, some 130 of whom reportedly were children (Human Rights Watch, 1991, pp. 129–130).

U.S. Media and Public Opinion Responses

U.S. Media. Although the reporting levels do not capture viewership and cannot adequately convey public sensitivities worldwide to the issue of civilian casualties,[35] the Iraqi leadership may have observed even before the Al Firdos incident that the issue of Iraqi civilian casualties was gaining increasing media attention (Figure 2.6). The data on reporting levels on the issue of civilian casualties suggest that the Al Firdos incident occasioned a fairly substantial, if short-lived, increase in U.S. media reporting on civilian casualties in the war.[36]

Figure 2.6 reports an increase in U.S. television reporting on civilian casualties beginning around February 7 that roughly corresponded with the growing Iraqi efforts to draw attention to the issue. The major U.S. newspapers did not show the same sort of response. Both U.S. newspaper and television reporting spiked after the incident.

Beyond the intrinsic newsworthiness of the subject, several other factors also may have contributed to the media's substantial coverage of civilian casualties during the Gulf War.

First of all, foreign journalists faced strong Iraqi pressure to file stories about civilian casualties. In addition to the limited access and heavy censorship practiced since the beginning of the war,[37] the Iraqi regime restricted foreign reporters to filing stories on civilian casualties and collateral damage in civilian areas to better ensure that their

---

[35] For example, on February 3, one journalist wrote,

> Since early last week, when refugees in Jordan first reported seeing dead civilians and smoldering autos along a highway in western Iraq, claims of U.S. and allied bombing of Iraqi civilians have increasingly been reported in televised scenes approved by Iraqi government censors. Vivid images on Cable News Network of injured children, flattened homes, and weeping families in towns such as Diwaniyeh, south of Baghdad, have raised concerns in Jordan and elsewhere in the Arab world that the massive U.S. and allied aerial bombardment is harming noncombatants. (Smith, 1991)

[36] No doubt this was in part due to the fact that reporters were taken to the Ameriyah area of Baghdad (Kellner, 1992, especially the discussion of the Al Firdos bunker bombing beginning on p. 297).

[37] On January 19, Iraq ordered foreign journalists out of the country, with the exception of one American correspondent in Baghdad—Peter Arnett of CNN—and another correspondent by the name of Rojes (Goodman, 1991).

Figure 2.6
U.S. Media Reporting on Civilian Casualties in Iraq During the Gulf War

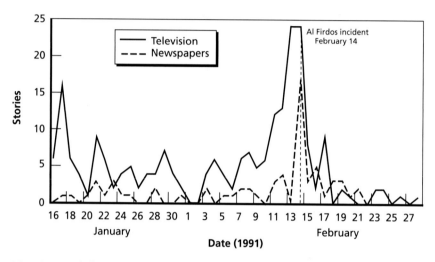

SOURCE: Search for "Iraq" and "civilian casualties," "civilian deaths," or "collateral damage" in *The Christian Science Monitor, Los Angeles Times, The New York Times, The Wall Street Journal*, and *The Washington Post* newspapers, and on ABC News, CBS News, CNN, and NBC News.

RAND *MG441-2.6*

reporting would be uniformly favorable to Iraq's cause.[38] The regime also provided foreign news crews unimpeded access to the sites of alleged attacks on civilian targets to better ensure that the graphic imagery of the dead would reach Arab, Western, and other foreign publics.[39] Thus, foreign reporting was, by Iraqi design, focused heavily on civilian casualties and collateral damage. It also is important to note that the Iraqis engaged in a variety of schemes to place innocents at risk, evidently in the hope of eroding the credibility of the U.S. coalition's claims that it was doing its utmost to avoid civilian casualties (Central Intelligence Agency, 2003).

---

[38] See Wittstock (1991). Although Iraqi censorship of news reporting predated the Al Firdos incident, it is not clear whether the regime's insistence that reporters write about collateral damage also predated the incident.

[39] CNN correspondent Arnett was taken on "guided tours" by Iraqi handlers in late January (Wittstock, 1991).

Although the study did not measure the frequency with which civilian casualties or collateral damage were mentioned, a content analysis of news reporting during the war conducted by Gannett suggested that the subject of "human shields"—the civilians and prisoners of war who, in contravention of the Geneva Conventions and other norms, the Iraqis placed at potential targets to deter attack—was one of the most frequently mentioned phrases used during the war, even exceeding references to U.S. military casualties (Figure 2.7).[40]

Of the 12 phrases included in Gannett's analysis, the most frequently mentioned one was "Vietnam," followed by "human shields" and "U.S. casualties." Although it is not known the extent to which reports on human shields presented the subject in a way that placed the moral burden on Iraq or the United States, it is quite striking that reporting on the human shields issue (2,588 mentions in total: 2,002 by the print media and 586 by television) actually eclipsed mentions of U.S. casualties (2,009 mentions: 1,492 by print media and 517 by television). Clearly, the matter of human shields was a prominent one in the media reporting, and although it seems not to have lowered support for the air war, it likely was on the minds of the public as well.

Taken together, it is clear both that civilian casualties were a prominent theme during the war, and that media reporting on the subject increased in response to the Al Firdos incident.

U.S. Public Opinion. As mentioned previously, prior to the war, most Americans seem to have expected civilian casualties and expressed the desire that efforts be made to avoid them.[41]

---

[40] See LaMay (1991). The analysis was based upon a search of the Nexis database of Mead Data Central, including AP, United Press International, Reuters, Gannett News Service, *Chicago Tribune*, *Los Angeles Times*, *Newsday*, *The New York Times*, *The Boston Globe*, *The Washington Post*, *Time*, *Newsweek*, and *The Christian Science Monitor*, and a search of Burrelle's Broadcast Database, including evening news programs on ABC, CBS, and NBC, as well as the Financial News Network (FNN), and National Public Radio. With a few exceptions, the search covered August 1, 1990, to February 28, 1991.

[41] For example, 86 percent of those polled in early January said that they expected that a war with Iraq would involve many civilian casualties in the Persian Gulf, whereas only 9 percent said that they expected mainly military casualties (Times Mirror poll conducted January 3–6, 1991, N = 1,208). Nevertheless, a plurality (48 percent) thought that if the United States became involved in a war against Iraq, it should restrict bombers only to targets in areas that

Figure 2.7
Key Terms and Phrases Used During the Gulf War

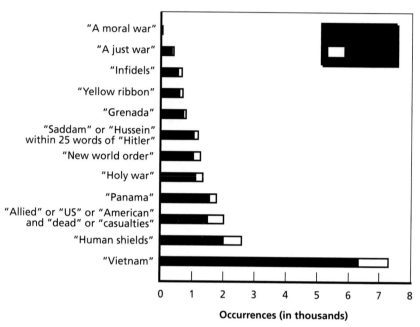

SOURCE: Gannett Foundation Media Center (1991).

RAND MG441-2.7

Although national political and military leaders seem to have feared that they were losing the public relations battle with Iraq, and that the Al Firdos incident would sap public support for the war, the public opinion data provide no evidence whatsoever that most Americans questioned the official U.S. explanation of the incident, that the incident made them believe inadequate attention was being paid to minimizing civilian casualties, or that the incident eroded support. Rather, U.S. public opinion on the matter suggested that most Americans accepted the official explanation of the Al Firdos incident that the

---

were not heavily populated, whereas four in ten (42 percent) thought U.S. bombers should be free to attack all targets (CBS News/*The New York Times* poll conducted January 5–7, 1991, N = 1,348). There appears to have been no polling on the question of civilian casualties from the onset of the war on January 16 until just before the Al Firdos incident.

Iraqi regime had allowed innocent civilians to take shelter at a military command-and-control facility, and that, while regrettable, responsibility for the incident lay with Iraq.[42]

Other polling also suggested that vast majorities of the American public were aware of the incident, accepted the coalition's explanations while rejecting Iraq's, and continued to believe that the coalition was doing its utmost to avoid civilian deaths. A selection of polling results on these matters follows:

- News of the incident moved quickly and had reached most Americans the day after the incident: On February 14, only one day after the incident, more than nine in ten (92 percent) said that they had heard or read something about the bombing (ABC News/*The Washington Post* poll conducted February 14, 1991, N = 772).

- Forty-three percent of those polled said that they thought that the Iraqi people supported Iraq's war with the United States and its allies, while 49 percent thought they did not (ABC News/*The Washington Post* poll conducted February 14, 1991, N = 772).

- The average (median) respondent seems to have believed that the number of Iraqi civilian deaths as a result of the war was in the hundreds or fewer,[43] and nearly three in four (73 percent) thought it either very likely (38 percent) or somewhat likely (35 percent) that thousands of civilians ultimately would be killed in the war zone (*Los Angeles Times*, 1991, N = 1,822).

- Respondents were evenly divided on the media's coverage of Iraqi claims of civilian casualties: Forty-seven percent said they thought the media had spent too much time showing film of Iraqi claims

---

[42] The most comprehensive analysis of American public opinion during the Gulf War concludes that "the well-publicized civilian casualties resulting from an attack on a Baghdad bomb shelter on February 13 inspired no notable change in this attitude [toward civilian casualties]. Overwhelmingly, Americans said the shelter was a legitimate military target and held Hussein and Iraq responsible for the civilian deaths there" (Mueller, 1994, p. 79).

[43] Forty-nine percent said they thought that civilian deaths were in the dozens (5 percent) or hundreds (44 percent), while 41 percent said they thought that deaths numbered in the thousands (37 percent) or tens of thousands (4 percent) (*Los Angles Times,* 1991, N = 1,822).

of civilian casualties, whereas 45 percent said that the media had done the right thing (Gallup poll conducted February 14–17, 1991, N = 1,009).

- Eighty-one percent of those polled on February 14 thought that the site was a legitimate military target, while only 9 percent did not (ABC News/*The Washington Post* poll conducted February 14, 1991, N = 772).

- Seventy-nine percent of respondents in one poll held Saddam Hussein or Iraq responsible for the deaths at the bombing site (ABC News/*The Washington Post* poll conducted February 14, 1991, N = 772). Another poll found 84 percent who held Saddam responsible (*USA Today* poll conducted February 14, 1991, N = 601).

- Ninety percent of those polled said they did not believe that the United States had intentionally bombed Iraqi civilians (ABC News/*The Washington Post* poll conducted February 14, 1991, N = 772).

- Nearly one in four (23 percent) thought that the Al Firdos bunker had been an Iraqi military command center, and another six in ten (59 percent) thought that it had been both a command center and a civilian shelter (*Los Angeles Times*, 1991, N = 1,822).

- Ninety-two percent agreed with the statement that the bombing of the shelter was a terrible tragedy, but such things were unavoidable in wartime, and 71 percent disagreed with the statement that by bombing the shelter, the allied military had made a terrible mistake that could have been avoided (*USA Today*/Gordon S. Black poll conducted February 14, 1991, N = 601).

- Fully nine out of ten Americans said that they believed the U.S. military was doing all it could to keep down the number of civilian casualties.[44]

- Three in four (75 percent) said they did not think that the United States should stop bombing the city of Baghdad in order to avoid

---

[44] *Los Angeles Times* (1991, N = 1,822). By comparison, nearly seven in ten felt that what had been accomplished had been worth the deaths among U.S. military personnel.

civilian deaths (ABC News/*The Washington Post* poll conducted February 14, 1991, N = 772).

- Seven in ten agreed that the United States was justified in attacking Iraqi forces in areas populated by civilians, while 22 percent disagreed (*Los Angeles Times*, 1991, N = 1,822).

- Seven in ten agreed that the deaths of civilians who were located close to military targets were worth it if American lives were saved (*USA Today*/Gordon S. Black poll conducted February 14, 1991, N = 601).

Polling Before and After the Al Firdos Incident. Polling by CBS News and *The New York Times* on the one hand, and ABC News and *The Washington Post* on the other, straddled the Al Firdos incident, enabling a comparison of attitudes before and after the incident on several key attitudes.

We begin with a poll by CBS News and *The New York Times* on February 12–13, 1991—the day before and day of the Al Firdos incident. Table 2.4 shows that there was no change in attitudes on the question of whether American bombers should attack military targets in heavily populated areas (about half approved of this policy on both days), although the percentage who believed that U.S. bombers were aiming only at military targets actually increased, from 71 to 76 percent; because of the composition of the samples in the two days, this probably is an underestimate of the actual change.[45]

There was a modest decline, however, in the percentage who thought that the damage the United States was inflicting on Iraq was what might be expected in wartime, from 84 to 80 percent; we cannot rule out that this might be the result of sampling error, however.[46]

---

[45] A higher incidence of blacks, liberals, and independents "leaned" Democrat on the second day, which would be expected to dampen any increase in support. It also is worth noting that relying upon the totals for the survey would mask the change over the course of the survey.

[46] The small sample sizes for each day make the margin of error for the first day (N = 479) about 4.5 points with a 95-percent confidence interval, meaning that differences of 4.5 points or less are not meaningful, as they could be entirely due to sampling error; the margin for the second day (N = 581) is about 4.1 points. Additionally, as was mentioned earlier, because the respondents on the second day of the poll would have been expected to have less

Table 2.4
Views on Avoiding Bombing Civilian Areas Before and After Al Firdos Incident

Response	Before 2/12/1991 (%)	After 2/13/1991 (%)	Total (%)
"Should American bombers attack *all* military targets in Iraq including those in heavily populated areas where civilians may be killed, *or* should American bombers attack only those military targets that are *not* in heavily populated areas?"			
Attack all targets	50	49	50
Only targets not in heavily populated areas	42	43	43
Don't know/no answer	8	8	8
"Do you think American bombers *are* aiming at only military targets in Iraq or do you think they are also *aiming* at some civilian locations?"			
Aiming at only military	71	76	74
Some civilian locations	18	15	16
Don't know/no answer	11	9	10
"Some other countries say United States forces are inflicting excessive damage on Iraq. Do you think the United States is causing excessive damage to Iraq, or is the damage about what should be expected in wartime?"			
Expected in wartime	84	80	81
Causing excessive damage	9	10	10
Less than expected (volunteered)	2	2	2
Don't know/No answer	5	8	7

SOURCE: CBS News/*The New York Times* poll conducted February 12–13, 1991, N = 1,060, with 479 respondents interviewed on February 12 and 581 respondents interviewed on February 13.

ABC News/*The Washington Post* polling—done just before and just after the Al Firdos incident—also provides some interesting results.

---

favorable attitudes toward the administration's policy of strategic bombing, any difference could be accountable to bias in the subsample.

Figure 2.8
Confidence That Al Firdos Bunker Was a Legitimate Military Target

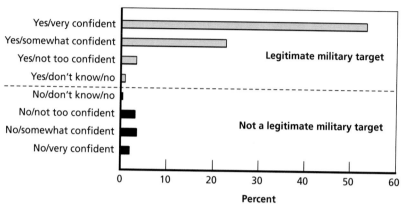

SOURCE: ABC News/*Washington Post* poll conducted February 14, 1991, N = 772.
NOTE: Question read, "Iraq says hundreds of civilians were killed when the U.S. bombed an air raid shelter in Baghdad on Wednesday. The U.S. says the site was being used as a military command bunker.) Do you think the site was a legitimate military target or not?" (Asked of respondents who said the air raid shelter the U.S. bombed in Baghdad was/was not a legitimate military target): "How confident of that are you: Very confident, somewhat confident, or not too confident at all?"

RAND *MG441-2.8*

The data from polling also show that most were pretty confident that the United States had struck a legitimate military target (Figure 2.8), and that the percentages who thought that the United States was making enough of an effort to avoid bombing civilian areas in Iraq actually swelled after the incident, from 60 to 67 percent (Figure 2.9), while those who thought the United States was making too much of an effort declined somewhat, and those who thought the United States should make a greater effort did not change at all.

Moreover, although the overall percentages approving and disapproving of the war did not really change after the incident (78 percent approving before and 77 percent after; see the question at the bottom of Table 2.5), there *might* have been a modest increase in polarization—strong opposition to the war increased modestly after the incident, but the change in the percentages strongly supporting was well within the margin of sampling error.

Figure 2.9
Views on Whether the United States Was Making Enough Effort to Avoid Bombing Civilian Areas Before and After Al Firdos Incident

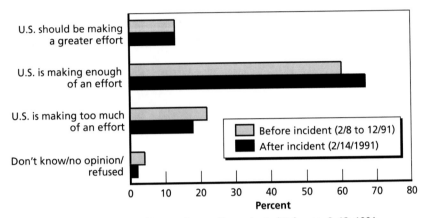

SOURCE: ABC News/*The Washington Post* polls conducted February 8–12, 1991, N = 1,011; February 14, 1991, N = 772.
NOTE: Question read, "Which of these statements comes closer to your own view?
   A. The U.S. should be making a greater effort…
   B. The U.S. is making enough of an effort…
   C. The U.S. is making too much of an effort…
…to avoid bombing civilian areas in Iraq."
RAND MG441-2.9

Finally, another question, asked only on February 14, found by a three-to-one margin (41 percent to 14 percent) that those who said that the bombing of the shelter made them more supportive outnumbered those who said it made them less supportive; 38 percent said it did not affect them one way or another (*USA Today*/Gordon S. Black poll conducted February 14, 1999, N = 601).

Table 2.6 reports that the percentage of Americans who believed that the damage inflicted by U.S. forces was "excessive" actually *declined* after the Al Firdos incident, from about 10 percent February 12–13 (the day before and day of the incident) down to 6 percent in late February, and thereafter to 3 percent by early April.

Finally, a comparison of polling done by the *Los Angeles Times* at the beginning of the war (January 17–18) and several days after the Al Firdos incident (February 17–19) showed no appreciable change in support: Eighty-two percent of those polled early in the war and

Table 2.5
Approval and Disapproval of Going to War with Iraq Before and After Al Firdos Bombing

"Do you approve or disapprove of the United States having gone to war with Iraq? (Is that approve/disapprove strongly/somewhat?)"	Before (%)	After (%)
Approve strongly	57	59
Approve somewhat	21	18
Disapprove somewhat	10	7
Disapprove strongly	7	11
Don't know/no opinion	5	4

SOURCE: *The Washington Post* poll conducted February 8–12, 1991, N = 1,011, and ABC News/*The Washington Post* poll conducted February 14, 1991, N = 772.

Table 2.6
Views on Whether U.S. Forces Were Inflicting Excessive Damage, February 12–13, 1991

"Some other countries say U.S. forces are inflicting (inflicted) excessive damage on Iraq. Do you think the United States is causing (caused) excessive damage to Iraq or is (was) the damage about what should be expected in wartime?"	Day Before/Day of Incident (February 12–13, 1991)	After Incident		
		February 24–March 1, 1991	March 4–6, 1991	April 1–3, 1991
U.S. damage to Iraq excessive	10	6	6	3
Damage expected	81	83	83	80
Damage less than expected (volunteered)	2	6	8	11
Don't know	7	6	3	6

SOURCE: CBS News/*The New York Times* poll conducted February 12–13, 1991, N = 1,060; and *The New York Times* polls conducted February 28, 1991, N = 528; March 4–6, 1991, N = 1,252; and April 1–3, 1991, N = 1,283.

NOTE: The difference between the February 12–13 and February 24–31 readings was statistically significant at the 0.01 level.

81 percent just after Al Firdos supported the war (Table 2.7). Moreover, the percentage strongly supporting the war actually grew modestly, from 59 to 63 percent.[47]

Taken together, these data suggest that U.S. leaders, who were extremely concerned about political fallout from the incident, should not have been unduly concerned about the impact of the Al Firdos incident on the American public's support for the war.[48]

Antiwar Demonstrations. The period just prior to the Al Firdos incident seems to have been a relatively quiescent one (Harris, 1991), and we found no evidence suggesting that the Al Firdos incident led to an increase in the frequency or size of antiwar

Table 2.7
Approval of the War in Iraq, January–February 1991

Response	Jan. 17–18, 1991 (%)	Feb. 17–19, 1991 (%)
Approve strongly	59	63
Approve somewhat	23	18
Disapprove somewhat	7	7
Disapprove strongly	9	10

SOURCE: *Los Angeles Times* poll conducted January 17–18, 1991, N = 1,406; *Los Angeles Times* (1991, N = 1,822).

NOTES: Wording of question in *Los Angeles Times* (January 17–18, 1991): "Generally speaking, do you now approve or disapprove of the decision to send American military troops to the Persian Gulf or not?" Wording of question in *Los Angeles Times* (1991): "Overall, do you approve or disapprove of the United States carrying on the war against Iraq?"

---

[47] The difference was statistically significant at the 0.05 level.

[48] See Gordon and Trainor (1995, pp. 340–343). The White House and Chairman of the Joint Chiefs of Staff Colin Powell seem generally to have been most concerned about the impact of such incidents on the ability to hold the coalition together. It is worth mentioning, however, that the incident did, nevertheless, affect the procedures for authorizing the attack of targets in central Baghdad, and at least temporarily halted strike operations against strategic targets there. Given the small percentage of sorties devoted to strategic attacks in central Baghdad, and the shift in emphasis that was already under way to conclude preparations of the battlefield for a ground attack, however, it is not clear how important the cessation of these attacks was (Gordon and Trainor, 1995).

demonstrations in the United States. In fact, some sources suggest that the demonstrations that took place after the Al Firdos incident actually were less well-attended and well-organized than those in the prior month:

- Nationally coordinated protests that were called for the weekend of February 16–17 reportedly were "still substantial in size and breadth, but there was a definite drop in momentum relative to the peak of activity in January" (Elbaum, 1991, p. 155).
- On February 21, U.S. college groups held demonstrations against the war, but reportedly failed to achieve a coordinated effort.
- On February 23, the day before the ground offensive began, antiwar organizers announced that demonstrations were planned for March 16 and April 6. Because the war was concluded on February 28, these demonstrations were never held.

Foreign Media and Public Opinion Responses

Foreign Media Reporting. Like U.S. media reporting, foreign media reporting on civilian casualties typically peaked after the Al Firdos incident.

Figure 2.10 shows that reporting on civilian casualties by *The Guardian* (London) began increasing after February 10 and peaked the day after the Al Firdos incident; by comparison, TASS and Xinhua reporting levels on civilian casualties were lower both before and after the incident.

Foreign Public Opinion. We found no additional data that would enable us to assess the specific impacts of the Al Firdos incident on foreign public opinion.

Antiwar Demonstrations. In the immediate aftermath of the incident, there were some reports of street demonstrations in Amman, Jordan, and elsewhere in the Middle East, but we found no compelling evidence suggesting that foreign demonstrations were more prevalent after the Al Firdos incident than before (see Andrew Rosenthal, 1991; Savva, 1991; and Watson, 1991).

Figure 2.10
Selected Foreign Reporting on Civilian Casualties, February 7–21, 1991

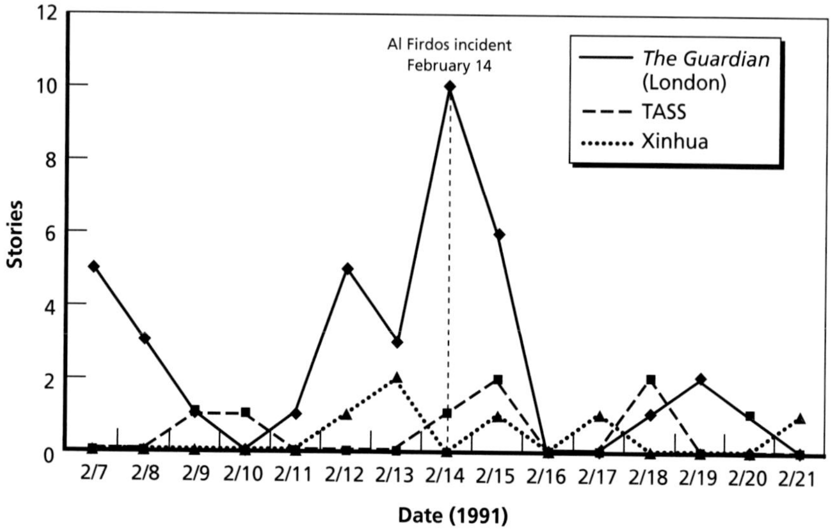

SOURCE: Search for "Iraq" and "civilian casualties," "civilian deaths," or "collateral damage" in *The Guardian*, TASS, or Xinhua.

RAND *MG441–2.10*

Key Lessons

Several key lessons that emerge from this case study. The first have to do with the United States' adversary, Iraq:

- Baghdad used "human shields" at strategic installations and located military capabilities in civilian areas to deter air attacks or otherwise complicate coalition planning.
- The Iraqi regime tightly controlled the foreign press in Baghdad and made it difficult for them to report on subjects other than civilian casualties and collateral damage.
- Iraq was able to exploit the Al Firdos incident to raise questions about the coalition's efforts to minimize casualties and to lend

credibility to its claims that thousands of Iraqi civilians were being killed in the air war.

Lessons regarding the media include the following:

- Although there appears to have been a delay of some hours between the incident and the first news reports on the incident, once news of the incident reached the press, it spread very quickly and was prominently reported by major news organizations, both at home and abroad.
- Given the fact that the Iraqis controlled the incident site and that even they had difficulties assessing the number of casualties, it seems unlikely that U.S. policymakers had any public affairs opportunities to manage the incident other than citing the evidence that the Al Firdos bunker was being used as a command-and-control facility, an argument that the vast majority of Americans accepted.
- Reporting on civilian casualties peaked at the time of the incident, and then quickly receded, with the incident seemingly becoming a part of the contextual fabric for subsequent reporting.

Lessons regarding the American public include the following:

- Public estimates that civilian casualties in the war in Iraq were in the hundreds to thousands just after the Al Firdos incident were generally in line with Iraqi claims and numbers that might have been inferred from press reporting.
- There is, however, little evidence of any adverse changes in U.S. attitudes toward the war following the Al Firdos incident, or more generally, as a result of civilian casualties; if anything, Americans' attitudes toward the war appear to have stiffened in the wake of the incident.
- Multivariate statistical modeling of respondent-level data suggests that concerns about civilian casualties were not particularly important in individuals' decisions about whether they supported or opposed the Gulf War when other variables that have been

shown to be important predictors of support and opposition were also included.

- The belief that the U.S. military was doing all it could to avoid civilian deaths was widespread, as was the view that any deaths that occurred were essentially misfortunes of war. A key finding is that the belief that the military was doing all it could to avoid casualties was a statistically significant predictor of support and opposition in two of our multivariate models, which controlled for many other factors that are known predictors of support and opposition. Subsequent chapters will demonstrate that this is the key belief that connects civilian casualties to support and opposition.

Because the public opinion data for foreign publics was rather sparser, it is hard to say exactly how the incident affected public attitudes abroad. The data on European attitudes, however, suggest that most European publics, at least retrospectively, viewed the war in a favorable light, and these judgments, it can plausibly be argued, almost necessarily factored in beliefs about whether the war was properly conducted. Nor did the Gulf War lead to "the Arab street" seriously threatening regimes in Arab nations. In many cases, demonstrations appeared to be only indirectly connected to the Gulf crisis and the war.

The lesson for military leaders and policymakers is that, despite the high level of media coverage and graphic imagery of death and destruction, the Al Firdos incident did not materially affect the high level of support for the war or the belief that the coalition was making efforts to avoid civilian casualties and collateral damage. Nor did the incident seem to give impetus to antiwar demonstrators, who already seemed to be losing their momentum by that time. Whether policymakers overestimated the prospects that civilian casualties would erode the coalition is unclear.

Finally, it also is clear that military planners and leaders involved in the Gulf War greatly regretted the Al Firdos incident, both because of the loss of civilian life and the judgment that the military value of its destruction actually was less than originally believed. Military planners and leaders would also regret other incidents of collateral damage in the war, such as the destruction of Iraqi power generators, which had much longer-term adverse consequences for the Iraqi civilian population and were a source of criticism of the conduct of the air war for more than a decade after the end of the war.

CHAPTER THREE

Operation Allied Force (Kosovo, 1999)

Operation Allied Force in Kosovo was the NATO air war to halt a Federal Republic of Yugoslavia (FRY) campaign of ethnic cleansing of Albanian Kosovars that already had killed an estimated 1,000 civilians in 1998 and resumed again in early 1999.[1] Although public attitudes toward the war appeared unaffected by the April 14, 1999, Djakovica convoy incident, following the mistaken bombing of the Chinese embassy, there was a significant decline in the belief that the U.S. coalition was doing everything it could to avoid civilian casualties. There is also some evidence that support for the war also may have declined.

Following the breakdown of peace talks and the withdrawal of the Organization for Security and Cooperation in Europe's (OSCE's) Kosovo Verification Mission on March 19, on March 20, the Serbs launched "Operation Horseshoe," a systematic campaign of destruction, rape, killing, and other actions designed to displace non-Serbs from Kosovo. The result was a massive humanitarian crisis involving an estimated 863,000 refugees (Kosovars displaced to adjacent countries), 100,000 missing, and perhaps another 590,000 internally displaced persons (IDPs) (Organization for Security and Cooperation in Europe, 1999).[2] It also involved a large but as-yet-uncertain number of deaths, primarily civilians killed by FRY forces, but also a smaller number who were killed by NATO bombs in collateral damage incidents. The irony

---

[1] Forty-five ethnic Albanians were killed by Serb forces at Racak on January 15, 1999.

[2] Data are from United Nations High Commissioner for Refugees (UNHCR) figures from October 15, 1999, presented in a NATO press briefing on May 13, 1999, cited in Organization for Security and Cooperation in Europe (1999, p. 167).

of the war, then, was that civilian deaths in the air war were incurred in pursuit of the overall humanitarian objective of saving lives.

Throughout the conflict, high-level policy attention was given to the issues of civilian casualties and collateral damage, reportedly including President Clinton's approval of targets on the target list, as the President was said to be profoundly averse to civilian casualties.[3] The rules of engagement (ROE) used by the U.S. military in Kosovo were correspondingly tight.[4] Media and public attention also showed significant concern for civilian casualties incurred in the conflict.

Civilian Casualty Estimates

Estimates of Civilian Deaths Due to NATO Action

With the exception of the FRY, whose estimates of civilian deaths accountable to NATO action ranged between 1,200 and 5,700,[5] most

---

[3]   According to one source, "President Clinton has vetted the entire list of targets, Secretary of Defense William S. Cohen said, but has focused on the most prominent ones, like President Slobodan Milosevic's party headquarters and a presidential palace in Belgrade, both of which were struck last week. Although Mr. Clinton has signed off on most targets, his aides say, he has vetoed others, always exhibiting what his aides describe as a profound aversion to unintended civilian casualties" (Myers, 1999).

[4]   Major General Charles Wald described the ROE in Allied Force as "as strict as I've seen in my 27 years in the military" (Lambeth, 2001, p. 136).

[5]   Seybolt (2000, p. 32) reports, "FRY Government sources claimed that at least 1,200 civilians were killed and possibly as many as 5,700." Human Rights Watch, which reviewed the FRY Ministry of Foreign Affairs publication *NATO Crimes in Yugoslavia*, estimated a total of 495 civilians killed and another 820 civilians wounded in specific documented instances, and was quite dismissive of the higher FRY estimates:

> The confirmed number of deaths is considerably smaller than Yugoslav public estimates. The post-conflict casualty reports of the Yugoslav government vary but coincide in estimating a death toll of at least some 1,200 and as many as 5,000 civilians. At the lower end, this is more than twice the civilian death toll of around 500 that Human Rights Watch has been able to verify.

> In one major incident—Dubrava prison in Kosovo—the Yugoslav government attributed ninety-five civilian deaths to NATO bombing. Human Rights Watch research in Kosovo determined that an estimated nineteen prisoners were killed by NATO bombs on May 21 (three prisoners and a guard were killed in an earlier attack on May 19), but at

estimates of civilian deaths accountable to NATO's bombing were in the 500 range. As in the 1991 Gulf War, the United States did not offer its own estimate of civilian deaths accountable to the air war. However, it did characterize independent estimates of about 500 civilian deaths as "reasonable."

The FRY claimed that NATO bombs had killed at least 1,200 and possibly as many as 5,000 civilians, although the FRY Ministry of Foreign Affairs' *White Book*, which documented alleged incidents of civilian casualties and collateral damage as a result of NATO bombing, listed only about 500 deaths, very close to some nongovernmental organizations' (NGOs') estimates (Federal Ministry of Foreign Affairs, 1999).

Human Rights Watch (HRW) documented 90 separate incidents involving civilian deaths that it said had resulted from the NATO bombing,[6] and estimated a total of 488 to 527 Yugoslav civilians killed as a result of the bombings:

> Human Rights Watch concludes on the basis of evidence available on these ninety incidents that as few as 488 and as many as 527 Yugoslav civilians were killed as a result of NATO bombing. Between 62 and 66 percent of the total registered civilian deaths occurred in just twelve incidents. These twelve incidents accounted for 303 to 352 civilian deaths. These were the only incidents among the ninety documented in which ten or more civilian deaths were confirmed. (Human Rights Watch, 2000)

HRW's estimate was cited favorably by Amnesty International, suggesting that it is a fairly widely accepted estimate of civilian deaths attributable to the NATO bombing campaign within the human rights community (Amnesty International, 2000).

---

least seventy-six prisoners were summarily executed by prison guards and security forces subsequent to the NATO attack. (See Human Rights Watch, 2000; see also *NATO Crimes in Yugoslavia*, 1999a, 1999b.)

[6] HRW reviewed the FRY Ministry of Foreign Affairs publication *NATO Crimes in Yugoslavia*. (See *NATO Crimes in Yugoslavia*, 1999a, 1999b.)

For its part, NATO and DoD publicly acknowledged only 20–30 incidents of "collateral damage" and did not offer any official estimates of the number of civilians killed (Seybolt, 2000, p. 32), but characterized as reasonable Human Rights Watch's figure of 500 civilians killed.[7]

The disparity between Human Rights Watch's estimate of 90 civilian casualty incidents and DoD's estimate of 20–30 incidents also is of some importance. On two occasions, DoD leaders estimated the number of collateral damage incidents that led to civilian deaths. In his May 11 testimony before the Defense Subcommittee of the Senate Appropriations Committee, Secretary of Defense William Cohen testified,

> Let me just point out, we've had 18,000 sorties, we've had 4,000 attack sorties, we've had 380 separate targets, we've had over 10,000 munitions that have been dropped, and out of all of that, roughly a dozen have involved unintended consequences.[8]

A little over two months later, in his July 22 testimony to the House Select Committee on Intelligence, Deputy Secretary of Defense John J. Hamre testified,

> [W]e flew over 9,300 strike sorties and attacked over 900 targets, dropping over 24,000 bombs or missiles. All together, we had 30 instances when we caused damage we did not intend. (U.S. House of Representatives, 1999)

Deputy Secretary Hamre broke these incidents out as follows:

---

[7]   Differences in the counts seem, at least in part, due to differences in DoD's and Human Rights Watch's assessments of which targets were legitimate; dual-use facilities were, for example, a contentious category of target. The authors are grateful to Bill Stanley for suggesting this point.

[8]   U.S. Senate Appropriations Committee (1999). By comparison, a May 7, 1999, AFP report documented seven instances involving a total of about 200 deaths, while a May 10 report in *The Guardian* documented 10 incidents possibly involving 227 deaths. Both reports relied heavily upon FRY estimates of deaths in a number of incidents. See AFP (1999d) and "Mounting Tally of Blunders" (1999).

Of the 30 instances of unintended damage, one third were instances where we damaged the target we wanted to destroy, but innocent civilians were killed at the same time. You will recall the time one of our electro-optically guided bombs homed in on a railroad bridge just when a passenger train raced to the aim point. We never wanted to destroy that train or kill its occupants. We did want to destroy the bridge and we regret this accident. As I said, 10 of the 30 instances of unintended damage fall in this category.

For the remaining 20 instances, 3 were caused by human error that identified the wrong target, and two were caused by mechanical error by our hardware. In 14 instances we have not yet determined whether the unintended damage was caused by human error or mechanical failure. We will determine that to the best of our ability during our after action assessment.

The one remaining case of course is the most dramatic and it is the subject of today's hearing. The bombing of the Chinese embassy was unique in that we had a legitimate target that we wanted to hit; the only problem is we had the target located in the wrong building. To my knowledge, this is the only example of this failing in all of our strike operations. Because it was such a tragedy, it merits special review and attention. (U.S. House of Representatives, 1999)

It thus appears that Human Rights Watch's independent estimates of civilian deaths may have included a much greater number of alleged incidents than DoD believed were warranted, but it still arrived at an estimate for civilian casualties that was not disputed by DoD as unreasonable.

Civilian Deaths Due to FRY Action

To provide a point of comparison, it is useful to compare the number of civilian deaths that were said to be accountable to NATO's bombing campaign to those that resulted from the FRY's campaign of ethnic cleansing.

For a variety of reasons—including the likelihood that many bodies were destroyed through burning or other means, and that some bodies were removed from Kosovo—the exact number of deaths accountable to FRY action may never be known with certainty. Even after acknowledging their imprecision, however, estimates of these deaths are generally an order of magnitude higher than those that have been attributed to NATO.

Estimates of possible dead from officials representing NATO and its members changed over the course of the war:

- In mid-April, based on interviews with refugees, NATO officials estimated that 3,200 Albanians had been killed in the ethnic cleansing campaign.
- At about the same time, U.S. Ambassador-at-Large for War Crimes David Scheffer reported that upwards of 100,000 Albanian men remained unaccounted for, and were feared also to have been victims.
- On May 10, State Department spokesman James Rubin invoked the 100,000 figure, and on May 16, Secretary of Defense Cohen said that he had seen reports of 4,600 Albanians killed. Cohen added that he suspected a much higher number due to the 100,000 military-aged men who were said to have gone missing.
- By June 1, NATO spokesman Jamie Shea claimed that 225,000 were missing and 6,000 were killed in summary executions.
- Several days later, British war crimes ambassador David Gowan suggested that the estimated number of dead was around 10,000.[9]

Postwar estimates of the dead from the ethnic cleansing campaign also vary. By the end of the war, FRY police, paramilitary, and military forces are estimated to have killed as few as 4,400 or as many as 10,000 Kosovar civilians:

---

[9]   Numbers cited in Mitchell (1999); see also Komarow (1999).

- On November 10, 1999, Chief Prosecutor Carla Del Ponte of the International Criminal Tribunal for the Former Republic of Yugoslavia (ICTY) reported to the UNSC that her office had received reports of 11,334 deaths in Kosovo.[10] However, ICTY forensic teams had by that time examined only 195 of 529 gravesites, and had actually exhumed only 2,108 of the 4,266 bodies reported to have been buried in those sites, meaning that 7,000–9,000 bodies remained to be found and exhumed (United Nations, 1999). In its 2001 report to the United Nations, moreover, the ICTY reported that it had completed its forensic work in 2000 and had exhumed a total of approximately 4,000 bodies or parts of bodies in Kosovo.[11]

- Citing the ICTY estimate, the U.S. State Department stated that "enough evidence has emerged to conclude that probably around 10,000 Kosovar Albanians were killed by Serbian forces" (U.S. Department of State, 1999, p. 3).

- A study by the American Association for the Advancement of Science (AAAS) and the American Bar Association's Central and East European Law Initiative (CEELI) also suggested approximately 10,000 deaths at FRY hands. Based upon interviews, their study documented 4,400 killings of unique, named individuals, and used a demographic statistical technique called "multiple systems estimation" to estimate the total number killed. Using this approach, their estimate was that 10,356 Kosovar Albanians were killed between March 20 and June 12, 1999, with a 95-percent confidence interval from 9,002 to 12,122.[12]

---

[10] The ICTY cited NATO as one source for the higher estimate.

[11] According to the ICTY, "The forensic work in Kosovo was completed in 2000. Over the two-year period in which exhumations were conducted in Kosovo, approximately 4,000 bodies or parts of bodies were exhumed. The work has provided the Prosecutor with an excellent picture of the extent and pattern of crimes committed in Kosovo during 1999" (International Tribunal for the Former Yugoslavia, 2001, p. 33).

[12] This represents a lower bound, as they did not include an additional 18,000 anonymous deaths reported (Ball et al., 2002). An earlier analysis had suggested 10,500 killed with a 95-percent confidence interval from 7,449 to 13,627 (American Bar Association and American Association for the Advancement of Science, 2000).

- The Independent International Commission on Kosovo estimated that FRY forces killed up to 1,000 civilians by September 1998, probably killed a smaller number between September 1998 and March 1999, and probably killed another 10,000 between March 24, 1999, and June 19, 1999.[13]
- Human Rights Watch documented a total of 3,453 extra-judicial executions, including 1,768 executions by the Serbian police, 1,173 by the Yugoslav Army, and 1,154 by Serb paramilitaries (Human Rights Watch, 2001). This number represents a lower bound for the organization's estimate due to the absence of interviews of displaced persons from some provinces, under-reporting for some municipalities, and dropping cases in which the number of executions was said to be more than ten but the exact number was imprecise.[14]
- The Congressional Research Service estimated that 2,500 civilians were killed between February 1998 and March 1999 and cited the State Department estimate that another 10,000 had been killed by FRY forces during the war (Woehrel, 2001).

Following its November 1999 estimate of approximately 10,000 killed by FRY forces, the ICTY seemed to take the position that the specific numbers mattered less than the estimated 4,000 executions that already had been documented, and were sufficient to demonstrate a clear pattern of war crimes on the part of Serb forces.

The United Nations Mission in Kosovo (UNMIK) Department of Justice Office on Missing Persons and Forensics (OMPF) has provided more recent, albeit still not conclusive, estimates of the number of civilians killed in the war. Based upon this source, the total could be

---

[13] The Commission was the initiative of Goran Persson, Prime Minister of Sweden, and the result of his concern regarding the absence of an independent analysis of the conflict in Kosovo (Independent International Commission on Kosovo, 2000).

[14] OSCE also issued a report on human rights violations by Serb forces based upon interviews with nearly 2,800 refugees, but did not venture an estimate of the total number of deaths that were accountable to the campaign of ethnic cleansing (Organization for Security and Cooperation in Europe, 1999).

as low as about 5,200[15] or as high as about 8,750.[16] The office has not, however, disavowed the early figure of 10,000 dead.

Estimates of FRY Military Deaths Due to NATO Action

Finally, the number of FRY troops killed also has been estimated:

> NATO gave no official estimate of the number of FRY troops killed but unofficially claimed that it was over 5,000. The FRY military stated that NATO bombs and engagements with the KLA [Kosovo Liberation Army] killed 524 soldiers and 114 policemen and wounded 2,000 and that a number of paramilitary were also killed. (Seybolt, 2000, p. 32)

Table 3.1 summarizes these disparate results and suggests that civilian deaths accountable to NATO's bombing campaign were a small fraction of the deaths that have been attributed to Serbian forces.

Handling of the Civilian Casualties Issue

The FRY's Handling of the Casualties Issue

The government of the Former Republic of Yugoslavia saw civilian casualties and collateral damage incidents as an effective means of splitting NATO's coalition through the corrosive effect that civilian casualties were presumed to have on moral judgments about the war, and it accordingly went to great lengths to publicize—and enhance the possibilities for—such incidents (Lambeth, 2001, p. 79).

There were numerous reports during the war of FRY forces using civilians as human shields, both to deter air attacks and to create

---

[15] In September 2002, the OMPF reported that 4,500 bodies of victims had been recovered, of which about half had been identified, and in March 2004, it reported that 699 additional remains had been exhumed in 2003, yielding a total of about 5,200, not including exhumations performed during the last quarter of 2002.

[16] In March 2004, the OMPF reported a total of 3,546 open and active cases of missing persons. If we assume that most of these are dead and add them to the 5,200 minimum, that would yield a total of as many as 8,750 dead.

Table 3.1
Comparison of Support for Air War and Ground Options

Poll Dates	Air War	Peacekeeping	Peace Enforcement	Ground Combat
	Average Percent Supporting Each Option			
March 24–31	52.8	54.8	38.0	N/A
April 1–30	59.5	65.2	45.9	46.4
May 1–31	51.4	N/A	45.5	28.5
June 1–13	62.0[a]	54.5[b]	N/A	27.0[c]
Overall average	56.4[d]	59.5[e]	43.1[f]	34.1[g]

NOTES: N/A = not available.

[a] Based on one question only, by Princeton Survey Research Associates (PSRA) between June 9, 1999, and June 13, 1999.

[b] Based on six questions asked between June 1, 1999, and June 10, 1999.

[c] Based on one question only, by Opinion Dynamics asked between June 2, 1999, and June 3, 1999.

[d] Average based on a total of 30 questions that were asked about support for the air war.

[e] Based on a total of 26 questions that asked about U.S. ground troops in a peacekeeping role.

[f] Based on a total of 15 questions that asked about U.S. ground troops in a peace enforcement role.

[g] Based on a total of nine questions that asked about U.S. ground troops in a combat role.

incidents in which civilians would be killed. In fact, efforts to protect facilities by putting civilians at risk began well before the war.

Even before the war, the Serb regime had created a range of dual-use facilities—with both military and civilian functions—that, if attacked, could be claimed to be purely civilian facilities: The Belgrade television and radio facility attacked on April 23, for example, was reported to have been used not just to transmit news and propaganda but also for communications for the command-and-control of fielded forces.

Once the war was under way, some so-called human shields appear to have been Serb volunteers. The extent to which these demonstrations of solidarity with the regime were in fact voluntary, or stage-managed by the FRY government, is not known. In any case, Serbian TV reported that large numbers of people had voluntarily formed human shields across bridges in Belgrade and at Grdelica in southern Serbia to protect them against NATO attacks, for example, while residents of Novi Sad formed a human shield on the only remaining bridge that was linking the city with Petrovardin. Protests by human shields taking place in the towns of Sabac and Cacak also were shown on TV, with some protesters wearing circular "targets" around their necks (BBC News, 1999a).

Most human shields seem, however, to have been innocent Kosovar Albanian civilians pressed into service by FRY forces. OSCE's report on human rights violations in the war in Kosovo, for example, provided numerous accounts of ways in which FRY forces used human shields: stashing ammunition in civilian locations, moving police administrative structures to civilian buildings, and conducting other activities to make targeting more difficult (OSCE, 1999, Chapter 13). OSCE described it as follows:

> Accusations quickly emerged from Kosovo Albanians and journalists that Yugoslav authorities were deliberately concealing their equipment in locations which jeopardized Kosovo Albanian civilians or detainees. Furthermore, movements, or restriction of movement, of the civilian population itself at times had at least the appearance of protecting military objects, sites or personnel. At a minimum, it was clear that armed forces were prepared to endanger civilians for their own objectives of military deterrence. (OSCE, 1999, Chapter 13, "Human Shields and Other Endangerment of Non-Combatants During Military Operations")

The issue of human shields accordingly became a recurring topic in Pentagon briefings. On May 17, several days after the May 14 bombing incident near the village of Korisa, for example, Pentagon spokesman Ken Bacon cited one survivor of the attack as having told a German radio interviewer that FRY forces had herded townspeople into an agricultural cooperative and then told them that they would "see what a NATO bombing strike is like."[17] Bacon further estimated that "[i]t may be that as many as half, or certainly a third of the people who may have been killed in NATO attacks, were put there specifically by Milosevic as human shields."

The FRY government also sought to extract as much public relations value from NATO's air campaign as possible. Serbian media heavily reported alleged incidents of NATO attacks on civilian targets and incidents involving civilian deaths or collateral damage,[18] provided foreign media with graphic footage of death and destruction it attributed to NATO and access to the sites of alleged incidents.[19]

Television footage also showed Serbian anti-NATO rallies and protesters holding signs in English making jokes about the civilian casualties attributable to NATO's air war.

The U.S. Coalition's Treatment of the Civilian Casualties Issue

In its handling of the issue, the NATO coalition generally emphasized its plans and efforts to avoid collateral damage, its regret for the deaths of innocent civilians that may have occurred, and its belief that collateral damage generally remained low, especially relative to the number of sorties flown. The coalition also contrasted civilian deaths resulting from the coalition's air war with Milosevic's deliberate policy of

---

[17] In response to a question about human shields, Bacon said, "First of all, there is stronger and stronger evidence that he [Milosevic] is in fact aggressively using Kosovar refugees as human shields. I think the most compelling report was a German radio report over the weekend, Deutsche Welle, which interviewed a witness of the Korisa event, and that witness said, and maybe you've seen this or heard it, that they were in fact herded into an area and in fact told before the event took place: 'Now you're going to see what a NATO bombing strikes is like'" (DoD, 1999j). On the issue of human shields, see also CNN (1999e) and White House (1999e).

[18] Various FRY sources routinely put out news reports of civilian damage and deaths attributable to the NATO air campaign. See, for example, Belgrade Tanjug (1999a, 1999b, 1999c), Yugoslav Army Supreme Command Headquarters (1999a, 1999b), Belgrade Radio Beograd Network (1999c), and Belgrade BETA (1999).

[19] For example, a day after the attacks on the convoys near Djakovica, the FRY government sponsored a media tour of the convoy area to the east-southeast of Djakovica. (See NATO, 1999g.)

genocide and targeting of Kosovar civilians in their homes.[20] President Clinton and his key aides also argued that it was unrealistic to expect that the sort of war the coalition was fighting, against an adversary that intentionally placed civilians at risk, could ever be fought without civilian casualties (see Clinton, 1999 and Berger, 1999). At the end of the day, however, NATO reported that "the actual toll in human lives will never be precisely known" (DeYoung, 2002).

The Arc of Media and Public Concern

U.S. Media and Public Opinion Responses

U.S. Media. Figure 3.1 reports a major increase in television and newspaper reporting on Kosovo from January 1999 until it peaked in April, when reporting levels declined. Major television reporting showed a second bump in June, when Milosevic acceded to NATO's demands and the conflict ended.[21]

Figure 3.2 reports the content of television news reporting during the war in Kosovo, as tabulated by the Center for Media and Public Affairs (CMPA). The figure shows that reporting on collateral damage was the sixth-ranked topic, just after reporting on Serbian ethnic cleansing and just before reporting on U.S. prisoners of war.

When CNN's reporting on civilian casualties is broken out by day and related to some of the more prominent incidents of civilian deaths in the war in Kosovo (Figure 3.3), the reporting appears to peak at the time of high-profile incidents of civilian deaths and fall off during other periods, providing some validation that the search terms actually are measuring reporting on civilian casualty incidents.

U.S. Public Opinion. Figure 3.4 shows that the percentage of Americans who were following Kosovo very or somewhat closely grew

---

[20] Among other sources, see North Atlantic Treaty Organization (1999a, 1999b, 1999g), UK Ministry of Defence (1999), Clinton (1999), DoD (1999e), and Hamre (1999).

[21] Although declines in reporting were evident even before the incident, the shootings at Columbine High School in Littleton, Colorado, on April 20 contributed to the drop in coverage of Kosovo from April to May.

Figure 3.1
Major News Reporting on Kosovo, January–July 1999

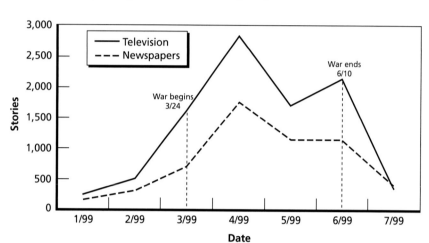

SOURCE: Search for "Kosovo" in *The Christian Science Monitor, Los Angeles Times, The New York Times, The Wall Street Journal, The Washington Post,* ABC News, CBS News, CNN, and NBC News.
RAND *MG441-3.1*

from about four in ten in February to about three out of four once the air campaign began in late March, and remained in the 70–80-percent range until the end of the war.[22] There is, however, some evidence that by mid-May, many Americans were becoming fatigued by the high reporting levels on the war and that both attention to and support for the war were flagging by that time.[23]

Although support for the various military options changed over time,[24] support for the air war and peacekeeping operations in Kosovo was substantially—and consistently—higher than support for peace

---

[22] The peak in attention to Kosovo as measured by this series was April 21–22, when 80 percent said they were following events in Kosovo very or somewhat closely.

[23] See for example, Pew Research Center for the People and the Press (1999).

[24] A running record of Gallup's analyses of changing public attitudes on the U.S. intervention in Kosovo can be found in Saad (1999), Gillespie (1999a, 1999b, 1999c), and Newport (1999a, 1999b, 1999c, 1999d, 1999e, 1999f, 1999g).

Figure 3.2
Number of Television News Stories by War Topic

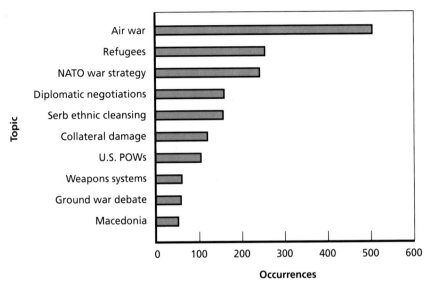

SOURCE: Center for Media and Public Affairs (1999).

RAND *MG441-3.2*

enforcement or combat operations (see Table 3.1).[25] (More broadly, this suggests that it is important for scholars who analyze marginals to understand the factors in support and opposition for military operations to differentiate more finely between types of military operations in coding the public opinion questions.)

A paired comparison of 20 questions that asked about support for air and ground options in the same poll produced results comparable to those in the table: Support for air options was anywhere from 7 to

---

[25] To construct the table, we calculated the average support in questions that asked about the air war, peacekeeping, peace enforcement, and ground combat in each month of the war. Questions were coded as being about the air war if they asked about approval for the air war or bombing; peacekeeping if they used the term "peacekeeping" or indicated that the question had in mind introducing U.S. troops following the establishment of a peace; peace enforcement if the question suggested that U.S. troops would be used to force the combatants to a peace agreement; and ground combat if the questions suggested that ground troops would be used in combat operations.

Figure 3.3
CNN Daily Reporting on Civilian Casualties and Collateral Damage

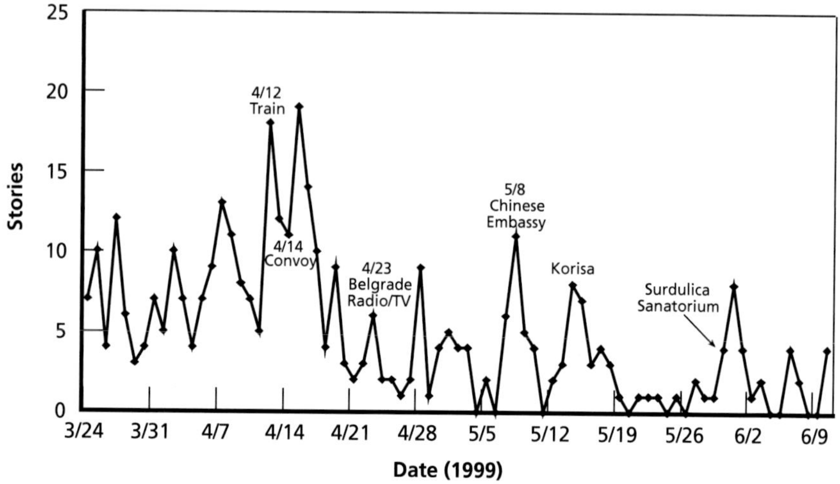

SOURCE: Search for "Kosovo" and "civilian casualties," "civilian deaths," civilians killed," or "collateral damage" on CNN.

RAND MG441-3.3

16 percentage points higher than that for ground options.[26] This generally reflected an aversion on the part of the public to placing U.S. troops in a combat situation that involves only secondary interests. (See Larson and Savych, 2005a, 2005b.)

Table 3.1 shows that support for the air war climbed in April and then fell back again, probably as a result of growing elite criticism of the air campaign in April, even before the high-profile incidents of collateral damage,[27] or possibly the result of a growing fear that an air war alone might not force Milosevic's capitulation, and

---

[26] Three questions were from ABC News/*The Washington Post*'s polling on the matter, five were from Gallup, and two were from PSRA.

[27] Growing bipartisan opposition to the war in Kosovo also may have contributed to declining support. For example, on April 20, Senators Joseph Biden and John McCain introduced a resolution that effectively declared a lack of confidence in the President's approach, and on April 28, the House voted to deny any use of U.S. funds to send ground troops to Kosovo; the House also refused to approve a measure approving of the bombing campaign. Data from the Center for Media and Public Affairs suggest that generally positive elite commentary car-

Figure 3.4
How Closely Was the Public Following Kosovo?

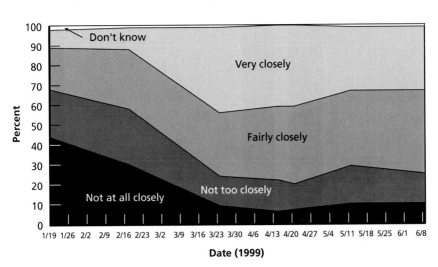

SOURCE: Pew Research Center/PSRA.

RAND MG441-3.4

that ground combat operations might therefore be needed. Support for the use of U.S. ground troops in peacekeeping and peace enforcement show the same basic pattern over time, although only the former was typically supported by a majority; support for using U.S. troops in a ground combat role showed a steep decline from April to May and remained below three in ten in May and June.

As might be inferred from this result, more Americans were concerned about U.S. military casualties than any of several other considerations, followed by the somewhat related possibility that U.S. troops could be in Kosovo for a long time. Figure 3.5 also shows that there was greater concern about innocent Kosovars being killed by the U.S.-NATO air strikes than Serb civilians being killed: Fifty percent were very concerned about the former, while only 37–40 percent were concerned about the latter.

---

ried by television news became extremely negative shortly after the bombing of the Chinese embassy.

Figure 3.5 shows that concern about civilian deaths—"innocent people" or "Serb civilians" being killed—were the second or third-ranked concerns in polling by Pew in mid-April and mid-May.

Finally, it is worth noting that although most were generally aware that civilians had been killed in the NATO bombing, Americans appeared to have had great difficulties estimating the actual number of civilian deaths (Table 3.2). Nearly four in ten said that they were incapable of estimating numbers, while those who ventured a guess cited numbers that were well below the 200 or so deaths that one might have surmised had occurred from press reporting up until that time.

Statistical Results. To understand the importance of civilian casualties and collateral damage in support for Kosovo when controlling for other factors that are predictors of support and opposition for U.S. military operations, we analyzed a respondent-level data set from

Figure 3.5
Americans' Concern About Various Costs in Kosovo, March–May 1999

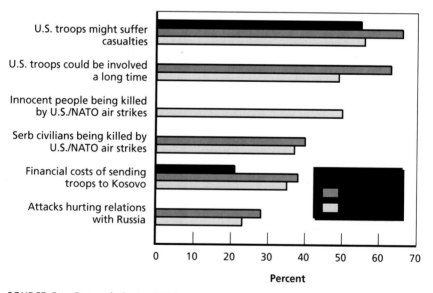

SOURCE: Pew Research Center/PRSA.
NOTE: Question read, "How worried are you (INSERT ITEM; ROTATE ITEMS) very worried, somewhat worried, not too worried, or not at all worried?"
RAND MG441-3.5

Table 3.2
Knowledge or Estimates of Civilian Casualties in Kosovo

Survey	Percent
As far as you know has the NATO bombing resulted in the killing of any civilians in Yugoslavia?	
Yes	80
No	9
No opinion	11
From what you've heard or read, about how many civilians have been killed?	
No casualties	20
50 or fewer	14
51–100	15
101 to 200	7
201 to 500	4
500 or more	1
Don't know, can't estimate casualties	39

SOURCE: Gallup poll conducted May 7, 1999–May 9, 1999, N = 1,025.

polling in May 1999 conducted by PSRA for the Pew Research Center that included these variables, as well as variables for civilian casualties. The poll that we analyzed had questions that could be used to populate a full model that predicted respondents' support or opposition from beliefs about the stakes, prospects, U.S. casualties, political party, race, and gender, as well as questions about civilian deaths. This model enabled us to estimate the importance of collateral damage while controlling for these other influences.

Based on our aggregate-level analyses, reported above, we expected that consideration of civilian casualties might have been an important factor in the May poll, which was conducted after the Chinese embassy incident, and during a time when elite commentary and media reporting seem to have turned against the operation. As a result, we expected that concern about civilian casualties would be a relatively salient concern. Our statistical modeling did not confirm these expectations.

Using probit regression modeling, we were able to predict approval or disapproval for the war correctly for 70 percent of the respondents based upon beliefs about the stakes, prospects for success, military casualties, party, and several other individual-level characteristics. The most important predictors of support were, in declining order of importance (valence of the coefficients in parentheses),

- beliefs about the importance of the moral stakes (+)
- beliefs about the prospects for success (+)
- U.S. military casualties (−)
- self-identified party (self-identification as a Republican [−], or as an Independent [−])
- race (−).

By comparison, our civilian casualties variable was neither a substantively nor statistically significant predictor of support and opposition to the war. Thus, both on the basis of the small coefficient values and the failure to attain statistical significance in the multivariate model, we judge that concern about civilian casualties did not much influence support and opposition to the war. Put another way, concern about civilian casualties a week after the bombing of the Chinese embassy was not an important predictor of support or opposition for the military campaign, when one would have expected the issues of collateral damage and civilian casualties to be highly salient. Instead, beliefs about the moral stakes and prospects for the campaign were the most important predictors of approval for the campaign.

We did, however, find other evidence of a bivariate relationship between support for the war and the belief that the United States and its allies were being sufficiently careful to avoid civilian casualties in two polls, each of which was conducted shortly after a high-profile incident involving civilian casualties, and the results of which are reported in Tables 3.3 and 3.4.

Table 3.3 reports the cross-tabulation of results from a late April 1999 poll by ABC News and *The Washington Post*, conducted a couple of weeks after the Djakovica convoy incident.

Table 3.3
Cross-Tabulation of the Approval of the Campaign in Kosovo and Beliefs
About Effort of the United States in Avoiding Civilian Casualties, April 1999

Q3. "Do you support or oppose the United States and its European allies conducting air strikes against Serbia?" Q6. "As you may know, some civilians have been killed in the air strikes against Serbia by the United States and its European allies. Do you think that the United States and its European allies are not being careful enough to avoid civilian casualties, or do you think these are just unavoidable accidents of war?"	Support (%)	Oppose (%)	N
Unavoidable accidents of war	71	26	593
Not being careful enough	44	51	140
Don't know/refused	48	16	23
Total	65	30	756

SOURCE: ABC/The Washington Post (April 25–26, 1999). Data set: ABC News "Nightline" Kosovo Poll #2, April 1999 (computer file), ICPSR version, Horsham, Pa.: Chilton Research Services (producer), 1999; Ann Arbor, Mich.: Inter-University Consortium for Political and Social Research (distributor), 1999.

NOTE: $p < 0.001$ in a Chi-square test of independence.

Table 3.3 shows that 71 percent of those who believed that civilian casualty incidents were unavoidable accidents of war supported the war, while only 26 percent opposed. By comparison, only 44 percent of those who thought the United States was not being careful enough supported the war, with 51 percent opposing. Moreover, the result of the Chi-square test suggests that the relationship between support and beliefs about whether the United States and its allies were being careful enough was statistically significant at the 0.001 level.

Table 3.4 presents a similar result from a poll by ABC News and *The Washington Post* on May 16, 1999, about a week after the Chinese embassy incident. The table shows that support and opposition were again closely associated with beliefs about whether the United States and its allies were being careful enough in avoiding civilian deaths, and this relationship was statistically significant. Thus, there is at least bivariate evidence suggesting that the linkage between support and opposition on the one hand and beliefs about civilian casualties on the other lies not in a respondent's level of concern about civilian

Table 3.4
Cross-Tabulation of the Approval of the Campaign in Kosovo and Beliefs
About Effort of the United States in Avoiding Civilian Casualties, May 1999

Q3. "Do you support or oppose the United States and its European allies conducting air strikes against Serbia?" Q9. "As you may know, some civilians have been killed in the air strikes against Serbia, and recently the NATO allies bombed the Chinese consulate in Serbia's capital. Do you think that the United States and its European allies are not being careful enough to avoid civilian casualties, or do you think these are just unavoidable accidents of war?"	Support (%)	Oppose (%)	N
Unavoidable accidents of war	68	30	496
Not being careful enough	43	56	240
Don't know/refused	27	37	16
Total	59	38	751

SOURCE: ABC/The Washington Post (May 16, 1999). Data set: ABC News/The Washington Post Kosovo Poll, May 1999 (computer file), ICPSR version, Horsham, Pa.: Chilton Research Services (producer), 1999; Ann Arbor, Mich.: Inter-University Consortium for Political and Social Research (distributor), 1999.
NOTE: $p < 0.001$ in a Chi-square test of independence.

casualties, but in his or her beliefs about whether the United States and its coalition are trying hard enough to avoid civilian deaths.

This result reinforces the finding from the multivariate model-ing of Americans' support for the Gulf War that the principal link-age between civilian casualties and Americans' support for a military operations is not concern about casualties, but rather the belief that the U.S. military is making every effort to avoid them.

Antiwar Demonstrations. Press reporting suggests that there was a fair amount of antiwar protest activity in New York City. On March 24, about 200 antiwar and Serb protesters demonstrated at Grand Central Station at rush hour to protest the air war, and on March 27, about 2,000 antiwar and Serb demonstrators marched from Grand Central Station to Union Square. (See United Press International, 1999a, 1999b.) Reporting on other antiwar demonstrations was very difficult to find.

Foreign Media and Public Opinion

Foreign Media. If the foreign news sources reported in Figure 3.6 are any indication, foreign (and especially European audiences) also were exposed to a significant amount of news reporting on Kosovo. The figure shows that the somewhat selective foreign news sources detailed in the figure peaked in April, the first full month of the war, and again in June when a peace settlement was reached, and then declined.

Foreign Public Opinion. We now summarize the public opinion data we found on European and Chinese attitudes toward the war.[28]

Tables 3.5 and 3.6 show that majorities of British, Germans, and, to a lesser extent, French, initially supported the war in Kosovo; some even argued that there was a bit of a "rally" in Europeans' support for the war at this time ("Not by Bombs Alone," 1999).

Figure 3.6
Selected Foreign Media Reporting on Kosovo, January–December 1999

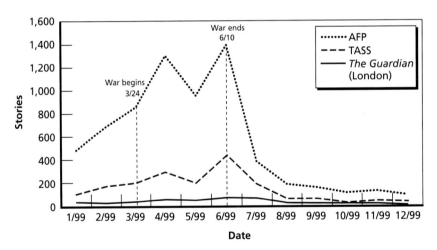

SOURCE: Search for "Kosovo" in AFP, *The Guardian* (London), and TASS.

RAND *MG441-3.6*

---

[28] As will be seen, support for the war varied greatly across the polls. This could be due to ambivalence or uncrystallized attitudes toward the war, differences in question wording, or other factors.

Table 3.5
U.S. and European Opinion on the War, March–April 1999

Population	% Support Air Strikes		% Support Ground Troops	
	First Poll	Second Poll	First Poll	Second Poll
United States	51	58	33	46
Britain	69	75	51	66
Germany	57	63	N/A	28
France	40	50	N/A	68
Italy	25	37	N/A	N/A

SOURCE: "Not by Bombs Alone" (1999), citing the following data sources and poll dates: U.S.: *The New York Times*/CBS (March 28 and April 6); Britain: Marplan (March 26 and April 2); Germany: ISIP (March 24 and April 1); France: CSA (March 27 and April 7); Italy: Forsa (March 24 and March 31).

And like their American cousins, Europeans were far less enthused about using ground troops than conducting an air war, probably due to the desire to avoid casualties; only a minority of Italians initially supported the war.

Another poll, conducted by the Angus Reid Group from late March through mid-April, found roughly comparable results: Majorities in most European countries supported the war in Kosovo (see Table 3.6). The table shows that clear majorities in 10 of the 16 countries polled approved of the war, two (Finland and Hungary) were on the fence, and clear majorities in four nations clearly opposed the war.

Finally, the March–April poll by the Angus Reid Group found substantial support for greater European independence on defense matters among Italians, French, Russians, Slovaks, and Ukrainians, but strong opposition among Germans, Danes, Norwegians, and Britons (Table 3.7).[29]

---

[29] It is not clear what lasting impact Kosovo might have had. According to polling by the U.S. Information Agency, the belief that NATO was essential rose by eight points between the spring and late fall of 1999 in Italy, fell in Great Britain by 14 points, and remained constant in Germany and France. See the data provided in Eichenberg (2003b, pp. 651–654).

Table 3.6
Support for War in Kosovo in 16 Countries, March–April 1999

Country	% Supporting
Croatia	82
Denmark	74
United States	68
Great Britain	68
Canada	68
Norway	64
Germany	57
France	54
Poland	54
Finland	50
Hungary	48
Italy	47
	% Opposing
Russia	94
Ukraine	89
Slovak Republic	75
Czech Republic	57

SOURCE: Dupin (1999), detailing polling conducted from March 25 to April 17, 1999, by the Angus Reid Group for *The Economist*. Sample size was 500 in each of 17 nations polled except Russia, where only urban population was polled. Exact question wording not provided.

According to polling by Ipsos/Sofres in early April (Table 3.8), while majorities in the United Kingdom, France, Germany, and Italy supported the war, fewer than half of Belgians, Portuguese, Spanish, and Greek citizens did so.

Table 3.7
Support for European Defense Independent of NATO, March–April 1999

Country	% Supporting
Italy	58
France	57
Russia	57
Slovak Republic	55
Ukraine	55
	% Opposing
Germany	71
Denmark	68
Norway	62
Britain	57

SOURCE: Dupin (1999), detailing polling conducted from March 25 to April 17, 1999, by the Angus Reid Group for *The Economist*. Sample size was 500 in each of 17 nations polled except Russia, where only urban population was polled. Exact question wording not provided.

Finally, a poll by the Angus Reid Group in late April (Table 3.9) showed support for the use of ground troops in only two nations (France and the United Kingdom), and strong opposition to the prospect of using ground troops among Italians and Germans. This result suggests that, with few exceptions, Europeans generally were no more enthusiastic than Americans about the possibility of using ground troops in a combat role in Kosovo.

Because of differences in question wording, polling organization, and other features, it is impossible to characterize any additional European-wide public opinion trends from this patchwork of results.

Polling of the British public by ICM Research for *The Guardian* newspaper (Figure 3.7) (see Little, 1999; Travis, 1999; Aitkenhead, 1999; Clarke, 1999; ICM Research, 1999),[30] and polling of the French public by Brulé Ville et Associé (BVA) (Figure 3.8) ("French

---

[30] ICM/*The Guardian* Poll, April 16–17, 1999, N = 1,205.

Table 3.8
European Support for the War in Kosovo in Early April 1999

Do you personally approve or disapprove of the NATO military intervention in Yugoslavia?	Approve (%)	Disapprove (%)	No Opinion (%)
Europe	53	41	6
United Kingdom	67	29	4
France	62	32	6
Germany	54	44	2
Italy	51	40	9
Belgium	42	45	13
Portugal	41	51	8
Spain	39	49	12
Greece	2	97	1

SOURCE: Ipsos/Sofres (1999).

NOTE: Country sample sizes as follows: Germany (949), Belgium (502), Spain (929), France (936), Greece (952), Italy (960), Portugal (572), United Kingdom (917). Polling dates not specified.

Table 3.9
European and U.S. Support for the War in Kosovo in Late April 1999

Now, if there's no settlement to end the war in Kosovo, would you support or oppose NATO sending ground troops in to fight against Yugoslav forces?	Approve (%)	Disapprove (%)	Don't Know/ Not Sure (%)
Europe	42	48	10
France	55	32	13
United Kingdom	54	30	15
Italy	33	63	3
Germany	27	63	9

SOURCE: Angus Reid Group (1999).

NOTE: Country sample sizes were 300 in all nations except Germany, which had a sample size of 476. Polling was conducted between April 22 and 25, 1999.

Figure 3.7
Polling on Kosovo by ICM for *The Guardian* Newspaper, March–April 1999

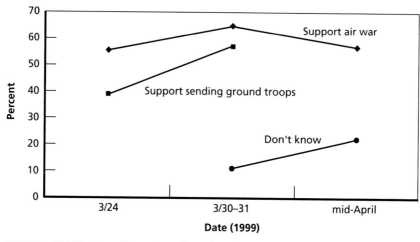

SOURCE: ICM/*The Guardian* poll conducted April 16–17, 1999, N = 1,205.
NOTE: Question wording unavailable.

RAND *MG441-3.7*

People's Warlike Spirit Flagging in Third Month of War," 1999), both suggested an initial increase in support for the war, followed by a decline. It is not at all clear how common this pattern may have been in other NATO publics (Travis, 1999).

For their part, polls taken in Russia and China in late March showed heavy opposition to NATO action.

For example, a late March poll by the Center for International Sociological and Marketing Research found that 97 percent of Russians polled had a negative attitude toward a NATO military solution to the Kosovo problem, and 91 percent sympathized with the Serbs, 3 percent with the Kosovar Albanians, and 4 percent with neither side. Ninety-three percent said that if the NATO bombing continued, Russia should break off relations with NATO, and 74 percent supported supplying Yugoslavia with missile launchers (Surovtseva, 1999).

Figure 3.8
French Support for Participation in NATO Intervention,
Late March–Mid-May 1999

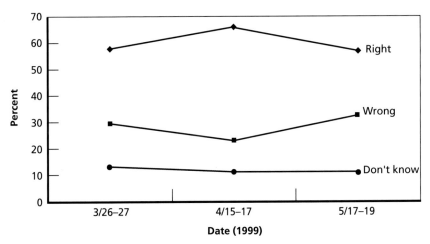

SOURCE: "French People's Warlike Spirit Flagging in Third Month of War" (1999).
NOTE: Question read, "Do you personally believe France was right or wrong to join in NATO air strikes on Kosovo and Serbia?"
RAND *MG441-3.8*

Polling of China's five biggest cities in late March by the Social Survey Institute of China similarly revealed strong Chinese opposition to the war even before the Chinese embassy incident:

- More than 71 percent were seriously concerned about the air strikes, while 44 percent identified the war as the first thing they read about in newspapers.
- Nearly 70 percent agreed that the United States was engaged in "sabre-rattling in its role as an international policeman" and is "hegemonism-motivated" in its dealings with Yugoslavia.
- More than 60 percent expressed satisfaction with the Chinese government's position against the U.S. and NATO air strikes.[31]

---

[31] Jingen (1999). One obviously needs to use more than the usual amount of caution in assessing public opinion polling from a non-democracy such as China.

Antiwar Demonstrations. Antiwar demonstrations were observed in a great many countries, including the United Kingdom, France, Germany, Canada, Belgium, Spain, Portugal, Russia, China (especially after the Chinese embassy bombing), Austria, Hungary, Sweden, the Czech Republic, Macedonia, Greece, Cyprus, Bosnia, Romania, Italy, The Philippines, Taiwan, and Sri Lanka. Particularly notable were demonstrations by Serbs who had emigrated abroad; Serbs in Johannesburg and Warsaw protested, for example ("RSA Serbian Demonstrators in Johannesburg Burn U.S. Flag," 1999), and France banned Serb demonstrations in Paris (AFP, 1999a).

We now turn to an examination of two of the most widely reported collateral damage incidents that occurred during the war in Kosovo: the April 14 bombing of two convoys outside Djakovica and the May 8 bombing of the Chinese embassy.

The April 14 Convoy Attacks Outside Djakovica

On April 14, NATO aircraft attacked convoys near Djakovica at two separate locations, one to the north, and one to the east-southeast.

The first attack, occurring at about 11:10 Greenwich Mean Time (GMT) on the Djakovica-Decane road northwest of Djakovica, involved two NATO F-16 aircraft, each dropping a single GBU-12 laser-guided bomb. The first F-16 observed three military vehicles that appeared to be involved in burning Kosovar houses as they moved southeast toward Djakovica and saw these vehicles join additional vehicles heading in a southeasterly direction. The F-16 attacked one of the military vehicles at the front of the convoy with a single GBU-12 500-lb laser-guided bomb close to a c-shaped building complex.[32] The video of this attack showed the bomb directly hitting the targeted vehicle, and a Predator unmanned aerial vehicle (UAV) imaged the attack site, and showed that the vehicle had been damaged and others had gathered around the damaged vehicle (NATO, 1999g). The second F-16 dropped a second

---

[32] A tape of the pilot describing the incident was played in NATO's April 15, 1999, daily press briefing.

GBU-12 on what appeared to the pilot to be a number of large military vehicles in the courtyard of the c-shaped complex at about 11:48 GMT, which set off a secondary explosion, possibly an accelerant such as gasoline that may have been present in the structure. That same day, on April 14, Serb television broadcast footage of the aftermath of the incident showing a number of destroyed tractors. It is unclear how many civilian deaths occurred in this incident.[33]

The second attack involved seven NATO aircraft expending a total of at least eight GBU-12s in four separate attacks on the lead elements of a second convoy beginning at about 12:19 GMT. This convoy, involving about 100 vehicles traveling east-southeast on the Djakovica-Prizren road, was very large and covered several kilometers. The first 20 or so vehicles, which were uniform in shape and color as seen from the air and maintaining a set spacing and pace that suggested a military movement, were believed to be military vehicles;[34] the convoy's status as a military convoy was confirmed by the Airborne Battlefield Command and Control Center (ABCCC) aircraft,[35] and one of the attacking aircraft was reported to have been fired upon by large-caliber antiaircraft artillery. An OA-10 brought in to verify the target observed military vehicles in the convoy, but others that might have been civilian vehicles also were present, whereupon the attacks were halted at about 13:20 GMT. Although this did not become clear for a number of days, most of the lives that were lost—and most of the media interest—was related to the attacks on this second convoy.

Table 3.10 provides the timeline of press and official reactions to the incident.

The timeline suggests that media reporting on the incident began about an hour after the incident ended:

---

[33] A witness interviewed by HRW estimated that 14 people in his tractor were killed (Human Rights Watch, 2000, Appendix A, Incident Number 19).

[34] According to one of HRW's (2000, Appendix A) interviewees, "[w]hen the aircraft were in the sky then the military vehicles mixed with the column. . . . No military vehicles were damaged. After the bombing, they [Serb forces] went into the hills."

[35] The ABCCC reported that it had received confirmation from intelligence or operational sources that the convoy was an Army of the Federal Republic of Yugoslavia military convoy and, therefore, a military target.

- AFP (1999b) broke the story at 1428 GMT (0928 Eastern Time [ET]).
- Belgrade Radio B92 (1999) reported the story at 1000 ET.
- Deutsche Presse-Agentur (1999a) broadcast a report at 1045 ET.
- Associated Press Worldstream picked up the story at 1135 ET.
- CNN picked up the report at 1201 ET (CNN, 1999b), ran the story several times thereafter, and provided live coverage of DoD's daily briefing that day.
- The ABC, CBS, and CNN evening news programs all led with the story, and ABC's *Nightline* program focused on the story as well.

The incident occurred too late in the day for it to be included in the April 14 NATO briefing on Operation Allied Force. Jamie Shea, NATO's spokesperson, first described the incident as follows in his April 15 daily briefing:

> I would like to comment first on yesterday's incident. NATO deeply regrets the loss of life to civilians from the attack yesterday on a convoy traveling between Prizren and Dakovica. As you all know, NATO pilots have orders to strike only at military targets. We have taken every possible precaution to avoid causing harm to civilians. Our Operation Allied Force was launched to save civilian lives, not to expend them. There has never been a military operation in history in which so many stringent measures have been taken to minimize harm to civilian lives and civilian property. We are using more precision-guided munitions than in any previous operation.
>
> Yesterday a NATO pilot was operating over western Kosovo. He saw many villages being burned. This is an area where the Yugoslav Special Police Forces, the MUP [Ministarstvo Unutrasnih Poslova], have been conducting ethnic cleansing operations in recent days. The 5,000 refugees that have arrived in Albania in the last 48 hours testify to that fact. The road between Prizren and Dakovica is an important resupply

Table 3.10
Postincident Timeline for Djakovica Convoy Incident

Media Reporting Highlights	Official Handling Highlights
4/14	**4/14**
0610: Incident begins.	0900: NATO gives daily briefing.
0820: Incident ends.	1435: DoD gives daily briefing, which
0928: AFP reports from scene.	airs on CNN.
1000: Belgrade Radio airs B91 story.	1640: Briefing by White House press
1045: Deutsche-Press Agentur reports.	secretary Joseph Lockhart.
1135: AP breaks story.	
1201: CNN breaks story.	
1436: CNN airs DoD briefing live.	
1700: *CNN Evening News* airs.	
1730: *ABC Evening News*, *CBS Evening News*, and *NBC Evening News* air.	
2337: ABC News *Nightline* airs.	
	4/15
	FRY media tour takes place.
	0900: NATO gives daily briefing.
	0949: Secretary of Defense William S. Cohen and Chairman of the Joint Chiefs of Staff Henry H. Shelton testify before the Senate Armed Services Committee; testimony airs on CNN
	1500: President Clinton gives address on Kosovo, which airs on CNN
	DoD gives daily briefing.
	4/16
	0900: NATO gives daily briefing.
	1430: DoD gives daily briefing.
	4/17
	0900: NATO gives daily briefing.
	1300: DoD gives daily briefing.
	4/19
	0900: NATO gives daily briefing.
	1000: Brigadier General Leaf gives briefing, which airs on CNN.
	1405: DoD gives daily briefing.

SOURCES: AFP (1999b), Belgrade Radio B92 (1999), Deutsche Presse-Agentur (1999a), CNN (1999a, 1999b), CBS News (1999), NBC News (1999), ABC News (1999a, 1999b), DoD (1999a, 1999b, 1999c, 1999d), U.S. Senate, Armed Services Committee (1999), White House (1999a, 1999b).

NOTE: All times Eastern.

and reinforcement route for the Yugoslav Army and the Special Police. The pilot attacked what he believed to be military vehicles in a convoy. He was convinced he had the right target. He dropped his bomb in good faith, as you would expect a trained pilot from a democratic NATO country to do. The pilot reported at the time that he was attacking a military convoy. The NATO bomb destroyed the lead vehicle, which we now believe to have been a civilian vehicle.

I again stress, NATO deeply regrets the loss of life from this tragic accident. But I also want to stress that no conflict in human history has ever been accident-free, or will ever be. We can reduce the risk of accidents but we cannot eliminate them altogether. (NATO, 1999e)

Several sources of confusion surrounded these incidents:

- First, although Shea was apologizing for an incident that took place on the road between Prizren and Djakovica, to the east-southeast of Djakovica, NATO's own map showed a strike to the northwest of Djakovica. It would, furthermore, later be determined that the description of the incident—a pilot dropping a single bomb on a military convoy—was part of the incident to the northwest of Djakovica, but not the one on the Prizren-Djakovica road.
- Second, multiple attacks on convoys had taken place that day, and for several days it was not clear that in fact two different convoys had been involved in separate incidents. In fact, for several days, NATO spokesman Shea reported that there was no information on Serb claims that a second attack was made on a convoy on the road to Prizren (Dovkants, 1999).
- On April 15, stating, "I cannot explain the NATO rendition" of the facts of the incident, Pentagon spokesman Ken Bacon contradicted NATO by stating that rather than one, in fact two attacks were made by NATO warplanes, and that neither of these attacks had been carried out by the American pilot whose description of the incident was played during NATO's daily press briefing that day (Williams, 1999).

- Accordingly, reporters (and others) had great difficulty correlating NATO's descriptions of the attacks with the footage being shown on Serbian television, because two different incidents were involved. On April 14, Serb television broadcast footage of the first incident, and the next day sponsored a media tour of the second convoy attack site.
- Additional confusion arose from the use of the audiotape in the April 15 briefing that was later determined to be unrelated to the second incident, which took place east-southeast of Djakovica and caused most of the civilian deaths that were of greatest interest.[36] The initial reports also suggested that a single F-16 had been involved, which also later proved to be incorrect. Two aircraft were involved in the first incident, while the second incident (which resulted in most of the deaths) involved more aircraft.
- Further confusion arose as a result of reports from witnesses that the second refugee column, which was east-southeast of Djakovica, had been attacked by Serb forces at the same time as the NATO attack.[37] Some reporters who were taken to the scene of the incident seemed to confirm this: They reported that some of the victims looked like they had been killed by machine guns and mortars rather than bombs.[38] Reporters taken to the scene of the second attack counted only about two dozen bodies, rather than the nearly 75 claimed by Serbia, which further muddied matters.

---

[36] The tape seems to have been of one of the pilots involved in the first incident.

[37] As Brigadier General Leaf described it, "In essence, this reported claim states after NATO aircraft attacked the front military vehicles, Serb aircraft attacked Kosovar Albanian refugees in the rear." In what appears to have been a separate incident, refugees arriving in Albania from Kosovo on April 14 reported that Serbian helicopters had attacked them, killing at least 40 people and wounding many others (see BBC News, 1999b).

[38] Dovkants (1999). Lambeth (2001, pp. 137–138) reported that

> [i]n the case of the Djakovica incident . . . , there were initial reports that Yugoslav aircraft had intentionally attacked the civilian tractors and wagons near Prizren. Those reports ultimately proved groundless, although Pentagon officials did confirm that the Yugoslav air force was still operating low-flying Galeb ground-attack jets and attack helicopters.

- Reporting that asserted that cluster bombs may have been used in the attacks also may have cast doubt on NATO's claims that GBU-12s with unitary warheads had been used (Watson, 1999).
- Lastly, the Serbs broadcast a tape that allegedly was of a conversation between a radar controller in an airborne warning and control system (AWACS) and the F-16 pilot who bombed one of the refugee convoys that NATO said had been remixed and in the end was completely fabricated (AFP, 1999c).[39]
- Finally, some missed opportunities to avoid the incident also were identified:
  - A Royal Air Force (RAF) GR-7 Harrier aircraft had radioed an ABCCC aircraft that the convoy included civilians minutes before it was attacked.[40] That the warning had never reached the aircraft responsible for bombing the convoy was a less-than-satisfactory explanation.[41]
  - An OA-10 forward air controller aircraft that had been sent to verify further the identity of the second convoy after the attacks had begun reported that, while there were military vehicles in the convoy, there could be civilians among them.[42]

While Brigadier General Leaf's April 19 detailed briefing on the incident received favorable coverage from many press sources, these facts, coupled with NATO's and the United States' apparently shifting explanations of the incident fostered doubts about credibility, at least in

---

[39] *Vecernje Novosti,* a Serb newspaper, claimed that the United States had decided to kill ethnic Albanian refugees and blame their deaths on the Serbs. The Serbs also claimed that Defense Secretary Cohen ordered NATO commander General Wesley Clark to choose personally a Dutch pilot to attack the convoy, and that President Clinton wanted to dismiss General Clark when the pilot failed to kill the refugees in sufficient secrecy. (See Erlanger, 1999.)

[40] See the questions to Major General Charles F. Wald, USAF (DoD, 1999d).

[41] See, for example, Walker and Norton-Taylor (1999).

[42] As Brigadier General Leaf put it, "witnesses believed that the Serbs used the convoy as a human shield, positioning some of their military vehicles and police vehicles at the front of the column" (NATO, 1999g).

some quarters of the media, and even Brigadier General Leaf's presentation failed to answer a number of important questions.[43]

In any event, as a result of criticism of the public affairs handling of this incident, UK Prime Minister Tony Blair's Press Secretary Alistair Campbell was called to NATO's Brussels headquarters to advise NATO on its public affairs strategy for the war.

U.S. Media and Public Opinion Responses

U.S. Media. From a quantitative viewpoint, as shown in Figure 3.9, television network news reporting on Kosovo generally declined after early April, but rose again following the April 12 incident involving a train crossing a bridge and the April 14 convoy incident.

From a qualitative viewpoint, the scale of the civilian losses and the graphic imagery of the aftermath of the convoy incident spurred major U.S. media to focus on several aspects of the story: the incident and the losses (see Michael Dobbs and Vick, 1999; and Gordon, 1999); U.S. and FRY efforts to implicate the other in the incident (Robbins, 1999); the confused explanations emanating from NATO and the Pentagon (Bradley Graham, 1999); the growing list of civilian casualty incidents in the war (Scarborough, 1999); and the possibility that the incident would erode the coalition's moral authority for conducting the war (Havemann, 1999). However, it is not clear that this reporting much affected American and European attitudes toward the war.

U.S. Public Opinion. The comparison of data on Americans' attention to Kosovo over time presented in Table 3.11 suggests that the April 14 convoy incident did not result in increased attention to the conflict in Kosovo. In fact, the data suggest that the percentage who were following Kosovo remained quite stable through April.

---

[43] See, for example, O'Donnell (1999), Evans (1999), Castle (1999), and CNN (1999d). *The Boston Globe* reported that "[y]esterday's appearance by Leaf, meanwhile, created as many questions as it answered" (Cullen, 1999).

Figure 3.9
U.S. Reporting on Civilian Casualties, Convoy Incident

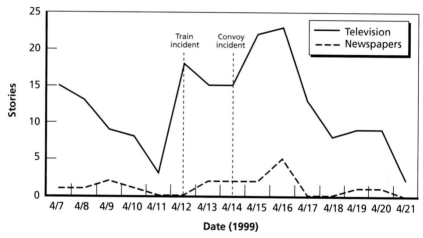

SOURCE: Search for "Kosovo" and "civilian casualties," "civilian deaths," or "collateral damage" in *The Christian Science Monitor, Los Angeles Times, The New York Times, The Wall Street Journal, The Washington Post,* ABC News, CBS News, CNN, and NBC News.

RAND *MG441-3.9*

Table 3.11
Attention Paid to Kosovo Before, During, and After Convoy Incident

Overall, how closely have you followed the situation in Kosovo—very closely, somewhat closely, not too closely, or not at all?	Survey: 4/6– 7/1999 (%)	Survey: 4/13– 14/1999 (%)	Survey: 4/26– 27/1999 (%)
Very closely	35	34	34
Fairly closely	49	50	48
Not too closely	12	13	14
Not at all closely	4	3	3
Don't know/refused	*	*	1

SOURCE: Gallup/CNN/*USA Today* polls conducted April 6–7, 1999, N = 1,055; April 13–14, 1999, N = 1,069; April 26–27, 1999, N = 1,073.

A comparison of public opinion polling before and immediately after the incident is somewhat inconclusive on the question of how the incident might have affected approval for the war (see Table 3.12); of four comparisons, three suggested a decline, though only one of these was statistically significant, while the fourth result showed a modest (albeit not statistically significant) increase in approval.

And Table 3.13 shows that far more respondents in polling just after the convoy incident were interested in the welfare of three captured U.S. servicemen than that of Kosovar or Serb civilians, and more were concerned about the fate of refugees and other victims in Kosovo than Serb civilians. Fewer than one in four mentioned air attacks and damage in Serbia as stories or images that had caught the respondent's attention, suggesting that the issue of civilian casualties was salient to fewer than one in four.

Table 3.12
Approval of War Before and After the Convoy Incident

Survey	Before	After	Change
Pew Research Center/PSRA: "Do you approve or disapprove of NATO forces, including the United States conducting air strikes against Serbia to force the Serbs to agree to the terms of the peace agreement to end the fighting in Kosovo?"	(N = 1,488) 3/24–28/1999 60%	(N = 1,000) 4/15–18/1999 62%	+2%
Gallup: "As you may know, the military alliance of Western countries called NATO has launched air and missile attacks against Serbian military targets in Yugoslavia. Do you favor or oppose the United States being a part of that military action?"	(N = 1,069) 4/13–14/1999 61%	(N = 659) 4/21/1999 51%	−10%***
CBS News/*The New York Times*: "Do you favor or oppose the United States and NATO (North Atlantic Treaty Organization) conducting air strikes against Yugoslavia?"	(N = 878) 4/13–14/1999 59%	(N = 450) 4/22/1999 55%	−4%
ABC News/*The Washington Post*: "Do you support or oppose the United States and its European allies conducting air strikes against Serbia?"	(N = 1,011) 4/6/1999 67%	(N = 757) 4/26/1999 65%	−2%

NOTE: * = p-value statistically significant at the 0.01 level. ** = p-value statistically significant at the 0.05 level. *** = p-value statistically significant at the 0.001 level.

Table 3.13
Which Kosovo Pictures and Stories Most Caught Respondents' Attention?
April 1999

"Thinking about the news coverage of the situation in Yugoslavia, which pictures
and stories have caught your attention most [ITEM ORDER ROTATED]?"
"And after that, which pictures and stories have caught your attention the next
most READ LIST except item selected in previous question; [ITEM ORDER ROTATED]"

Pictures and stories about	1st Choice (%)	2nd Choice (%)	Total (%)
the three captured U.S. soldiers	35	29	64
the refugees leaving Kosovo	30	26	56
the victims of violence in Kosovo	24	25	49
the air attacks and damage in Serbia	8	15	23
Don't know/refused	3	5	8

SOURCE: Pew Research Center/PSRA poll conducted April 15-18, 1999, N = 1,000.
NOTE: "Item Order Rotated" means that the order in which question options were
presented to respondents was randomized to avoid response-order effects.

Nor did polling by the Pew Research Center just after the incident suggest that concern about Serb civilians being hurt or killed was
a particularly good predictor of approval or disapproval of the war
(Table 3.14): About six in ten of those who were very or somewhat
worried about Serb civilians being hurt or killed approved of the war,
not terribly different from those who were not too worried or not at all
worried; the Chi-square test of independence did not suggest any systematic relationship between the two variables.

There is, moreover, little evidence that the incident led a majority
of Americans to believe that NATO's efforts to avoid civilian casualties
were inadequate or that the bombing should be stopped:

• Sixty-five percent of those polled between April 15 and 16 said
  that in spite of the civilian deaths and casualties that the air strikes
  were too important to stop despite the chances of civilian casualties (Pew Research Center/PSRA poll conducted April 15–16,
  1999, N = 751).

Table 3.14
Cross-Tabulation of Approval and Concern About Serb Civilians Being Hurt or Killed

"Do you approve or disapprove of NATO forces, including the United States, conducting air strikes against Serbia to force the Serbs to agree to the terms of the peace agreement and end the fighting in Kosovo?"
"How worried are you [ITEM ORDER ROTATED]: very worried, somewhat worried, not too worried, or not at all worried that Serbian civilians are being hurt or killed by U.S. and NATO air strikes?"

Worried About Civilian Casualties	Approval of Air Strikes (%)			
	Approve	Disapprove	Don't Know	Row Total
Very worried	58	33	9	100
Somewhat worried	63	27	10	100
Not too worried	60	31	10	100
Not at all worried	53	45	2	100
Don't know	48	21	31	100

SOURCE: Pew Research Center/PSRA poll conducted April 15-18, 1999, N = 1,000.
NOTE: p-value in Chi-square test of independence was 0.5436.

- Seventy-eight percent of those polled April 25–26 said that civilian casualties that resulted from NATO's air strikes were "unavoidable accidents of war," while 19 percent said they thought the United States and its allies were not being careful enough (ABC News/*The Washington Post* poll conducted April 25–26, 1999, N = 757).

Table 3.14 reports that a Chi-square test of the bivariate relationship between approval of the war and concern about Serb civilians being hurt or killed indicated that there was no systematic relationship between the two variables: The Chi-square test of independence failed to achieve even the most modest level of statistical significance.

Finally, Table 3.15 shows that there were some modest partisan differences regarding beliefs about whether civilian deaths in the air strikes were due to carelessness, or were simply unavoidable accidents of war: Although strong majorities in each group subscribed to the latter view, Republicans were somewhat more likely to believe that any

Table 3.15
Are We Being Careful Enough to Avoid Civilian Casualties?
By Party, April 1999

"As you may know, some civilians have been killed in the air strikes against Serbia by the United States and its European allies. Do you think the United States and its European allies are not being careful enough to avoid civilian casualties, or do you think these are just unavoidable accidents of war?"	Not Careful Enough (%)	Unavoidable Accidents (%)	Don't Know (%)
Republican	13	85	2
Democrat	18	78	3
Independent	20	77	3
All	19	78	3

SOURCE: ABC News/*The Washington Post* poll conducted April 25–26, 1999, N = 757.

civilian deaths were unavoidable accidents of war, although nearly eight in ten Democrats and Independents also felt that way.

Taken together, these data suggest that there is little evidence suggesting that the convoy incident affected Americans' basic attitudes toward the war or its conduct.

Antiwar Demonstrations. Xinhua reported a small protest involving over 200 antiwar protesters who rallied outside the White House on April 17 (Xinhua General News Service, 1999a). Beyond this relatively small event, we found little evidence in the press that antiwar demonstrations in the United States increased following the convoy incident.[44]

Foreign Media and Public Opinion Responses

Foreign Media. As was described previously, foreign media were among the first to pick up the story of the convoy incident. From a quantitative viewpoint, the convoy incident appears to have resulted in higher levels of media reporting on civilian casualties in AFP, although it does not appear to have affected reporting on civilian casualties in *The Guardian* (London) (Figure 3.10).

---

[44] Anecdotally, however, many Serbian-Americans appear to have opposed the war against Serbia (see CNN, 1999b).

Figure 3.10
Selected Foreign Media Reporting on Civilian Casualties, Convoy Incident

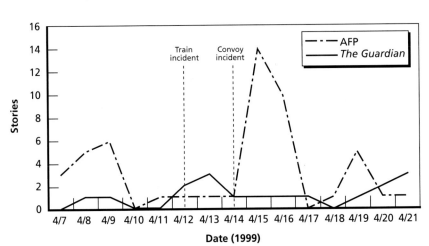

SOURCE: Search for "Kosovo" and "civilian casualties," "civilian deaths," or "collateral damage" in AFP or *The Guardian* (London).

RAND MG441-3.10

Figure 3.10 shows that AFP's reporting on civilian casualties spiked the day after the incident, climbing from two stories on April 14 to 14 stories on April 15, before falling off to the levels observed before the incident.

Foreign Public Opinion. We did not find any public opinion data on how foreign publics viewed civilian deaths in the war in Kosovo after the convoy incident; however, a poll of five European nations by the Angus Reid Group in late April suggested that majorities of each of the five nations approved of the way NATO had been managing its military campaign (Table 3.16).

The poll reported in Table 3.16 was conducted a little over a week after the convoy incident, and shows that about six in ten in each country expressed the belief that NATO had done a very good or good job managing the military campaign against Yugoslavia. The poll suggests that these publics had not lost heart for the Kosovo campaign as a result of the convoy incident, and that, despite the civilian casualties, they continued to have confidence in the way it was being waged. Put another way, these data would seem to suggest that the convoy incident

Table 3.16
European Support for the War in Kosovo in Late April 1999

"Overall, do you feel that NATO has done a very good, good, poor, or very poor job of managing its military campaign against Yugoslavia?"	Very Good/Good (%)	Poor/Very Poor (%)	Don't Know/ No Opinion
Europe	60	26	14
United Kingdom	64	26	10
France	60	26	13
Germany	59	21	20
Italy	59	34	8

SOURCE: Angus Reid Group (1999). Sample sizes were 300 in each nation except Germany, which had a sample size of 476. Polling was conducted between April 22 and 25, 1999.

did not lead to the wholesale withdrawal of support from major European publics.

Antiwar Demonstrations. Reporting suggests that antiwar protests in Greece may have become increasingly militant following the convoy incident (see AP, 1999; Associated Press Worldstream, 1999b, 1999c), but we found little evidence to suggest a more general increase in antiwar protest activity.

The May 7 Chinese Embassy Bombing

In what some have described as the most consequential instance of unintended bomb damage in Operation Allied Force (Lambeth, 2001, p. 144), on May 7, 1999, three Joint Direct Attack Munitions (JDAMs) from a U.S. B-2 bomber struck the Chinese embassy in Belgrade, killing four and injuring 26. The postincident timeline is provided in Table 3.17.

Table 3.17
Postincident Timeline for Chinese Embassy Incident

Media Reporting Highlights	Official Handling Highlights
5/7 1646: Incident occurs 1722: Deutsche Presse-Agentur breaks story 1800: Belgrade Radio and SAT RTS break story 1800: *CNN Evening News* breaks story 1843: *CBS Evening News* breaks story 1921: AFP reports China confirms bombing	
5/8 0938: NATO daily briefing airs on CNN 1107: DoD news briefing airs on CNN 1507: President Clinton's comments air on CNN	**5/8** 1100: DoD news briefing airs on CNN 1435: President Clinton expresses regret 1500: NATO daily briefing. NATO Secretary General Javier Solana expresses regret
	5/9 0900: NATO daily briefing; no DoD briefing
	5/10 0900: NATO gives daily briefing 1543: White House press secretary Lockhart gives briefing 1619: Secretary of Defense Cohen briefing on embassy attack airs on CNN
	5/11 0900: NATO gives daily briefing; no DoD briefing
	5/12 0900: NATO gives daily briefing 1620: DoD gives news briefing (Cohen and Shelton)
	5/13 0900: NATO gives daily briefing 1500: DoD gives news briefing
	5/14 1500: DoD gives news briefing (USAF General John P. Jumper and Joint Staff Vice Director for Strategic Plans and Policy Major General Charles F. Wald)

SOURCE: Deutsche Presse-Agentur (1999b), Belgrade Radio Beograd Network (1999a, 1999b), Rather (1999).

NOTE: All times Eastern. SAT RTS = Radio-Televizija Srbije.

News of the incident appears to have reached the national media relatively soon after it occurred (roughly 1646 ET):

- Deutsche Presse-Agentur (1999b) reported the incident at 1722 ET.
- At 1800 ET, Belgrade Radio Beograd Network (1999a, 1999b) reported that NATO had hit the Chinese embassy in Novi Beograd.
- At 1800 ET, CNN's evening news program reported the incident.[45]
- At 1843 ET, *CBS Evening News* reported the incident (Rather, 1999).
- At 1921 ET, AFP reported that China was confirming the bombing.

In the days following the attack, the incident was given very high levels of attention in various news conferences and briefings:

- The attack was a prominent and recurring topic of questions in the May 8 DoD news briefing, as well as those on May 10, 12, 13, and 14, and at NATO's daily press conference on May 8 and subsequent days.
- On May 8, President Clinton, NATO Secretary General Solana, Secretary of Defense Cohen, and Central Intelligence Agency (CIA) Director George Tenet all issued statements of regret, but also explained that the risks of such incidents could never be eliminated (White House, 1999c; NATO, 1999j; DoD, 1999f).
- On May 10, 11, and 12, White House spokesman Joe Lockhart fielded questions on the incident and its consequences for U.S. relations (White House, 1999d).
- Also on May 10, Secretary of Defense Cohen gave a briefing on the embassy attack; on May 12, Secretary Cohen and Chairman Shelton briefed on Kosovo; and on May 14, General Jumper, then-

---

[45] LexisNexis reports that the story was broadcast at 6:00 p.m., whereas the Vanderbilt Television News Archive transcript reports that the story was broadcast at 5:00 p.m. ET.

commander of the U.S. Air Forces in Europe (USAFE) gave a Pentagon briefing on the incident (DoD, 1999g, 1999h, 1999i).

U.S. Media and Public Opinion Responses

U.S. Media. From a quantitative perspective, U.S. major television and newspaper reporting on the errant bombing of the Chinese embassy grew slowly, peaked three to four days after the incident, and then fell to earlier levels (Figure 3.11). And Figure 3.12, which reports the number of stories mentioning the Chinese embassy incident in 53 major newspapers in the United States and abroad, suggests that this general pattern was common in newspaper reporting at home and abroad.

Figure 3.11
Media Reporting on Civilian Casualties, Chinese Embassy Incident

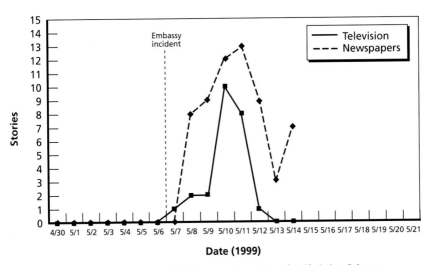

SOURCE: Search for "Kosovo" and "Chinese embassy" in *The Christian Science Monitor, Los Angeles Times, The New York Times, The Wall Street Journal, The Washington Post,* ABC News, CBS News, CNN, and NBC News.

RAND MG441-3.11

Figure 3.12
Reporting on Chinese Embassy Incident in 53 Major Newspapers

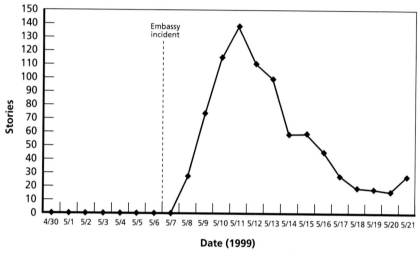

SOURCE: Search for "Kosovo" and "Chinese embassy" in *The Christian Science Monitor, Los Angeles Times, The New York Times, The Wall Street Journal, The Washington Post,* ABC News, CBS News, CNN, and NBC News.
RAND *MG441-3.12*

Qualitatively, the growth in reporting on the incident seems to have been accountable to the wide range of stories that resulted: FRY government claims that the bombing had been "deliberate" (RTS, 1999); the increasingly strident reaction of the Chinese, including mass demonstrations at the U.S. embassy in Beijing, which Beijing officials allowed to fester for several days before seeking to calm the Chinese public (see Eckholm, 1999b; Xinhua General News Service, 1999b, 1999c, 1999g, 1999h; Hong Kong Agence France Presse, 1999); concern that the incident might affect the possibilities for a diplomatic solution to the Kosovo crisis (Perlez, 1999) or that the broader U.S.-Chinese relationship would be affected by the incident (Mufson, 1999; Sanger, 1999); rising doubts among the coalition's European allies (Drozdiak, 1999); and criticism from various quarters.[46]

---

[46] For example, FBIS reported official condemnations of NATO's attack on the Chinese embassy from Vietnam, Burma, and Mozambique, as well as from mass organizations and

In addition to an increase in reporting on civilian casualties following the embassy bombing incident (Figures 3.11 and 3.12), according to data from the CMPA, the tenor of U.S. television news reporting changed dramatically following the attack on the Chinese embassy.

According to these data, the tone of media reporting on the war was both increasingly negative (Figure 3.13) and increasingly focused on civilian casualties of the air war (Figure 3.14).[47]

Figure 3.13 shows that following the attack on the Chinese embassy, the focus of television news reporting shifted from the plight of Kosovar refugees to civilian damage from the air war: Refugee-related stories constituted 31 percent of all stories on Kosovo before the incident but only 18 percent after, whereas stories on civilian damage grew from 8 to 37 percent of television news stories on Kosovo.

Figure 3.13
Focus of News Reports Before and After Chinese Embassy Incident

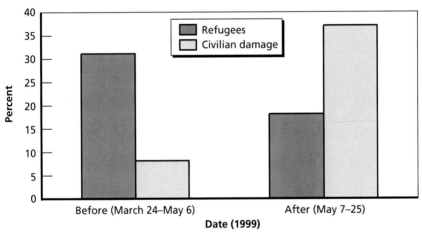

SOURCE: Center for Media and Public Affairs (1999).

RAND *MG441-3.13*

---

deputies of the Chinese People's Political Consultative Conference in Hong Kong, the French and Japanese communist parties, a member of the Ukrainian parliament, and Thai and foreign journalists in Thailand.

[47] News stories on Kosovo were the most frequently reported television news story in 1999 (see CMPA, 2000).

Figure 3.14
TV News Evaluations of U.S. Policy Before and After Chinese Embassy Incident

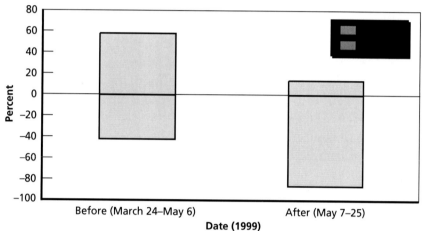

SOURCE: Center for Media and Public Affairs (1999).
RAND MG441-3.14

In a similar vein, the mix of positive and negative evaluations of U.S. policy also shifted from a predominantly positive tone to a predominantly negative one (Figure 3.14). The figure shows that positive evaluations of the war comprised 58 percent of all evaluations of U.S. policy before the incident but only 14 percent after, whereas negative evaluations grew from 42 to 86 percent of all evaluations.

Taken together, the Chinese embassy incident appears to have been a turning point for television news reporting on the war.

U.S. Public Opinion. Although question wording or other differences may partially account for the change, there appears to have been a decline in the U.S. public's attention to Kosovo after the incident (Table 3.18).

Table 3.18 reports that whereas 82 percent told Gallup that they were following the situation in Kosovo very or fairly closely before this incident, only 70 percent of those polled by PIPA said that they were following the situation very or fairly closely after the incident, a decline of 12 percentage points.

Table 3.18
Attention Paid to Kosovo Before and After May 7 Chinese Embassy Incident

"Overall, how closely have you followed the situation in Kosovo—very closely, somewhat closely, not too closely, or not at all?" (Gallup poll conducted April 26–27, 1999, N = 1,073) "As you may know, NATO (North Atlantic Treaty Organization) is bombing Serb targets to pressure Yugoslav President (Slobodan) Milosevic to stop ethnic cleansing in Kosovo. How closely are you following the situation in Kosovo? Very closely, somewhat closely, not very closely, not at all closely" (Program on International Policy Attitudes [PIPA] poll conducted May 13–17, 1999, N = 1,206)	Date Before 4/26–27/1999 (%)	Date After 5/13–17/1999 (%)
Very closely	34	24
Fairly closely	48	46
Not too closely	14	20
Not at all closely	3	10
Don't know/refused	1	1

In light of the increase in negative reporting on Kosovo in the media, it should be little surprise that there is somewhat stronger evidence of a decline in support for the war following the May 8 bombing of the Chinese embassy than in the other cases, but even here the evidence is not entirely conclusive (Table 3.19).

The data in Table 3.19 report polling results by day from a three-day poll conducted by Gallup that spanned the embassy bombing incident. These results do not suggest either a decline in support or any change in those who said that the military action had been too aggressive, following the incident.

When we compare the results of four polls conducted before and after the Chinese embassy incident (Table 3.20), we can see that, in three polls, a statistically significant decline in approval was evident, while the fourth poll, although not statistically significant, also showed a decline. This suggests a much greater drop in support than was observed in the comparison of polling before and after the convoy incident, although it is impossible to state with any degree of assurance that the Chinese embassy incident was responsible for the change. The

Table 3.19
Approval and Beliefs About Aggressiveness of War by Day, May 7–9, 1999

Survey	May 7 (%)	May 8 (%)	May 9 (%)	Total (%)
Next, we have a few questions about the situation in the Yugoslavian regions of Kosovo, Serbia, and other areas of the Balkans. As you may know, the military alliance of Western countries called NATO has launched air and missile attacks against Serbian military targets in Yugoslavia. Do you favor or oppose the United States being a part of that military action?				
Favor	53	55	59	55
Oppose	41	38	33	38
Don't know/refused	6	7	8	7
So far, do you think the military action against Yugoslavia by the United States and NATO: (a) has been too aggressive; (b) has been about right; (c) has not been aggressive enough?				
Too aggressive	26	23	24	24
About right	42	47	44	44
Not aggressive enough	26	26	29	27
Don't know/refused	6	4	3	5

SOURCE: Gallup poll conducted May 7–9, 1999, N = 1,027.

low loss of life in the incident suggests that the principal issue was not so much civilian casualties as potentially provoking the Chinese.

Moreover, this appears to be a robust finding. Gallup's polling three weeks after the incident also shows that doubts had emerged about the air war and NATO's efforts to avoid civilian casualties: By May 23–24, 1999, fewer than half (48 percent) said they thought the United States and NATO were doing everything possible to conduct the air strikes in a way that minimized the number of civilian casualties, whereas 46 percent said the they could do more to minimize civilian casualties caused by the air strikes (Gallup/CNN/USA Today poll conducted May 23–24, 1999, N = 1,050).

Taken together, these two results suggest both that public reactions to the incident may have taken time to crystallize and that the shift in the tone of media reporting on Kosovo reflected in the CMPA

Table 3.20
Approval of the War Before and After the May 7 Chinese Embassy Incident

Poll	Before	After	Change
Pew Research Center/PSRA: "Do you approve or disapprove of NATO forces, including the United States conducting air strikes against Serbia to force the Serbs to agree to the terms of the peace agreement to end the fighting in Kosovo?"	(N = 1,000) 4/15–18/1999 62	(N = 1,179) 5/12–16/1999) 53	–9***
Gallup: "As you may know, the military alliance of Western countries called NATO has launched air and missile attacks against Serbian military targets in Yugoslavia. Do you favor or oppose the United States being a part of that military action?"	(N = 1,025) 5/7–9/1999 55	(N = 1,050) 5/21–23/1999 49	–6*
CBS News/The New York Times: "Do you favor or oppose the United States and NATO (North Atlantic Treaty Organization) conducting air strikes against Yugoslavia?"	(N = 1,151) 5/1–2/1999 53	(N = 578) 5/11/1999 49	–4
ABC News/The Washington Post: "Do you support or oppose the United States and its European allies conducting air strikes against Serbia?"	(N = 757) 4/26/1999 65	(N = 761) 5/16/1999 59	–6**

NOTES: * = p-value statistically significant at the 0.01 level. ** = p-value statistically significant at the 0.05 level. *** = p-value statistically significant at the 0.001 level.

data actually may have contributed to that shift, i.e., as news reports increasingly cited critics of the war, and as this criticism went beyond the incident that precipitated it to raise questions about the larger conduct of the war, the increasingly negative reporting filtered through the media to the public.

Antiwar Demonstrations. We found no evidence that the Chinese embassy incident resulted in additional antiwar protest activity in the United States.

Foreign Media and Public Opinion Responses

The main effect of the Chinese embassy incident was a crisis in U.S.-Chinese relations that was, in part, accountable to China's efforts to exploit fully the incident for its own purposes, possibly including deflecting attention from a spying scandal involving alleged Chinese efforts to acquire U.S. nuclear secrets that had emerged in early March 1999 (Pincus, 1999; Risen, 1999).

Foreign Media. Figure 3.15 shows that foreign media reporting on the Chinese embassy incident varied dramatically by source, with AFP showing the heaviest reporting of the three available sources, followed by TASS; *The Guardian*'s reporting on the incident shows peaks on May 10 and 12.[48] A small amount of this reporting appears to have been devoted to a review of other incidents of collateral damage and civilian deaths in the war (AFP, 1999d; "Mounting Tally of Blunders," 1999).

Importantly, Chinese state-controlled media, which had not reported on Yugoslavia's campaign of ethnic cleansing in Kosovo during the seven weeks preceding the embassy incident, did not immediately report President Clinton's apology and expression of profound sorrow for the unintentional bombing of China's embassy in Belgrade ("China Puts Gas on the Fire," 1999).

Foreign Public Opinion. A pan-European poll by ICM Research conducted between May 6 and 22, 1999, found a majority supporting the war in six of twelve nations polled (Denmark, France, Luxembourg, the United Kingdom, Belgium, and Germany), and somewhat slim majorities supporting the use of ground troops in only three (France, Denmark, and the United Kingdom, Table 3.21). We uncovered no additional foreign public opinion data on the matter.

Antiwar Demonstrations. The bombing of the Chinese embassy sparked a fair amount of protest activity among Chinese, both in China proper and in the larger Chinese diaspora. The Chinese government choreographed large demonstrations involving tens of thousands near the U.S. embassy in Beijing until about May 10, after which only scattered protesters remained.[49] These protests included the

---

[48] We found no articles on the embassy incident in the LexisNexis online service's Xinhua file; this may reflect a gap in the data.

[49] On the Chinese government's efforts to orchestrate the protest activity, see Eckholm (1999a, 1999b), Pollack (1999), and Platt (1999).

Figure 3.15
Foreign Media Reporting on Civilian Casualties, Chinese Embassy Incident

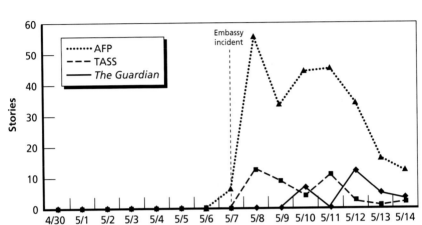

SOURCE: Search for "Kosovo" and "Chinese embassy" in AFP, *The Guardian* (London), and TASS.

RAND *MG441-3.15*

stoning, and even the use of gasoline bombs, against the U.S. embassy (Elisabeth Rosenthal, 1999). Citing the "volatile" conditions, the U.S. Department of State suspended official travel to China by U.S. employees and urged Americans to defer personal travel to China.[50]

Following the bombing of the Chinese embassy, Chinese expatriates abroad also engaged in anti-NATO demonstrations (see, for example, Xinhua General News Service, 1999d, 1999e, 1999f, 1999i; GMA Network, 1999; Central News Agency–Taiwan, 1999). Cambodian police fired shots in the air after hundreds of ethnic Chinese demonstrators stormed a security cordon outside the U.S. embassy in Phnom Penh, for example ("Shots Fired as Protestors Storm US Embassy in Phnom Penh," 1999). Some pro-NATO demonstrations also were held in Albania after the incident (Çani, 1999; AFP, 1999e).

---

[50] Kilborn and Carden (1999). Also, on the hostile environment for Americans in China after the incident, see Brauchli (1999).

Table 3.21
European Support for the War in Kosovo in Mid-May 1999

Country	Approve (%)	Disapprove (%)	Don't Know (%)
"Do you personally support or oppose the NATO military actions in Serbia?"			
Denmark	70	20	10
France	68	27	5
Luxembourg	61	30	9
United Kingdom	54	33	13
Belgium	53	35	12
Germany	52	40	8
Ireland	46	42	12
Finland	44	43	13
Austria	41	43	16
Italy	37	46	17
Spain	34	48	18
Greece	2	97	1
"Do you personally support or oppose the use of ground forces in Kosovo?"			
France	53	42	5
Denmark	52	37	11
United Kingdom	51	36	13
Ireland	45	41	14
Belgium	41	48	11
Finland	40	45	15
Luxembourg	38	52	10
Spain	28	54	18
Austria	27	58	15
Italy	26	59	15

Table 3.21—Continued

Country	Approve (%)	Disapprove (%)	Don't Know (%)
"Do you personally support or oppose the use of ground forces in Kosovo?"			
Germany	18	78	4
Greece	3	96	1

SOURCE: ICM Research (1999).

Conclusions

As described in this chapter, civilian casualties and collateral damage were a fairly prominent, if second-tier, theme in U.S. press reporting during Operation Allied Force, and CNN reporting on civilian casualties appears to have been highly responsive to new civilian casualty incidents. And as in the case of the Al Firdos incident and the 1991 Gulf War, collateral damage incidents led to increased reporting. No doubt due to the large number of civilian deaths, the convoy incident sparked more reporting on the civilian casualties issue, but the Chinese embassy incident appears to have had a greater impact on overall reporting levels.

The public opinion data on Americans' attitudes suggest that Americans paid fairly close attention to the war in Kosovo but had great difficulty estimating civilian deaths in the war. Americans also were generally more concerned about U.S. casualties and the Kosovar victims of the FRY government than civilian casualties of the air war, which were generally viewed as regrettable but ultimately unavoidable accidents of war. The public opinion data are somewhat difficult to summarize:

- Comparisons of polling results before and after each incident suggested that there is stronger evidence that the Chinese embassy incident may have reduced Americans' approval for the war than that the convoy incident did, but the evidence is still rather weak. This is especially so in light of the various other factors that probably were contributing to a decline in support: especially growing doubts as to whether an air war alone would achieve campaign objectives and whether ground troops might need to be employed, an option most Americans resisted.

• Statistical evidence from bivariate analyses of data from two different polls, one a week after the convoy incident and one a week after the Chinese embassy incident, suggested that beliefs about whether the coalition was being careful enough were related to overall approval and disapproval.

• Multivariate statistical modeling of respondent-level data from polling about a week after the Chinese embassy incident suggested that Americans' concerns that innocents might be dying as a result of the air war did not affect their overall support for the war.

Whether the relationship between support and beliefs about whether the coalition was being careful enough would have held up in multivariate statistical analyses cannot be said, but it certainly is plausible, given three additional pieces of data: (1) there does seem to have been some erosion in approval for the war, and (2) concern about Serbian civilians being killed did not change much between the convoy and Chinese embassy incidents, but (3) there were declines in the prevalence of the belief that the coalition was being careful enough after the Chinese embassy incident that could have contributed to the erosion in approval.

Table 3.22 presents data on Americans' concerns about Serb civilian casualties before and after the Chinese embassy incident, and shows virtually no change in concern about Serb civilians.[51]

However, Table 3.23 shows that there was a statistically significant increase in the percentage of respondents who said they thought the coalition was not taking enough care to avoid civilian casualties, and a decline in those who thought civilian deaths were unavoidable accidents of war.

---

[51] Note that the "before" poll was conducted just after the April 14 convoy incident.

Thus, although we were not able to confirm this in our multivariate statistical modeling, there is some reason to believe that declining approval for the war may in part have been caused by the increasing prevalence of the view that NATO was not being careful enough to avoid civilian casualties. Nevertheless, it is impossible to isolate the effects of civilian casualties from growing elite criticism, coupled with declining beliefs that the air war alone would be successful and growing concern that ground troops might be needed.

Our analysis of foreign attitudes suggested fairly strong support for the war in Europe and strong opposition in Russia and China, even before the Chinese embassy incident; the absence of time series data made it impossible to assess the impact of civilian casualty incidents on support and opposition, though a five-country poll conducted a week after the convoy incident provided indirect evidence that European support held up in the face of civilian casualties: The poll showed that about six in ten of those polled in the United Kingdom, France, Germany, and Italy thought that NATO had done a very good or good job managing the military campaign.

Table 3.22
Americans' Concern About Civilian Casualties, April–May 1999

"How worried are you that that Serbian civilians are being hurt or killed by U.S. and NATO air strikes—very worried, somewhat worried, not too worried, or not at all worried?"	April 15–18 (%) (N = 500)	May 12–16 (%) (N = 599)
Very worried	40	37
Somewhat worried	37	40
Not too worried	16	13
Not at all worried	5	6

SOURCES: Pew Research Center polls conducted April 15–18, 1999; and May 12–16, 1999.
NOTE: Question was asked of half of respondents.

Table 3.23
Comparison of Beliefs About Coalition Efforts to Avoid Casualties, Post–Convoy Incident and Post–Chinese Embassy Incident

"As you may know, some civilians have been killed in the air strikes against Serbia by the United States and its European allies. Do you think that the United States and its European allies are not being careful enough to avoid civilian casualties, or do you think these are just unavoidable accidents of war?" (ABC News/ The Washington Post poll conducted April 25–26, 1999, N = 757). "As you may know, some civilians have been killed in the air strikes against Serbia, and recently the NATO (North Atlantic Treaty Organization) allies bombed the Chinese consulate in Serbia's capital. Do you think that the United States and its European allies are not being careful enough to avoid civilian casualties, or do you think these are just unavoidable accidents of war?" (ABC News/The Washington Post poll conducted May 16, 1999, N = 761)	April 25–26 (%)	May 16 (%)
Not being careful enough	19	32
Unavoidable accidents of war	78	66
No opinion	3	2

From the vantage point of policymakers and military leaders, the handling of the Djakovica convoy incident—in which partial and ultimately inaccurate information was provided to the press over the days leading up to the April 19 briefing on the incident—should be read as an object lesson in how not to respond to civilian casualty incidents. There were, no doubt, pressures to provide a timely response to FRY charges that the allies had attacked a purely civilian convoy. But the confusion resulting from making statements before actually knowing the relevant facts seems to have clouded the larger moral framing of the incident: FRY forces in the convoy had been observed burning buildings, they were using civilians as human shields, and the allied attack was called off as soon as it became clear that the convoy also included many civilian vehicles. The convoy incident also led some news organizations to review the record of civilian casualty incidents and provided a graphic backdrop for subsequent reporting on the matter.

By comparison, although it involved only a relatively small number of deaths, the Chinese embassy incident was a watershed event in the war. It led to a major crisis in U.S.-Chinese affairs, temporarily disrupted negotiations to end the conflict, and resulted in a two-week pause in attacks on strategic targets in Belgrade, the latter of which no doubt gave some welcome relief to the beleaguered Milosevic regime. Whether or not this ultimately delayed Milosevic's decision to withdraw FRY troops from Kosovo cannot be said. The embassy incident also appears to have led to a shift in the focus of television news reporting on the war, from stories about the plight of refugees to stories about collateral damage and civilian deaths, which also may have opened the door for broader criticisms of the strategy and conduct of the campaign. Finally, the incident was the first instance we have seen in which a civilian casualty incident may have contributed to declining support for the war, though it is impossible to separate out the effects of the Chinese embassy incident from declining confidence that an air war alone would succeed, concern that ground troops might need to be employed in a combat role, and other factors.

CHAPTER FOUR

Operation Enduring Freedom (Afghanistan, 2001–)

Operation Enduring Freedom was the name given to military operations conducted in support of the U.S. global war on terrorism following the September 11, 2001 ("9/11") terrorist attacks on New York City and Washington, D.C. After 9/11, the United States demanded that Afghanistan's ruling Taliban give up Osama bin Laden and his al Qaeda followers. When the Taliban failed to comply, on October 7, 2001, military operations began in Afghanistan with the aim of defeating Taliban and al Qaeda forces and changing the regime. This chapter shows that, although the evidence suggests that Americans became less comfortable about civilian casualties as the war proceeded, the exceedingly high support for the war remained essentially unaffected by civilian casualties.

Civilian Casualty Estimates

As in the other military operations we examined, DoD has not, as of this writing, offered its own estimates of civilian casualties in the war in Afghanistan.

Taliban claims of civilian deaths were higher than most others'. For example, on October 31, 2001, Taliban ambassador to Pakistan Abdul Salam Zaeef claimed that airstrikes had killed 1,500 to 1,600 civilians (Associated Press Worldstream, 2002). An AP report in February 2002 would later report that Afghan journalists had claimed that "Taliban officials systematically doctored reports of civilian deaths to push their estimate to 1,500 in the first three weeks of the war" (King, 2002a).

By early 2002, press reporting suggested that estimates of civilian deaths due to the war in Afghanistan generally ranged between 1,000 and 1,300 at the low end and 3,767 and 5,000 at the high end. Among the estimates at that time were the following:[1]

- In January 2002, Human Rights Watch was cited as estimating that 1,000 Afghan civilians had died in the war, and the Reuters news agency was cited as estimating that perhaps 982 people had died in 14 incidents (Campbell, 2002).
- Based on a review of selected Western media and discounting any reports based on Taliban figures, the Project on Defense Alternatives estimated that between 1,000 and 1,300 Afghan civilians had died in the war by January (King, 2002a).
- A February 2002 review of the air war by the Associated Press that detailed the results of its investigation of civilian casualty incidents suggested that Afghan civilian deaths were in the hundreds, not the thousands, as claimed by the Taliban (Associated Press Worldstream, 2002; King, 2002a, 2002b), and probably were in the 500–600 range (Table 4.1).

As in the other military operations we examined, between the United States frequently not having direct access to the alleged location of civilian casualty incidents and the Taliban's intentional policy of exaggerating the number of deaths accountable to these incidents, the actual numbers probably will never be known with any certitude.

---

[1] According to Seybolt (2002, p. 44),

> The number of civilians killed by U.S. actions was difficult to determine. The Taliban alleged that the casualty rates were high, but few people regarded this claim as credible. The U.S. Government acknowledged that the operations had killed civilians but insisted that the number of casualties was low and offered no total figure. Independent estimates of the number of Afghan civilians killed by early December range from a conservative 1,000–1,300 to 3,767–5,000.

Table 4.1
AP Estimate of Civilian Casualties, February 2002

Location	Estimated Deaths
Kabul	70
Kandahar	81
Jalalabad	55
Mazar-e-Sharif	10
Herat	18
Spinboldak, south of Kandahar	25
Karam, near Jalalabad	55
Kama Ado, Tora Bora region	155
Agom, Tora Bora region	5
Pacir, Tora Bora region	7
Paktia province, December 2001 convoy incident	27
Niazi, Paktia's Zawar district	18
Subtotal	526

SOURCE: King (2002a).

Handling of the Civilian Casualties Issue

As described previously, the Taliban sought to exaggerate the number of deaths in civilian casualty incidents. An Associated Press analysis of hospital records, visits to bomb sites, and interviews with eyewitnesses and officials suggested that the Taliban regime had distorted casualty reports, yielding inflated estimates, and that the toll in civilian deaths at that time probably was in the range of 500–600 people (King, 2002a). The United States also was criticized by international and nongovernmental organizations for the civilian casualties that were resulting from the war.[2]

For its part, DoD acknowledged that Afghan civilians were unintended casualties of the air war.[3] Nevertheless, DoD simultaneously stressed that many of the reports of casualties in these incidents may have been inaccurate, that some incidents may have been the result of misinformation provided to the United States for the purposes of score-settling, and that, by any measure, incidents of civilian casualties in Afghanistan have been relatively rare.[4] DoD also stressed that it was impossible to count civilian casualties without on-site investigations, which usually cannot be carried out in wartime or can be carried out only with great difficulty (King, 2002a).

In testimony before the Senate Armed Services Committee in early February 2002, General Tommy Franks, commander of U.S. Central Command (CENTCOM), commented that "any loss of innocent life is a shame," that that the war in Afghanistan "[had] been the most accurate war ever fought in the nation's history" (King, 2002a), while noting that of the 18,000 bombs that were dropped in Afghanistan, 10,000 were precision munitions, but also that some had still gone awry (King, 2002a).

---

[2]   For example, the United Nations High Commissioner for Human Rights, Mary Robinson, charged that the U.S. military action had led to excessive civilian casualties (Associated Press Online, 2002). See also Lobe (2002).

[3]   On October 15, 2001, Secretary of Defense Donald Rumsfeld acknowledged that Afghan civilians had been unintended casualties.

[4]   As Secretary Rumsfeld put it in an interview with National Public Radio in February 2002,

> We know of the thousands of sorties and the tens of thousands of weapons dropped and efforts on the ground. We know of less than a handful of instances where in fact there was a mistake made. There is very, very, very little that anyone could characterize as a mistake. (National Public Radio, 2002)

The Arc of Media and Public Concern

U.S. Media and Public Opinion Responses

U.S. Media. As in the other cases, media attention greatly increased in anticipation of military action in Afghanistan, and peaked when military operations actually began (Figure 4.1).

Figure 4.1 shows an increase in U.S. major media reporting on Afghanistan in September (most of which occurred after the 9/11 attacks), a peak in October 2001 for the major newspapers, and another in November 2001 for the major television news organizations.[5]

Figure 4.2 shows that major newspaper reporting on the topic of civilian casualties also peaked in October 2001, receded, and then resurfaced at the time of claimed civilian casualty incidents.[6]

Figure 4.1
Major U.S. Newspaper and Television Reporting on Afghanistan, August 2001–March 2004

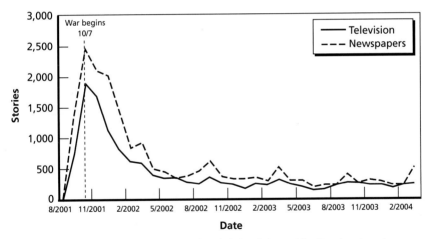

SOURCE: Search for "Afghanistan" in *The Christian Science Monitor, Los Angeles Times, The New York Times, The Wall Street Journal, The Washington Post,* ABC News, CBS News, CNN, and NBC News.

RAND *MG441-4.1*

---

[5]   The correlation between major U.S. newspaper and television reporting was 0.97.

[6]   The correlation between major U.S. newspaper and television reporting was 0.85.

Figure 4.2
Major U.S. Newspaper Reporting on Afghanistan and Civilian Casualties, August 2001–March 2004

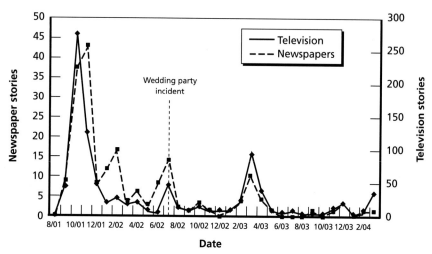

SOURCE: Search for "Afghanistan" and "civilian casualties," "civilian deaths," or "collateral damage" in *The Christian Science Monitor, Los Angeles Times, The New York Times, The Wall Street Journal, The Washington Post*, ABC News, CBS News, CNN, and NBC News.

RAND *MG441-4.2*

In February 2002, for example, several developments related to civilian casualties seem to have combined to bring the issue to the forefront.[7] In July 2002, there was an incident involving an Afghan wedding party (described in greater detail in this chapter), and in March 2003, the topic resurfaced with the onset of the war in Iraq. By February 2002, the result was said to be that, in contrast to the generally upbeat reporting that had come before, the media climate surround-

---

[7] These included allegations that those killed by a missile fired from a CIA Predator in early February were innocent civilians; the release of 27 people mistakenly captured in a commando raid in late January that reportedly killed 18; renewed questions about a controversial air strike on a convoy near the city of Khost that reportedly killed at least 12 people, and in which the 27 released Afghans claimed that they were kicked and beaten; a February 13 *New York Times* editorial titled "Afghanistan's Civilian Casualties"; and a report by the Associated Press that civilian deaths were lower than had originally been believed. See Cummins (2002), Vogel and Loeb (2002), King (2002b), "Afghanistan's Civilian Casualties" (2002), and Kurtz (2002).

ing the war had turned sharply negative (Kurtz, 2002). Qualitatively, the media only occasionally appear to have discussed the difficulties of assessing civilian deaths in the war (Bearak, 2002).

U.S. Public Opinion. The American public paid consistently high attention to the developments in Afghanistan (Figure 4.3): Nearly 90 percent said that they were watching developments very or somewhat closely from October 2001 to well into 2002. This high level of attention to Afghanistan had tapered off only modestly by July 2002.[8]

The public opinion data from the war in Afghanistan demonstrate that concerns about civilian casualties had little if any impact on support for the war. Indeed, Americans' concern about civilian casualties in Afghanistan appears to have been much lower than that observed during the war in Kosovo and possibly as low as (or lower than) that observed during the 1991 Gulf War.

Figure 4.3
Americans' Attention to Afghanistan, October 2001–July 2002

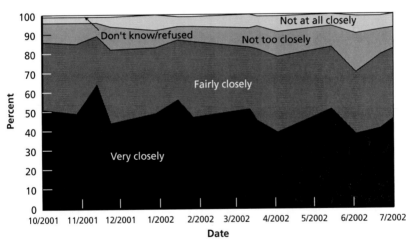

RAND *MG441-4.3*

---

[8] Note, however, the decline in June and recovery in July, which straddled the July 1 wedding party incident: Whereas 70 percent had been following events very or somewhat closely in Pew Research Center/PSRA's poll conducted June 19–23, 2002, 79 percent were doing so according to the poll conducted July 8–16. The wedding party incident may have resulted in renewed interest in Afghanistan.

Figure 4.4 shows that support for military action against Afghanistan was high—67 percent strongly supported military action in this case and another 14 percent somewhat supported military action— even when it was suggested that civilian casualties might result. This support was nearly as high as that from a poll by ABC News/*The Washington Post* at about the same time that asked about support but did not mention the possibility of civilian casualties: It found 72 percent strongly supporting military action and another 13 percent somewhat supporting military action, only about six percentage points higher. This suggests that the possibility of civilian casualties had little effect on support.

Table 4.2 shows that about eight in ten of those polled by *Newsweek*/PSRA in September 2001 thought that military strikes against

Figure 4.4
Support for Military Action in Afghanistan Even with Civilian Casualties, Mid-September 2001

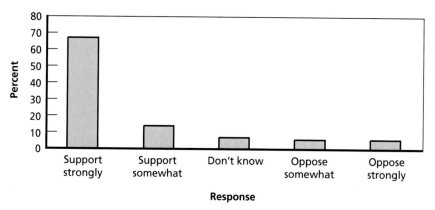

SOURCE: *Los Angeles Times* poll conducted September 13–14, 2001, N = 1,561.
NOTE: Question read, "The United States is saying that it is fairly certain that Osama bin Laden was responsible for the attack on the World Trade Center buildings and the Pentagon last Tuesday (September 11, 2001). Bin Laden is an exiled Saudi militant with extreme anti-American views who is allegedly being protected by the Taliban regime in Afghanistan...If it is also determined that the Taliban ruling party in Afghanistan is harboring Osama bin Laden, would you support the United States and its allies retaliating with military action against Afghanistan, even if it could result in civilian casualties, or would you oppose that? (If support/oppose, ask:) Would you support/oppose that strongly, or support/oppose it somewhat?"
RAND *MG441-4.4*

terrorist targets would be a very or somewhat effective means of preventing future attacks, even if civilian casualties resulted.

As shown in Figure 4.5, nearly two in three of those surveyed said that they would support military action even if it meant that innocent civilians in other countries might be hurt or killed.

There is some evidence of erosion in Americans' willingness to support military operations in Afghanistan if they resulted in civilian casualties (Table 4.3): The percentage who told *Newsweek*/PSRA that they would favor attacking terrorist bases abroad even if there were a high likelihood of civilian casualties slipped from 71 percent in the September 13–14 and September 20–21 polls, to 65 percent in the September 27–28 poll.

And polling by Fox News/Opinion Dynamics suggests that most Americans were undeterred in their support for war, even if it resulted in thousands of deaths among civilian noncombatants, though there was some movement in this belief as well. The September and October 2001 and March 2002 results from Fox News/Opinion Dynamics, which asked about support for military action even if it resulted in thousands of civilian lives being lost, show that the percentage saying they would still support such a war increased slightly from September

Table 4.2
Judgments About Effectiveness of Military Strikes if Civilian Casualties

"(How effective do you think each of the following would be in preventing terrorist attacks in the future?) What about . . . military strikes against terrorist targets, even if there might be civilian casualties? Would this be very effective, somewhat effective, not too effective, or not at all effective?"	9/13–14/2001 (%)	9/20–21/2001 (%)
Very effective	49	46
Somewhat effective	33	31
Not too effective	7	11
Not at all effective	6	8
Don't know	5	4

SOURCE: *Newsweek*/PSRA polls conducted September 13–14, 2001, N = 1,001; and September 20–21, 2001, N = 1,005.

Figure 4.5
Support for Military Action in Afghanistan Even with Civilian Casualties,
Late September 2001

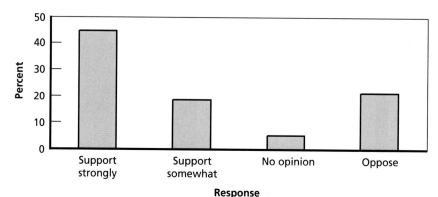

SOURCE: *The Washington Post*/TNS Intersearch poll conducted, September 25–27, 2001, N = 1,215.

NOTE: Question read, "Asked of the 90 percent who supported taking action against the groups or nations responsible for the attack: What if it meant innocent civilians in other countries might be hurt or killed—in that case would you support or oppose taking military action (against the groups or nations responsible for the recent terrorist attacks on the World Trade Center and Pentagon, September 11, 2001)? (If support, ask:) Do you feel that way strongly or somewhat?"

RAND MG441-4.5

to October 2001, and then fell back somewhat by March 2002, while still hovering around six in ten.

Several polling organizations asked Americans whether they believed that the military was doing all it could to avoid civilian casualties, or whether they thought that they were regrettable but ultimately unavoidable results of modern warfare.

Table 4.4 reports that 85 percent of those polled by ABC News/ *The Washington Post* in mid-October 2001 thought that the United States was doing all that it reasonably could to try to avoid civilian casualties in Afghanistan, and polling by Gallup/CNN/*USA Today* at about the same time showed an identical result: Eighty-five percent considered civilian casualties to be an unavoidable aspect of war.

When asked, most Americans indicated that it was more important to achieve victory than avoid civilian casualties when using force; note that the question did not ask specifically about Afghanistan, but

Table 4.3
Approval of Military Action if Civilian Casualties Would Result

Survey	First Poll (%)	Second Poll (%)	Third Poll (%)
"Thinking about a possible US (United States) military response to the terrorist attacks on (New York City and Washington, DC) September 11th (2001), would you favor or oppose attacking terrorist bases and the countries that allow or support them even if there is a high likelihood of civilian casualties?" (*Newsweek*/PSRA polls conducted September 13-14, 2001, N = 1,001; September 20-21, 2001, N = 1,005; and September 27–28, 2001, N = 1,000)	9/13–14/2001	9/20–21/2001	9/27–28/2001
Support	71	71	65
Oppose	21	21	24
Not sure	8	8	11
"Would you support or oppose the military action (in Afghanistan in response to the terrorist attacks on the World Trade Center and the Pentagon, September 11, 2001) even if it cost the lives of thousands of civilians in the countries we attack?" (Fox News/Opinion Dynamics polls conducted September 19–20, 2001, N = 900; October 17–18, 2001, N = 900; and March 12–13, 2002, N = 900)	9/19–20/2001	10/17–18/2001	3/12–13/2002
Support	63	66	59
Oppose	26	21	22
Not sure	11	13	19

NOTE: The second question was asked of those who supported the military action being taken in Afghanistan in response to the terrorist attacks on the World Trade Center and the Pentagon or were not sure. In all cases, that was 94 percent of the respondents. Sixty-six percent of 94 percent is 62 percent, 59 percent of the 94 percent is 55.5 percent, and 63 percent of 94 percent is 59 percent.

Table 4.4
United States Doing All It Reasonably Can to Avoid Casualties?

Survey	Percent
"Do you think the United States is doing all it reasonably can do to try to avoid civilian casualties in Afghanistan, or do you think it should do more?" (ABC News/ *The Washington Post* poll conducted October 15, 2001, N = 509).	
United States is doing all it can	85
United States should do more	12
No opinion	2
"There have been reports recently about civilian casualties in Afghanistan as a result of the US (United States) military action there. Which comes closer to your view—these civilian casualties are an unavoidable aspect of war, or these civilian casualties could have been avoided if the US took proper care?" (Gallup/CNN/*USA Today* poll conducted October 19–21, 2001, N = 1,006).	
Casualties are unavoidable	85
Casualties could be avoided	13
No opinion	2

Table 4.5
Greater Concern About Civilian Casualties or Achieving Victory?

"What do you worry about more when the United States uses military force? That the U.S. doesn't do enough to avoid civilian casualties or that the U.S. doesn't go far enough to achieve military victory?"	Percent
That the U.S. doesn't do enough to avoid civilian casualties	25
That the U.S. doesn't go far enough to achieve military victory	56
Don't know/refused	19

SOURCE: Pew Research Center/PSRA poll conducted November 13–19, 2001, N = 1,500.

rather, more generally about how the United States manages its conflict. The result in Table 4.5, from polling in November 2001 by the Pew Research Center, found that by a margin of more than two to one, a majority, 56 percent, thought that the United States did not go far enough to achieve military victory when it went to war, while only one in four said that it did not do enough to avoid civilian casualties.

And Table 4.6 shows that fewer than one in five thought that the information the U.S. government was providing on civilian casualties in Afghanistan was very accurate, while a little over half thought that it was somewhat accurate.

In light of these results, in which very large majorities stated the belief that the U.S. military was doing all it could to avoid civilian casualties and most thought the United States should try harder to achieve victory than to avoid civilian casualties, this result should not be read as suggesting government deception or the absence of full disclosure. Rather, it seems likely that it has to do with the difficulties of confirming civilian casualties in situations in which the United States does not actually control the ground where incidents are alleged to have occurred. Lacking accurate information itself, the U.S. government is incapable of providing accurate information to the public.

Finally, although it does not address civilian casualties resulting directly from U.S. military operations, nearly nine in ten of those polled by Ipsos Reid in September 2001 who supported an all-out commitment to a war on terrorism said that they would still be prepared to join in such a war even if it could expose Americans to further attacks (Table 4.7).

Table 4.6
Accuracy of Information Government Is Providing About Civilian Casualties

"How accurate do you think the information the government is providing about the number of civilian casualties in Afghanistan is? Would you say very accurate, somewhat accurate, not very or not at all accurate?"	Percent
Very accurate	16
Somewhat accurate	53
Not very accurate	19
Not at all accurate	6
Not sure	4

SOURCE: Harris poll conducted November 14–20, 2001, N = 1,011.

Table 4.7
Approval of Military Action if Civilian Casualties Would Result

"I'm now going to read you some statements about the terrorist attacks (on the World Trade Center and the Pentagon, September 11, 2001) and the United States' declaration of war on terrorism. For each one, I'd like you to tell me if you strongly agree, somewhat agree, somewhat disagree, or strongly disagree. Would you still be prepared to join the all-out war on international terrorism if you knew that it could expose civilians in the US (United States) to attack by terrorists?"	Percent
Yes	88
No	11
Not sure	1

SOURCE: Ipsos Reid (poll conducted September 21–23, 2001, N = 1,000) asked of the 86 percent who agreed that the United States should commit to an all-out war on international terrorism.

NOTE: Asked of the 90 percent who supported taking military action against the groups or nations responsible for the attack. Fifty percent of 90 percent is 45 percent.

Taken together, these results suggest the following:

- The war in Afghanistan enjoyed some of the highest public support measured since the 1991 Gulf War, and at most, only about one in ten Americans said they would withhold their support for the war if there was a strong possibility of civilian deaths.
- More generally, when asked to weigh possible tradeoffs between ensuring military victory and avoiding civilian deaths in its wars, more than half said that the United States generally does not go far enough to ensure military victory.
- Although there appears to have been some slight erosion in the willingness to support a war involving large numbers of civilian deaths, at least six in ten said that their support for the war would be unaffected by civilian casualties.

Again, these attitudes suggest much lower sensitivity to civilian casualties than was observed in the 1999 war in Kosovo, perhaps rivaling attitudes toward casualties in the 1991 Gulf War.

Statistical Results. We were unable to find a data set that would enable us to estimate a multivariate model that included a civilian casualties variable along with variables indicating respondents' views on factors that have in the past been shown to be excellent predictors of support and opposition: the perceived importance of the stakes, prospects for success, U.S. military casualties, and party orientation.

However, our multivariate probit model correctly predicted approval or disapproval for about 84 percent of the respondents in the poll based solely upon their beliefs about whether the United States' security interests demanded a leading role for the United States in taking action against al Qaeda, the prospects for success, and U.S. military casualties, suggesting that fairly good predictions were possible even without considering the issue of civilian casualties.[9] Put another way, it is difficult to imagine that a variable for civilian casualties could have much improved our predictions of support and opposition in this case.

Antiwar Demonstrations. Planning for antiwar protest activity started even before the war began on October 7, 2001, and college campuses were riven by both antiwar and prowar demonstrations.[10] Most of this protest activity seems to have receded by the end of December 2001, although as late as April 2002, protesters gathered in Washington, D.C., to demonstrate against a litany of issues, including globalization, the World Bank, Israeli policy toward the West Bank, and the war in Afghanistan, and there was some reporting of antiwar activity through the end of 2002 as the United States appeared to be moving toward war in Iraq (Sanchez, 2001; Harmon, 2001; Maureen O'Hagan, 2001; "Protests in Nation's Capital Remain Peaceful," 2002; "Second Day of Protests Getting Underway in Washington," 2002; Alan C. Miller, 2002; Neuman, 2002; Trejos, 2002; O'Neill, 2002).

---

[9] The President also may have benefited from his still-preternaturally high approval rating: ABC News/*The Washington Post* (poll conducted November 27, 2001, N = 759) found 80 percent approved of the President's job handling in the poll we used for our statistical modeling.

[10] Reports that a Washington protest group was planning an antiwar march in the capital emerged on September 21, 2001 (Lou Dobbs, 2001). See also Alexandra Marks (2001), Mehren (2001), Niebuhr (2001), and Wilgoren (2001).

Foreign Media and Public Opinion

Foreign Media. Foreign reporting on Afghanistan showed the same general pattern (Figure 4.6): a peak occurring with the onset of military operations in October 2001, followed by an equally dramatic decline.

Foreign Public Opinion. As with the other cases we examined, it was more difficult to find public opinion data on foreign attitudes, and most of the data we were able to find were from European publics.

We found only one question that asked foreign publics about their attitudes toward potential civilian casualties: Gallup International's mid-September 2001 poll asked respondents in 36 countries whether the United States should attack only military targets, or whether it should attack both military and civilian targets, if it decided to launch an attack (Figure 4.7).

Figure 4.6
Selected Foreign Media Reporting on Afghanistan,
August 2001–March 2004

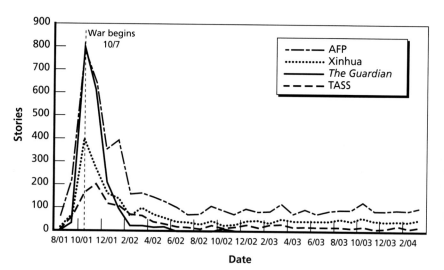

SOURCE: Search for "Afghanistan" in AFP, *The Guardian* (London), TASS, and Xinhua.
RAND *MG441-4.6*

Figure 4.7
Should the United States Attack Military and Civilian Targets?
Mid-September 2001

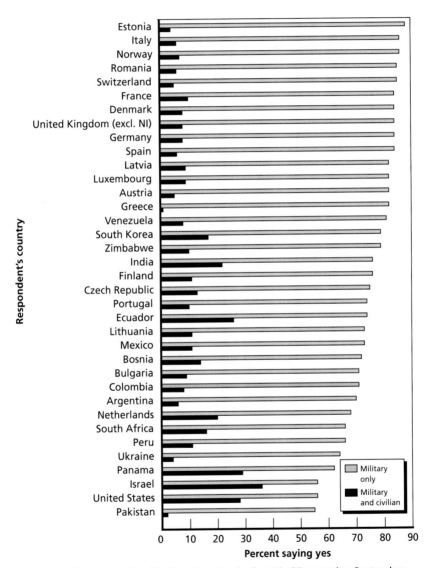

SOURCE: Gallup International Poll on Terrorism in the U.S., 37 countries, September 14–17, 2001.
NOTE: Question read, "If the United States decides to launch attack, should the American government attack military targets only or both military and civilian targets?"
RAND *MG441-4.7*

Not surprisingly, most foreign publics overwhelmingly preferred that the United States restrict itself to military targets. Only small percentages said they thought the United States should attack both military and civilian targets.

Gallup International's International Poll on Terrorism surveyed respondents in 37 countries during the week after the September 11 attacks and asked questions about support for U.S. military action and participation of their country's military in the U.S. military action (Figure 4.8).

The figure shows that majorities in only three of the 37 countries polled—Israel, India, and the United States—supported a U.S. military attack on the countries harboring the terrorists, which, at the time, were not definitively known.[11] And when asked whether they thought their country should participate in U.S. military action, majorities in only 13 of the 35 countries that were asked this question responded affirmatively (Figure 4.9).

Ipsos Reid's November 2001 poll of 20 countries found majority support for the U.S.-led air strikes in Afghanistan in only nine countries; fewer than a majority backed the United States in the other 11 (see Figure 4.10).

A November–December 2001 Flash Eurobarometer poll found that majorities in 12 of the 15 European publics surveyed supported sharing intelligence with the United States, majorities in 10 supported giving permission to use military bases, while majorities in only five supported sending troops (European Commission, 2001).

The Chicago Council on Foreign Relations and the German Marshall Fund Transatlantic Trends polled residents of six European countries and the United States in June and July 2002 and asked them to rate the Bush administration's handling of the war in Afghanistan (Figure 4.11).[12]

---

[11] Most preferred that the United States seek the extradition of the terrorists.

[12] Approval of the war on terrorism was somewhat higher; the percentages saying that the administration was doing a good or excellent job were as follows: Britain (38 percent); France (26 percent); Germany (51 percent); Netherlands (45 percent); Italy (50 percent); Poland (53 percent); United States (55 percent).

Figure 4.8
Support for U.S. Military Action, Mid-September 2001

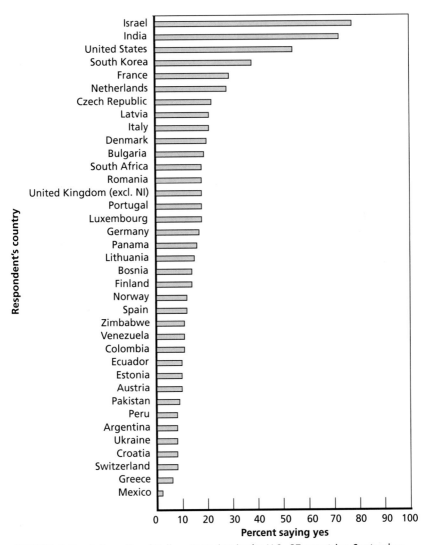

SOURCE: Gallup International Poll on Terrorism in the U.S., 37 countries, September 14–17, 2001.
NOTE: Question read, "In your opinion, once the identity of the terrorists is known, should the American government launch a military attack on the country or countries where the terrorists are based or should the American government seek to extradite the terrorists to stand trial?"

RAND *MG441-4.8*

Figure 4.9
Approval of Own Country's Military Participating in U.S. Military Action, September 2001

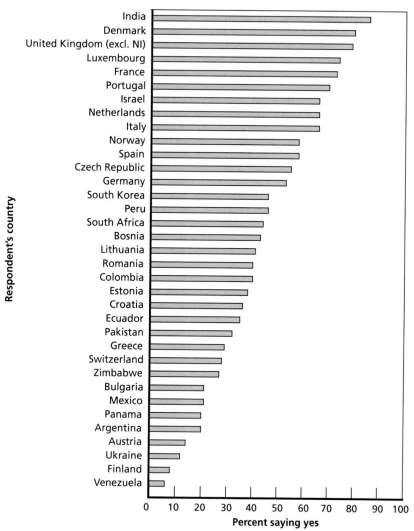

SOURCE: Gallup International Poll on Terrorism in the U.S., 37 countries, September 14–17, 2001.

NOTE: Question read, "Some countries and all NATO member states have agreed to participate in any military actions against the terrorists responsible for the attacks or against those countries harbouring the terrorists. Do you agree or disagree that <your country> should take part in military actions against terrorists with the United States?"

RAND MG441-4.9

Figure 4.10
Support for U.S. Air War in Afghanistan in 20 Countries,
November–December 2001

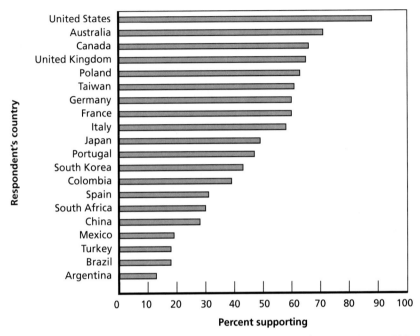

SOURCE: Ipsos Reid survey of 20 countries, November 19–December 17, 2001, N = 500
in all countries except the United States, where N = 1,000.
NOTE: Question read, "As you know, the United States has launched military strikes on
targets in Afghanistan—including military sites of the Taliban government and training
camps of the Al Qaeda group led by Osama Bin Laden. All things considered, do you
support or oppose these U.S.-led air strikes on Afghanistan? "
RAND MG441-4.10

Figure 4.11 shows that only in the United States did a majority
say that the administration's handling of the war in Afghanistan was
good or excellent. Although the reluctance of the six foreign publics to
credit the administration's handling of Afghanistan could be due in
part to the record of civilian deaths in Afghanistan, there is no direct
evidence that that is the case.

Figure 4.11
Rating of Bush Administration Handling of the War in Afghanistan in the United States and Six European Countries, June–July 2002

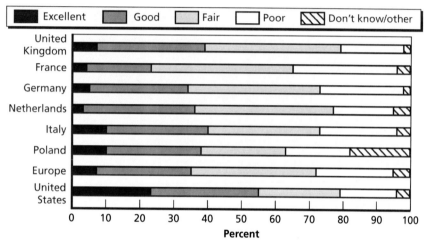

SOURCE: Chicago Council on Foreign Relations, Transatlantic Trends polls conducted June–July 2002.
NOTE: Question read, "IN EUROPE: How do you rate the George W. Bush administration's handling of the following problems? Would you say the American administration's handling of the war in Afghanistan has been excellent, good, fair, or poor? IN THE U.S.: How do you rate the Bush administration's handling of the following problems? Would you say the administration's handling of the war in Afghanistan has been excellent, good, fair, or poor?"
RAND MG441-4.11

Although the question did not ask directly about U.S. military operations in Afghanistan, polling by the Pew Research Center's Global Attitudes Project in the summer and fall of 2002 shows that majorities in about three-fourths (32 of 43) of the countries polled approved of the U.S.-led efforts to fight terrorism at the time (Figure 4.12), while less than a majority approved in the remaining 11 countries, many of which were Islamic countries.

Although there are some differences in question wording or other technical factors that suggest we should be careful in making comparisons between the results of the two polls, we compared the percentage approving of military action in three polls (Gallup International's mid-September 2001 and November–December 2001 polls, and Ipsos Reid's November–December 2001 poll) with the percentage approving

Figure 4.12
Support for U.S.-Led War on Terrorism in 43 Countries, July–October 2002

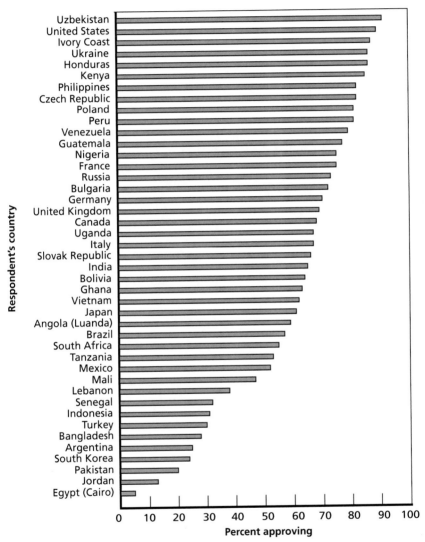

SOURCE: Pew Research Center for People and the Press (2002).

NOTE: While polling in most countries took place in July and August 2002, in some countries, polling took place as late as September–October. These included the United States, Angola (Luanda only), Egypt (Cairo only), India, Ghana, Lebanon, Ivory Coast, Mali, Jordan, Nigeria, Kenya, Pakistan, South Africa, Senegal, and Uganda.

RAND MG441-4.12

of the war on terrorism from the Pew Research Center's July–October 2002 poll, which was fielded after the wedding party incident.

Table 4.8 suggests that an increasing number of foreign publics polled approved of U.S. military action in Afghanistan or the war on terrorism, though the Transatlantic Trends survey is an exception.

And as shown in Table 4.9, we calculated the average increase in support for the U.S. military operation in Afghanistan from the first to the last poll to be 29.4 points. Although wording differences prevent

Table 4.8
Number of Foreign Publics Polled and Number Where Majority Supported United States

Poll	Countries Polled	Majorities Supporting United States
Gallup International, International Poll on Terrorism, mid-September 2001: "In your opinion, once the identity of the terrorists is known, should the American government launch a military attack on the country or countries where the terrorists are based or should the American government seek to extradite the terrorists to stand trial?"	37	2
Ipsos Reid, November–December 2001: "As you know, the United States has launched military strikes on targets in Afghanistan—including military sites of the Taliban government and training camps of the Al Qaeda group led by Osama Bin Laden. All things considered, do you support or oppose these U.S.-led air strikes on Afghanistan?"	19	8
Chicago Council on Foreign Relations (CCFR)–German Marshall Fund Transatlantic Trends, June–July 2002	6	0
Pew Research Center, July–October 2002: "And which comes closer to describing your view? I favor the US-led efforts to fight terrorism, OR I oppose the US-led efforts to fight terrorism."	42	31

Table 4.9
Differences in Support,
November–December 2001 and July–October 2002 Polls

Country	Gallup Int'l Mid-Sep 01 (%)	Gallup Int'l Nov–Dec 01 (%)	Ipsos Reid Nov–Dec 01 (%)	Pew Jul–Oct 02 (%)	Change (%)
Argentina	8	14	13	25	+17
France	29	73	60	75	+46
Germany	17	65	60	70	+53
Italy	21	60	58	67	+46
Mexico	2	21	19	52	+50
South Korea	38	43	43	24	-14
United Kingdom	18	68	65	69	+51
United States	54	88	88	89	+35
Japan		33	49	61	+28
Poland		61	63	81	+20
Turkey		16	18	30	+14
Brazil			18	57	+39
Canada			66	68	+2
South Africa			30	55	+25
				Average:	29.4

NOTES: Wording for questions: Gallup International International Poll on Terrorism mid-September 2001: "In your opinion, once the identity of the terrorists is known, should the American government launch a military attack on the country or countries where the terrorists are based or should the American government seek to extradite the terrorists to stand trial?" Gallup International International Poll on Terrorism November–December 2001: "Do you personally agree or disagree with the United States military action [in Afghanistan]?" Ipsos Reid November–December 2001: "As you know, the United States has launched military strikes on targets in Afghanistan— including military sites of the Taliban government, and training camps of the Al Qaeda group led by Osama Bin Laden. All things considered, do you support or oppose these U.S.-led air strikes on Afghanistan?" Pew Research Center July–October 2002: "And which comes closer to describing your view? I favor the US-led efforts to fight terrorism, OR I oppose the US-led efforts to fight terrorism."

any definitive conclusions, the result does not suggest diminished support over time.[13]

Taken together, except for the tepid reading on the Bush administration's handling of the war on terrorism from the CCFR Transatlantic Trends survey, the data on foreign attitudes that we found did not suggest that civilian casualties in Afghanistan had had an impact on support from foreign publics for the U.S. war in Afghanistan and the larger war on terrorism.

Antiwar Demonstrations. Antiwar demonstrations abroad were reported in Amsterdam, London, Paris, Rome, Berlin, and Bern shortly after the war began, even as many European governments—including the United Kingdom, France, Germany, Spain, and Italy—pledged support for the U.S. military campaign in Afghanistan (Daley, 2001; Boston, 2001; Winestock, 2001). Thousands of antiwar demonstrators also were reported as late as June 2002, during President Bush's visit to Germany and just after his speech at West Point outlining his doctrine of preemptive military action against terrorism (Chen, 2002).

The Wedding Party Incident

Background on the Incident

On July 1, 2002, U.S. aircraft attacked six sites in an Afghan village in the Oruzgan province, which most considered a Taliban stronghold where the Taliban enjoyed a great deal of popular support (CENTCOM, 2002).

Afghan villagers claimed that celebratory fire from a wedding party had led to an errant attack by U.S. AC-130 aircraft. According to the unclassified summary of the official CENTCOM investigation into the incident, however, it was only after several days of hostile

---

[13] Moreover, between May 2001 and July 2002, the belief that NATO was essential to one's country's defense increased by 14 points in France and Germany, 15 points in Italy, and 11 points in the United Kingdom. While it is not clear the extent to which the war in Afghanistan may have been responsible for these changes, it does not suggest reduced support for NATO as a result of the way the war in Afghanistan was prosecuted (Eichenberg, 2003b, pp. 651–654).

fire from anti-aircraft artillery (AAA) weapons that Operation FULL THROTTLE was conducted to eliminate the threat to coalition aircraft (CENTCOM, 2002). CENTCOM described the circumstances of the incident as follows:

> There were people within this area of Oruzgan Province that regularly aimed and fired a variety of weapons at coalition aircraft. These weapons represented a real threat to coalition forces. As [Operation FULL THROTTLE] commenced, AAA weapons were fired and, as a result, an AC-130 aircraft, acting properly and in accordance with the rules, engaged the locations of those weapons. Great care was taken to strike only those sites that were actively firing that night. While the coalition regrets the loss of innocent lives, the responsibility for that loss rests with those that knowingly directed hostile fire at coalition forces. The operators of those weapons elected to place them in civilian communities and elected to fire them at coalition forces at a time when they knew there were a significant number of civilians present. (CENTCOM, 2002)

Estimates of the human toll of the attack also varied. The Afghan government would later estimate that 48 people were killed and 117 wounded in the attack, including many women and children; although not challenging this estimate, U.S. forces were only able to confirm 34 dead and approximately 50 wounded (Rubin, 2004).

The timeline following the incident is reported in Table 4.10. The timeline suggests that hours passed before the incident was first reported by DPA, which shortly thereafter cited CNN reporting on the incident.[14] It subsequently was on CNN and *CBS Evening News*. As shown in the right side of the table, reporters asked about the incident in the DoD's news briefings on July 2, 3, and 8.

---

[14] A report from Deutsche Presse-Agentur time-stamped 1712 Central European Time cited a U.S. spokesman in Kabul reporting about 40 deaths when U.S. planes struck a wedding party in southern Afghanistan. A report 21 minutes later cited CNN reporting on the incident. (See Deutsche Presse-Agentur, 2002a, 2002b.)

Table 4.10
Postincident Timeline for Wedding Party Incident

Media Reporting Highlights	Official Handling Highlights
6/30	
1530: Incident occurs (0100 7/1 local)	
7/1	
1042: Deutsche Presse-Agentur reports	
1103: Deutsche Presse-Agentur cites CNN	
1700: CNN airs *Wolf Bliitzer Reports*	
1830: *CBS Evening News* airs	
7/2	7/2
0458: Voice of Islamic Republic of Iran reports	1230: Secretary of Defense Rumsfeld takes questions in DoD news briefing (airs on CNN)
0500: *CNN Daybreak* reports	
0700: NBC *Today* airs	
1230: CNN airs DoD news briefing	
7/3	7/3
1830: *CBS Evening News* and *NBC Evening News* air	1130: DoD gives news briefing and takes questions
	7/4
	DoD holds no news briefing
	7/8
	1230: DoD gives news briefing and takes questions

NOTE: All times are Eastern unless otherwise indicated.

U.S. Media and Public Opinion Responses

U.S. Media. As shown in Figure 4.13, both major U.S. newspaper and television reporting increased following the incident, with television showing the highest reporting levels.

U.S. Public Opinion. Table 4.11 shows that there was a statistically significant increase in the percentage who said that they were following the U.S. military effort in Afghanistan after the July 1 wedding party incident: It rose from 70 percent in Pew Research Center's June 19–23 poll to 79 percent in its July 8–16 poll. It is impossible to determine whether this is accountable to the wedding incident or not, however, as other developments—the assassination of Vice President Abdul Qadir,

Figure 4.13
Reporting on Civilian Casualties in Afghanistan in Major Papers and on Television

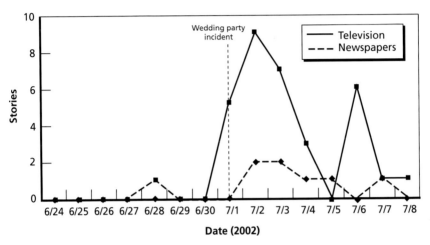

SOURCE: Search for "Afghanistan" and "civilian casualties," "civilian deaths," or "collateral damage" in *The Christian Science Monitor, Los Angeles Times, The New York Times, The Wall Street Journal, The Washington Post,* ABC News, CBS News, CNN, and NBC News.

RAND *MG441-4.13*

Afghan president Karzai's efforts to challenge the warlords, continued military action against al Qaeda, and the John Walker Lindh trial—also occurred in July. It is also noteworthy that the increased attention in July represented a partial recovery to the attention levels at the end of May 2002.

The only question on approval for U.S. military action in Afghanistan that appears to have been asked before and after the wedding party incident was a question asked by Gallup/CNN/*USA Today* in March and September 2002 (Table 4.12), which showed a decline of eight points in support for military action in Afghanistan. Given the poor timing of the polling—the question was first asked nearly four months before the wedding party incident, and then again about two months after the incident—it is impossible to rule out that many factors other than the wedding party incident may have played in this decline.

Table 4.11
Attention Paid to Afghanistan Before and After July 1 Incident

"Now I will read a list of some stories covered by news organizations this past month. As I read each item, tell me if you happened to follow this news story very closely, fairly closely, not too closely, or not at all closely: the US (United States) military effort in Afghanistan?" (Pew Research Center/PSRA, 6/19–23/2002, N = 1,212, and 7/8–16/2002, N = 1,365) "Now I'm going to read you a list of some stories covered by news organizations in the last month or so. As I read each one, tell me if you happened to follow this news story very closely, fairly closely, not too closely, or not at all closely. How closely did you follow this story: the U.S. (United States) military efforts in Afghanistan?" (Henry J. Kaiser Family Foundation/Harvard School of Public Health/PSRA, 7/18–20/2002, N = 1,208)	5/31–6/3/2002 (%)	6/19–23/2001 (%)	7/8–16/2001 (%)	7/18–20/2001 (%)
Very closely	51	38	41	46
Fairly closely	32	32	38	36
Not too closely	11	20	13	11
Not at all closely	6	9	7	7
Don't know/refused	1	1	1	—

NOTE: Change in very and fairly closely was statistically significant at the 0.001 level. — = increase of less than 0.5 percent.

As Table 4.12 also shows, questions were asked about respondents' approval of the president's handling of the war on terrorism before and after the incident by four different polling organizations. In three of these four cases, there actually appears to have been a statistically significant *increase* in support for the war on terrorism between the two polls, while in one case, there was a slight (but not statistically significant) decline. If we assume that the polling on the question of support for the war on terrorism is in fact tapping support for the war in Afghanistan, and that polling done closer to the incident is likely to be

Table 4.12
Approval Before and After the July 1 Wedding Party Incident

Poll	Before	After	Change
"Do you approve or disapprove of U.S. military action in Afghanistan?" (Gallup/CNN/ *USA Today*)	3/8–9/2002 91%	9/2–4/2002 83%	–8%****
"Do you approve or disapprove of the (George W. Bush) is handling the U.S. campaign against terrorism?" (ABC News/*The Washington Post*)	5/18–19/2002 78%	7/11–15/2002 82%	+4%***
"Do you approve or disapprove of the job President Bush is doing on the following issues: handling terrorism?" (Fox News/ Opinion Dynamics)	6/4–5/2002 73%	7/23–24/2002 77%	+4%*
"When it comes to dealing with the war on terrorism, do you approve or disapprove the job George W. Bush is doing?" (*The Wall Street Journal*/Hart and Teeter)	6/8–10/2002 75%	7/19–21/2002 73%	–2%
"Do you approve or disapprove of the way George W. Bush is handling the campaign against terrorism?" (CBS News)	6/18–20/2002 72%	7/8–9/2002 77%	+5%*

NOTES: * = p-value statistically significant at the 0.05 level. ** = p-value statistically significant at the 0.01 level. *** = p-value statistically significant at the 0.005 level. **** = p-value statistically significant at the 0.001 level.

more reliable in indicating changes that might have been accountable to the wedding party incident, then these results suggest an increase in support following the incident, though again, it is impossible to rule out the possibility that other factors also may have been at work. In any event, there is scant evidence that the incident led to an observable decline in support.

Antiwar Demonstrations. We found no evidence that the wedding party incident led to an increase in antiwar demonstration activity in the United States.

Foreign Media and Public Opinion Responses

Foreign Media. Foreign media responses to the wedding party incident were mixed. Figure 4.14 shows that only AFP dramatically increased its reporting on civilian casualties in the wake of the

Figure 4.14
Selected Foreign Media Reporting on Civilian Casualties in Afghanistan,
Wedding Party Incident

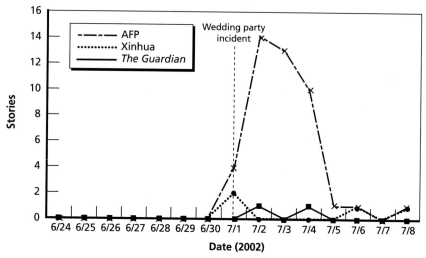

SOURCE: Search for "Afghanistan" and "civilian casualties," "civilian deaths," or "collateral damage" in AFP, *The Guardian* (London), and Xinhua.
RAND MG441-4.14

incident, while Xinhua and *The Guardian* devoted only a small amount of additional coverage to the subject.

Foreign Public Opinion. We found no adequate time series for foreign polling that would enable us to understand how the attitudes of foreign publics might have changed in response to the July 1 incident.

Antiwar Demonstrations. We found no evidence that the incident led to an increase in antiwar demonstration activity abroad.

Key Lessons

As described in this chapter, civilian casualties again were a relatively prominent, if somewhat secondary theme in U.S. and foreign media reporting on the war in Afghanistan, but the wedding party incident led to increased media attention to the subject of civilian casualties. It also seems that reporting on Afghanistan fell after the Taliban and al

Qaeda were routed in late 2001 and early 2002; with less reporting on Afghanistan, few were likely to be able to closely follow developments there.

The public opinion data on Americans' attitudes toward the war show that Americans paid very close attention to the war in Afghanistan but showed relatively little concern about civilian casualties incurred in the war. This seems to have been the result of a combination of beliefs, including the importance that they attached to defeating al Qaeda and the Taliban in Afghanistan, as well as continued faith that, in any case, the U.S. military was making sufficient efforts to avoid civilian casualties and that any casualties that did occur were unavoidable, if regrettable. Support for the war from foreign publics was, by comparison, quite mixed—strong in some countries, weak in others. Although we lack foreign public opinion data on this question, Americans' high and unflagging support and apparently low sensitivity to civilian casualties suggests that many foreign publics probably were far more sensitive to civilian casualties.

For policymakers and military leaders, the war in Afghanistan provides the second clear case—the other was the 1991 Gulf War—in which civilian casualties appear to have been of only modest concern to the American public, apparently eclipsed by its views of the stakes engendered in the conflict and the need to punish those responsible for the attacks of 9/11.[15] It also represents another case, however, in which Americans' beliefs that the U.S. military was doing everything that it could to avoid civilian casualties helps to explain what some might otherwise see as a rather callous portrait of ordinary Americans' views of human suffering by innocents during wartime.

---

[15] For a detailed analysis of how Americans viewed the stakes and other characteristics of Operation Enduring Freedom in Afghanistan, see Larson and Savych (2005a, 2005b).

CHAPTER FIVE

Operation Iraqi Freedom (Iraq, 2003–)

Following about six months of heightened diplomatic and military activity, Operation Iraqi Freedom—the invasion of Iraq and overthrow of Saddam Hussein's regime—began on March 19, 2003. President Bush announced the conclusion of major combat operations on May 1, although an insurgency involving remnants of Saddam's regime, disenfranchised Sunnis, foreign jihadists, and others, has since continued to plague the coalition's postwar occupation. This chapter will show that, although Americans appear to have been more sensitive to civilian casualties in this war than in the 1991 Gulf War or the more recent war in Afghanistan, the very high level of support that the combat phase of the war enjoyed seems to have been generally unaffected by civilian casualty incidents.

Civilian Casualty Estimates

The Department of Defense did not issue its own estimates of Iraqi civilian deaths from the 2003 war in Iraq. Estimates of Iraqi civilian deaths incurred during major combat operations in Iraq by others have varied:

- In mid-May 2003, the *Los Angeles Times* published the results of a survey of 27 hospitals in and around Baghdad and estimated that at least 1,700 civilians had died and another 8,000 were injured in the capital during combat operations conducted during the war (King, 2003).

- In late May 2003, *The Guardian* reported an estimate from an organization called Iraq Body Count that between 5,425 and 7,041 civilians had died as a result of the war and postconflict instability (see Steele, 2003, and Sloboda, 2003).[1] In June 2003, the organization summarized 15 separate efforts to estimate civilian casualties in Iraq, and estimated that there had been significantly more than 5,000 civilian deaths reports that were well founded (see Sloboda and Dardagan, 2003).[2]

- In June 2003, the Associated Press estimated at least 3,240 civilian deaths based on a survey of 60 Iraqi hospitals (see Price, 2003).[3]

- In October 2003, the Project on Defense Alternatives estimated between 3,200 and 4,300 civilian deaths (Conetta, 2003).

- In October 2003, Human Rights Watch claimed that thousands of Iraqi civilians had been killed in the war, basing this on estimates that there were 678 deaths in three Iraqi towns where hospital records were examined.

- In November 2003, a British group called Medact used Iraq Body Count's estimate that between 5,708 and 7,356 Iraqi civilians had been killed during the invasion, and between 7,757 and 9,565 Iraqi civilians had been killed through October 20, 2003.[4]

---

[1] According to Iraq Body Count's Web site: "In the current occupation phase this database includes all deaths which the Occupying Authority has a binding responsibility to prevent under the Geneva Conventions and Hague Regulations. This includes civilian deaths resulting from the breakdown in law and order, and deaths due to inadequate health care or sanitation." Thus, its totals include deaths that are not claimed to have resulted directly from U.S. military action.

[2] While it may be useful for setting an upper-bound estimate on civilian deaths, the methodology of relying heavily on press reports for estimates of civilian dead tends to overestimate the toll in civilian war dead (Suarez, 2004). For scathing indictments of antiwar critics' reliance on press accounts and adversaries' claims of civilian casualties, see Muravchik (2002) and Chafetz (2003).

[3] A breakdown of civilian deaths by city can be found in AP (2003).

[4] Medact used an estimate from Iraq Body Count that, as of October 2003, between 13,500 and 45,000 Iraqi military personnel were killed in the war, for a total of 21,700 and 55,000 Iraqi deaths between March 20 and October 20, 2003 (Farooq et al., 2003).

Medact's first report, issued in November 2002, projected that major combat operations would lead to 2,000 to 50,000 civilian deaths in Baghdad alone, and another 1,200 to

- Before being captured, Saddam Hussein charged that somewhere between 13,000 and 45,000 Iraqi civilians had died as a consequence of the U.S. attack (Joya, 2004).

Our analyses suggest that despite the prominence of the issue in media reporting and public opinion questions, Iraqi civilian deaths did not particularly affect Americans' support for or other key attitudes toward the war, though they may have strengthened preexisting opposition to the war among American war opponents and foreign audiences.

Handling of the Civilian Casualties Issue

Baghdad sought to convince the world that the United States was not only careless in its targeting, but that the United States was "killing civilians wherever they can," and provided details on alleged incidents of civilian deaths that were resulting from "criminal bombardment of Americans and British" (see, for example, Federal News Service, 2003g, 2003h; "Iraq's al-Sahhaf Briefs Press on War Activities," 2003) and claimed that the death toll was in fact much higher than the coalition was acknowledging. The Baghdad regime also ensured that civilian casualties were reported in Iraqi-controlled media, although the air war seems to have halted the operations of some state-controlled radio and television facilities.[5]

By comparison, from the earliest days of the war, members of the coalition stressed their commitment to minimizing civilian casualties:

30,000 civilian deaths in the Iraqi cities of Basra, Diyala, Kirkuk, and Mosul. Within three months of the end of the conventional war, Medact further predicted an additional 60,000 or more deaths, including 4,000–6,000 Iraqi civilians; 20,000 Iraqi civilian deaths in civil war; 15,000–30,000 refugee deaths; and 23,500 additional deaths among children under age five. Thus, the low end of its prediction for the war was about 3,200 civilian deaths, and its prediction for the postwar period was more than another 60,000 (Salvage et al., 2002, p. 10).

[5] For example, the last time Baghdad Republic of Iraq Television broadcasting was observed by FBIS was on March 24, 2003 (Foreign Broadcast Information Service, 2003a).

- The White House stressed the President's commitment to the principle that the military's planning and operations sought to minimize Iraqi civilian casualties. For example, White House spokesman Ari Fleischer stated on March 20, 2003, "Throughout the process, the President has stressed, going way back as the military planning began, that all actions taken by the military need to be done in a way to minimize civilian causalities, and that is also something the United States military takes very seriously and carries out on their own as well" (Federal News Service, 2003c).
- The United States' British allies similarly stressed their commitment to avoiding civilian deaths.[6]
- The commander of CENTCOM, General Tommy Franks, also highlighted the importance of protecting innocent lives, both coalition and civilian, during the war (Federal News Service, 2003e).
- The Pentagon briefed on its efforts to reduce the potential for collateral damage and civilian casualties, even as the U.S. military stressed that civilian casualties were unavoidable in war (Federal News Service, 2003a, 2003i, 2003l).

During the war, the United States routinely expressed deep regret for possible incidents of civilian deaths that might have occurred as a result of U.S. military action, while stressing the difficulties of actually confirming the facts regarding alleged incidents of civilian deaths.[7] The United States also disparaged Iraqi claims of high civilian losses while at the same time pointing to the Iraqis' use of human shields and their policy of ordering death squads to conduct executions of Iraqi civilians (Federal News Service, 2003k).

---

[6]   See, for example, Federal News Service (2003b, 2003d).

[7]   See, for example, Federal News Service (2003f, 2003j).

The Arc of Media and Public Concern

U.S. Media and Public Opinion

U.S. Media Reporting. As described in the other cases we examined, there was a build-up in U.S. media reporting on Iraq prior to the onset of hostilities that peaked with the onset of military operations and then fell off dramatically with the conclusion of major combat operations in early May 2003 (see Figure 5.1).

Figure 5.1 describes media reporting levels on Iraq by four major U.S. television networks and five major national newspapers. Media reporting on Iraq increased shortly after the administration began pressing the issue of Iraqi compliance with past UN resolutions on its weapons of mass destruction programs in August 2002 and increased dramatically in the months leading up to the war, peaking in April 2003 and falling afterward.

Figure 5.1
U.S. Major Television and Major Reporting on Iraq,
August 2002–March 2004

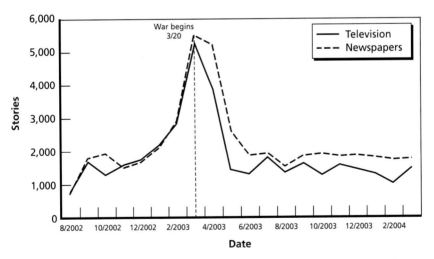

SOURCE: Search for "Iraq" in full text of *The Christian Science Monitor, Los Angeles Times, The New York Times, The Wall Street Journal, The Washington Post,* ABC News, CBS News, CNN, and NBC News.

RAND *MG441-5.1*

Figure 5.2 reports the weekly number of news stories in newspapers and on major television networks from the beginning of March 2003 into early June; it shows that news reporting peaked in the first week of the war.[8]

Figure 5.3 suggests that the topic of civilian casualties was a recurring one in U.S. media reporting, but it followed the general arc of overall reporting levels on Iraq: The topic of civilian casualties received a small amount of reporting through the fall of 2002, became much more prominent once the war actually was under way in March 2003, and, with the conclusion of major combat operations on May 1, dropped back to prewar levels.

Figure 5.2
Weekly Major News Reporting on Iraq, March–June 2003

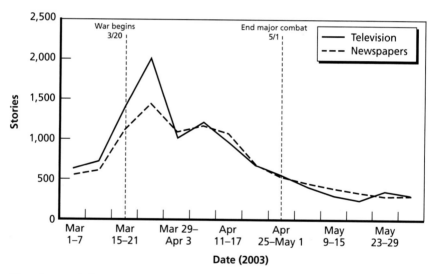

SOURCE: Search for "Iraq" in full text of *The Christian Science Monitor, Los Angeles Times, The New York Times, The Wall Street Journal, The Washington Post,* ABC News, CBS News, CNN, and NBC News.
RAND *MG441-5.2*

---

[8] The war began on March 20, 2003, and major combat operations were declared concluded on May 1, 2003.

Figure 5.3
Major U.S. Media Reporting on Iraq and Civilian Casualties,
August 2002–March 2004

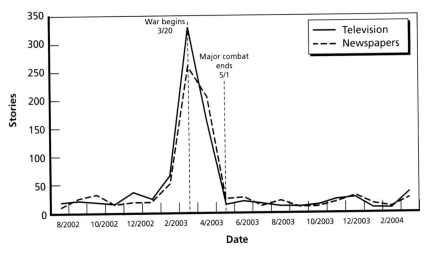

SOURCE: Search for "Iraq" and "civilian casualties," "civilian deaths," or "collateral damage" in *The Christian Science Monitor, Los Angeles Times, The New York Times, The Wall Street Journal, The Washington Post,* ABC News, CBS News, CNN, and NBC News.

RAND *MG441-5.3*

It is somewhat more difficult to get a sense of the content and tone of news reporting. However, the CMPA analyzed content in television news reporting during major combat operations in Iraq from March 19 to April 14 (when Saddam's hometown of Tikrit fell), and from May 1 to October 31, 2003 (Figure 5.4) (CMPA, 2003a, 2003b).

CMPA's study included a tabulation of the video content of television news stories and distinguished between those that involved footage of combat, civilian damage, and other themes. The figure shows that stories about civilian damage typically comprised only about 15–25 percent of all war stories, fewer than the number of stories with combat footage or featuring other topics. The figure also shows that footage of civilian damage accounted for about 15–25 percent of the stories that were broadcast, while stories involving footage of combat accounted for about 20–35 percent.

Figure 5.4
Percentage of Television News Stories by Subject, March 19–April 14, 2003

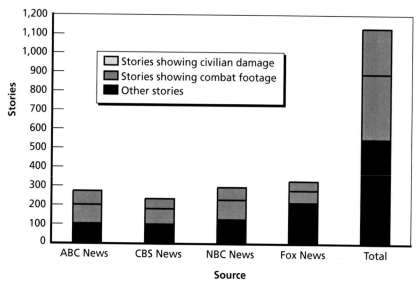

SOURCE: CMPA (2003b).

RAND *MG441-5.4*

It also is interesting to note that stories that failed to show either footage of combat or civilian damage predominated across all four television news organizations; many of these stories presumably were interviews with military experts, reporting on military strategy, and other matters related to the conduct of the war.

CMPA's content analyses of 1,100 television news stories on the war also suggested the following:

- Overall, television news media coverage during the war was fairly balanced: On average, 50 percent of the combined on-air evaluations of Bush administration policy, the military, and whether the United States was justified in going to war that were broadcast on four network television news organizations were positive, while 50 percent were negative.[9]

- There were, however, important differences across the networks in the percentage of positive evaluations: CBS News (74 percent positive, 26 percent negative), Fox News (60 and 40 percent, respectively), NBC News (53 and 47 percent), and ABC News (34 and 66 percent) (CMPA, 2003a, 2003b). Put another way, one could come away with very different impressions of the war depending on which television news channel one watched.

U.S. Public Opinion. Figure 5.5 shows that from August 2002 to March 2004, Americans consistently paid fairly close attention to developments in Iraq.

Figure 5.5 shows that the percentage following the debate about the war and the actual war very closely generally was in the 50–60-percent range; the percentage paying close attention to the UN inspectors prior to the war was substantially lower, while attention to the stability operations conducted since May 2003 generally has been in the 40–50-percent range, a fairly high level of attention from a historical perspective, but lower than during combat operations.

Public Views of Press Reporting on Civilian Casualties. Of some interest is how the American public viewed the press' reporting on civilian casualties; several questions plumbed attitudes on this matter.

For example, fewer than one in five of those polled by the Pew Research Center in early April 2003 said that there was too much coverage of the issue of civilian casualties, a little over half said that coverage of civilian casualties was about right, and fewer than three in ten said that there was too little coverage (Table 5.1).

---

[9] Whereas 49 percent of the evaluations of Bush administration policy toward Iraq from March 19 to April 14, 2003, were favorable, only 23 percent of the evaluations from May 1 to October 31, 2003, were. In a similar vein, positive evaluations of President Bush fell from 56 percent during the war to 32 percent after the war (Center for Media and Public Affairs, 2003a, 2003b).

Figure 5.5
Attention to Iraq, August 2002–March 2004

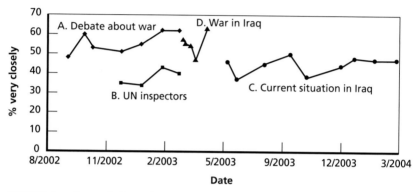

SOURCE: Pew Research Center/PSRA.

NOTE: Question read, "A. (Now I will read a list of some stories covered by news organizations this past month. As I read each item, tell me if you happened to follow the news story very closely, fairly closely, not too closely, or not at all closely.)...

A. ...Debate over the possibility that the U.S. (United States) will invade Iraq

B. ...The work of United Nations weapons inspectors in Iraq?

C. ...News about the current situation in Iraq

D. How closely have you been following news about the war in Iraq—very closely, fairly closely, not too closely, or not at all closely?"

RAND *MG441-5.5*

And Figure 5.6 reports that while 40 percent thought that anti-war sentiment was being covered too heavily, fewer than 20 percent said that about civilian casualties: Interest in reports about the personal

Table 5.1
Assessment of Press Coverage of Civilian Casualties in Iraq, Early April 2003

"Now thinking specifically about the war in Iraq, please tell me if you think the press is giving too much, too little, or about the right amount of coverage to Iraqi civilian casualties?" (Pew Research Center/PSRA poll conducted April 2–7, 2003, N = 912)	Percent
Too much coverage	17
About the right amount	51
Too little coverage	28
Don't know/refused	4

Figure 5.6
Adequacy of Press Attention to Civilian Casualties and Other Iraq Issues

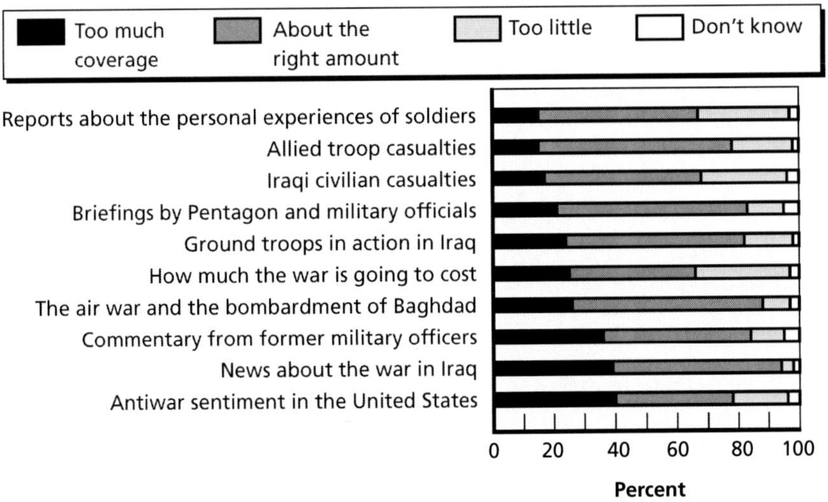

■	Too much coverage	▓	About the right amount	▨	Too little	☐	Don't know

Reports about the personal experiences of soldiers
Allied troop casualties
Iraqi civilian casualties
Briefings by Pentagon and military officials
Ground troops in action in Iraq
How much the war is going to cost
The air war and the bombardment of Baghdad
Commentary from former military officers
News about the war in Iraq
Antiwar sentiment in the United States

0   20   40   60   80   100
Percent

SOURCE: Pew Research Center/PSRA poll conducted April 2–7, 2003, N = 912.
NOTE: Question read, "As I read a short list of issues and topics, please tell me if you think the press is giving it too much coverage, too little coverage, or about the right amount of coverage . . . [ITEM] . . . Is the press giving this too much, too little, or about the right amount of coverage?"
RAND MG441-5.6

experiences of soldiers, allied troop casualties, and the likely cost of the war modestly exceeded interest in the civilian casualties issue.

Views on Avoiding Civilian Casualties. Several polling questions asked respondents about the importance of avoiding civilian casualties in a war with Iraq.

When respondents were asked to identify what worried them most about a war with Iraq (see Table 5.2), their greatest concern was about the prospects for U.S. military casualties (mentioned by 45 percent, more than twice as many as the next most frequently mentioned concern). By comparison, civilian casualties were a second-order concern: They were mentioned by fewer then one in five, less than half of those who expressed concern about U.S. casualties. In fact, civilian casualties were mentioned by about as many as mentioned the costs of rebuilding Iraq, lack of support from the UN, creating lasting resentment in

Table 5.2
Greatest Worries About War in Iraq, March 2003

"Which one or two of the following worry you most about the likely war against Iraq: the probability of U.S. (United States) military casualties, the political and economic costs of occupying and rebuilding Iraq, the lack of support from the United Nations, the probability of Iraqi civilian casualties, creating a lasting resentment in the Arab world against the United States, the negative effect on United States' reputation internationally, the fact that the United States is starting the war first without being attacked? (If All, ask:) Well, if you had to choose just one or two, which would you say worry you the most?" (NBC News/*The Wall Street Journal*/Hart and Teeter Research poll conducted March 17, 2003, N = 506)	Percent
The probability of U.S. military casualties	45
The political and economic costs of occupying and rebuilding Iraq	21
The lack of support from the United Nations	20
The probability of Iraqi civilian casualties	18
Creating a lasting resentment in the Arab world against the U.S.	18
The negative effect on U.S.' reputation internationally	17
The fact that the U.S. is starting the war first without being attacked	13
None/other (volunteered)	2
Not sure	5

the Arab world, and the potential negative effect on the United States' international reputation.[10]

On average, about four in ten expressed a great deal of concern about civilian casualties in the war, and another three in ten expressed a fair amount of concern (Table 5.3). There is, moreover, some evidence that once military action had begun in Iraq, expressions of concern about civilian casualties may have diminished.

Table 5.3 shows that polling by the Pew Research Center suggests that concern about civilian casualties peaked at 47 percent in its February 12–18, 2003 poll, and then fell to the 37–42-percent range once the war was underway.

---

[10] As a practical matter, given the small sample size, the differences between the responses in the 17–21-percent range are not statistically significant.

Table 5.3
Concern About Iraqi Civilians Being Killed, 2002 and 2003

Poll	A Great Deal (%)	A Fair Amount (%)	Not Much (%)	Don't Know/ Refused (%)
"How worried are you that many Iraqi civilians might be killed (in the war with Iraq) a great deal, a fair amount, or not much?" (Pew Research Center/PSRA polls conducted October 17–27, 2002, and February 12–18, 2003)				
10/17–27/2002, N = 1,751	40	30	27	3
2/12–18/2003, N = 1,254	47	28	23	2
"Thinking about a possible war with Iraq, how worried are you that many Iraqi civilians might be killed, a great deal, a fair amount, or not much?" (Pew Research Center/CCFR/PSRA, all other polls)				
3/20–22/2003, N = 903	38	33	26	3
3/20–25/2003, N = 1,600	38	34	25	3
3/20–24/2003, N = 1,495	37	34	26	3
3/23–24/2003, N = 592	38	34	26	2
3/25–27/2003, N = 539	37	28	23	3
3/28–4/1/2003, N = 674	41	33	24	2
Average	40	32	25	3

When these results are compared with a similar question asked during the first Gulf War (Table 5.4), it provides further evidence that Americans were somewhat more concerned about civilian casualties in the 2003 war in Iraq than during the 1991 war over Kuwait: Whereas an average of 40 percent of those polled worried "a great deal" about civilian casualties during the 2003 war, only 33 percent did so during the 1991 war.

Put another way, cross-case comparisons can reveal significant differences in concerns about civilian casualties.

War Strategy and Civilian Casualties. Polling organizations also asked several questions that illuminate how concern about civilian casualties affected preferences regarding war strategy and especially the relative importance of avoiding U.S. military casualties and Iraqi civilian casualties.

Table 5.4
Concern About Iraqi Civilians Being Killed, 1991

"How worried are you that many Iraqi civilians might be killed (in the Gulf War) a great deal, a fair amount, or not much?"	Percent
A great deal	33
A fair amount	35
Not much	28
Don't know/refused	4

SOURCE: Times Mirror/PSRA poll conducted January 25–27, 1991, N = 924.

There is some evidence that more Americans were worried that the United States might not go far enough to achieve victory in Iraq than that it would fail to do enough to avoid civilian casualties. Nevertheless, this represented a decline in that sentiment from earlier polling conducted during Operation Enduring Freedom in Afghanistan in November 2001 (Table 5.5).

Table 5.5 reports that although concern about civilian casualties in Iraq was low relative to fears of failing to achieve military victory, concern about casualties was still somewhat higher than it had been during Operation Enduring Freedom in Afghanistan.

Figure 5.7, reporting data from an early April 2003 poll, shows a similar result. Concern about minimizing U.S. casualties and

Table 5.5
Greatest Worries About U.S. Uses of Military Force,
November 2001 and March 2003

"What do you worry about more when the United States uses military force? That the U.S. doesn't do enough to avoid civilian casualties or that the U.S. doesn't go far enough to achieve military victory?"	11/13–19/01 (%)	3/13–16/03 (%)
That the U.S. doesn't do enough to avoid civilian casualties	25	32
That the U.S. doesn't go far enough to achieve military victory	56	47
Don't know/refused	19	21

SOURCE: Pew Research Center/PSRA polls conducted November 13–19, 2001, N = 1,500; and March 13–16, 2003, N = 1,032.

Figure 5.7
Preferred Priority for Minimizing Civilian Casualties and Other Desiderata, Early April 2003

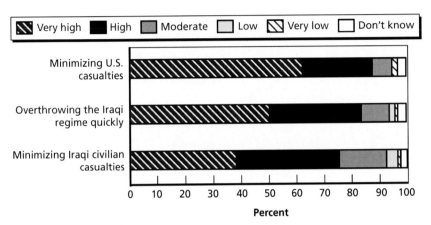

SOURCE: *Investor's Business Daily/The Christian Science Monitor*/TechnoMetrica Institute of Policy and Politics poll conducted April 1–6, 2003, N = 906.
NOTE: Question read, "What level of priority would you say U.S. (United States) troop commanders should put on the following objectives in Iraq. As I read each one, please tell me if the level of priority should be very high, high, moderate, low, or very low. OK?"
RAND *MG441-5.7*

ensuring a successful outcome in Iraq were viewed as higher priorities than minimizing civilian casualties: Whereas six in ten gave minimizing U.S. casualties a high priority, half gave a quick victory a high priority, and fewer than four in ten gave minimizing civilian casualties a high priority.

Table 5.6, which reports the results of the March 20, 2003, ABC News/*The Washington Post* poll, shows that a plurality of 49 percent of those polled said that the United States should strike military targets even if they were located in civilian areas where civilians might be killed; 42 percent did not think so.

Despite these beliefs, in a poll conducted by *Newsweek*/PSRA after the March 26, 2003, Baghdad marketplace incident (described in more detail later in this chapter), 50 percent of those polled said they continued to favor safeguards to reduce civilian casualties over more aggressive action, even if that meant a longer war (Table 5.7).

Table 5.6
Should the United States Strike Targets Even in Civilian Areas in Iraq?
March 2003

"(As you may know, the United States went to war with Iraq last night [March 19, 2003].) Do you think the United States should strike Iraqi military targets even if they're located in areas where civilians might be killed, or should the United States avoid striking Iraqi military targets located in civilian areas?"	Percent
Strike	49
Avoid	42
No opinion	3

SOURCE: ABC News/*The Washington Post*, March 20, 2003, N = 506.

Table 5.7
Assessment of U.S. Efforts to Minimize Civilian Casualties in Iraq,
March 2003

"Please tell me which one of the following two options you would choose for U.S. (United States) military action in the Iraq war, if it were up to you? More aggressive military action that would increase the risk of high Iraqi civilian casualties but might lead to a shorter war. More safeguards that would reduce the risk of high Iraqi civilian casualties but might lead to a longer war."	Percent
More aggressive military action that would increase the risk of high Iraqi civilian casualties	40
More safeguards that would reduce the risk of high Iraqi civilian casualties but might lead to a longer war	50
Don't know	10

SOURCE: *Newsweek*/PSRA poll conducted March 27–28, 2003, N = 1,004.

Despite wording differences, the conclusion that there was greater concern about civilian casualties in the 1991 war than in the 2003 war also seems supported by the data in Table 5.8: Whereas 75 percent of those polled just after the Al Firdos incident approved of continuing the bombing of Baghdad even if it meant more civilian deaths, only 51–65 percent approved of such attacks in the 2003 war.[11]

---

[11] As the poll was done the day before and the day of the March 26 marketplace incident, many of those polled on the 26th probably were aware of the incident. The lower bound on

Table 5.8
Willingness to Bomb Baghdad in Two Wars, 1991 and 2003

Survey	Percent
"If Iraqi troops retreat into Baghdad and use the civilian population as human shields, would you approve or disapprove of U.S.-led troops bombing and shelling the Iraqi troops even if civilian casualties were likely?" [Asked of those who said they would disapprove of bombing and shelling]: "If bombing and shelling could save the lives of U.S. troops by making house-to-house fighting unnecessary, then would you approve or disapprove of bombing Iraqi troops who have retreated into Baghdad and are using the civilian population as human shields even if civilian casualties were likely?" [combined results of two questions] (Fox News/Opinion Dynamics poll conducted March 25–26, 2003, N = 900)	
Approve	51
Disapprove, but would approve if it could save lives of U.S. troops	14
Disapprove, even if could save U.S. lives	14
Not sure	21
"Do you think the United States should stop bombing the city of Baghdad in order to avoid civilian deaths or not?" (ABC News/*The Washington Post* poll conducted February 14, 1991, N = 772)	
Yes	20
No	75
Don't know/no opinion	5

SOURCE: Fox News/Opinion Dynamics poll conducted March 25–26, 2003, N = 900.

Polling done the day after the March 26 marketplace incident by *Time*/CNN/Harris shows that half of those polled thought that the military should do everything it could to avoid civilian casualties (Table 5.9).

However, as late as August 2003, slightly more than half supported more aggressive action in Iraq, even if it meant a higher risk of civilian casualties (Table 5.10). One reasonable conjecture is that the U.S. military deaths that were occurring as a result of the insurgency may have diminished Americans' sensitivity to Iraqi casualties.

---

this range is not terribly different from the 49 percent mentioned earlier who responded to a March 20 ABC News/*The Washington Post* poll that the United States should conduct strikes even if it meant civilian casualties.

Table 5.9
Assessment of U.S. Efforts to Minimize Civilian Casualties in Iraq, March 2003

"Which comes closest to your view—the U.S. (United States) military should do everything it can to avoid killing Iraqi civilians, even if that makes it more difficult to defeat the Iraqi military, or, the U.S. military should do everything it can to defeat the Iraqi military even if that means additional Iraqi civilians are killed?"	Percent
U.S. military should do everything it can to avoid killing Iraqi civilians	50
U.S. military should do everything it can to defeat the Iraqi military	43
Not sure	7

SOURCE: *Time*/CNN/Harris poll conducted March 27, 2003, N = 1,014.

Table 5.10
Support for More Aggressive Action Even if Civilian Casualties Result in Iraq, August 2003

"(Which of the following steps, if any, would you support in response to the attacks on U.S. military personnel and other targets by anti-American forces in Iraq since major combat ended?) Would you support more aggressive action by U.S. forces to stop the violence, even if it means greater risk of civilian casualties or not?"	Percent
Yes	52
No	42
Don't know	6

SOURCE: *Newsweek*/PSRA poll conducted August 21–22, 2003, N = 1,011.

Assessments of Efforts to Avoid Civilian Casualties. Polls conducted during the war asked a number of questions that suggest a widespread belief that the U.S. military was doing everything it could to avoid civilian casualties.

Table 5.11 reports four different polls by four different organizations conducted between late March and early May that found that more than eight in ten Americans thought that the United States was doing all it reasonably could to try to avoid civilian casualties, whereas only 11–15 percent thought that it should do more.

Table 5.11
Assessment of U.S. Efforts to Minimize Civilian Casualties,
Late March–Early April

Survey	Percent
"Do you think the United States is doing all it reasonably can do to try to avoid civilian casualties in (the war with) Iraq, or do you think it should do more?" (ABC News/*The Washington Post* poll conducted March 23, 2003, N = 580)	
U.S. doing all it can	82
U.S. should do more	15
No opinion	4
"Do you think the U.S. military is doing everything it can to avoid killing Iraqi civilians or don't you think so?" (*Time*/CNN/Harris poll conducted March 27, 2003, N = 1,014)	
Yes	86
No	11
Don't know/no answer	3
"Do you think the U.S. is doing all it can to avoid harming Iraqi civilians, or not?" (CBS News poll conducted April 2–3, 2003, N = 950)	
U.S. doing all it can	85
U.S. not doing all it can	12
Don't know/no answer	3
"(Now I'm going to read you some goals that the United States had in the war with Iraq. For each, please tell me whether you think that the United States has been successful in that goal.) Minimizing Iraqi civilian casualties (NBC News/*The Wall Street Journal*/Hart and Teeter Research poll conducted April 12–13, 2003)	
Successful	82
Not successful	11
Not sure	7

Table 5.11—Continued

Survey	Percent
"Did the U.S. and its allies try very hard to avoid civilian casualties in Iraq or didn't they try hard enough?" (Pew Research Center/PSRA poll conducted April 30–May 4, 2003, N = 1,201)	
Tried very hard	82
Didn't try hard enough	14
Don't know/refused	4

NOTE: The Pew Research Center also asked this question in its polling of 20 other countries in April and May 2003.

When Gallup asked in late March about the U.S. military's precautions to avoid civilian deaths (Table 5.12), just over half (53 percent) said that such efforts had been "about right," while a surprisingly high one in three (35 percent) said that the military was taking too many precautions. In comparison, only one in ten said that there were too few precautions being taken to avoid civilian deaths.

The data in Table 5.13 suggest that there actually was an increase in late March and early April in the percentage who believed that the United States was making the right amount of effort to avoid

Table 5.12
Assessment of U.S. Efforts to Minimize Civilian Casualties in Iraq, March 2003

"Which comes closer to your view about the U.S. (United States) military's approach to avoiding Iraqi civilian casualties? The U.S. military is taking too many precautions and as a result [is] putting U.S. troops at unnecessary risk. The U.S. military is taking too few precautions and is causing unnecessary Iraqi civilian deaths. Do you think the U.S. is taking about the right approach in avoiding civilian casualties?"	Percent
Too many precautions	35
About right	53
Too few precautions	9
No opinion	3

SOURCE: Gallup/CNN/*USA Today* poll conducted March 29–30, 2003, N = 1,012.

Table 5.13
Assessment of U.S. Efforts to Minimize Civilian Casualties in Iraq,
Late March–Early April 2003

"In its efforts to try to avoid civilian casualties in Iraq, do you think the United States is doing too much, too little, or about the right amount?"	3/27/2003 (%)	4/3/2003 (%)	4/9/2003 (%)
Too little	12	10	7
Right amount	68	74	82
Too much	16	12	9
No opinion	4	4	2

SOURCE: ABC News/*The Washington Post* polls conducted March 27, 2003, N = 508;
April 3, 2003, N = 511; and April 9, 2003, N = 509.

civilian casualties, and a decline in both the percentage who thought the United States was making too much of an effort and those who felt it was making too little effort.

In a similar vein, polling by the Pew Research Center in early April (Table 5.14) found that 73 percent of those polled felt that the U.S. coalition was doing an excellent (39 percent) or good (34 percent) job at avoiding civilian casualties, while about one in four thought it was doing a fair or poor job.

Table 5.14
Assessment of U.S. Efforts to Minimize Civilian Casualties in Iraq,
Early April 2003

"In general, how would you rate the job that coalition military forces (in the war with Iraq) have done in avoiding civilian casualties? Excellent, good, only fair, poor?"	Percent
Excellent	39
Good	34
Only fair	17
Poor	6
Don't know/refused	4

SOURCE: Pew Research Center/PSRA poll conducted April 8–9, 2003, N = 809.

One of the reasons for the favorable judgments about how well the U.S. military was doing to avoid casualties may lie in the public's expectations regarding civilian casualties. According to polling by *Newsweek*/PSRA in early April (Table 5.15), nearly three in four (72 percent) believed that the civilian casualties that had been incurred to date had been what they had expected (45 percent) or lower than expected (27 percent). In comparison, fewer than one in five said civilian casualties had been higher than expected.

Polling by NBC News and *The Wall Street Journal* suggests that there was a decline in the belief that the United States had been successful in minimizing Iraqi civilian casualties between April and December 2003 (Table 5.16), although it is likely that judgments in July and December 2003 were more reflective of views on civilian deaths incurred during the ongoing stability operations rather than the major combat operations that ended on May 1, 2003.

Taken together, these results suggest an important and quite robust finding: Most Americans believed that the military was making the sorts of efforts to avoid civilian casualties that they favored.

Prospective Civilian Casualties and Support. Some questions also were asked that enable inferences about the relationship between prospective civilian casualties and support for the war.

According to polling by CBS News and *The New York Times*, for example, prior to the war, fewer than half typically said that they would still favor military action if it resulted in "substantial" civilian

Table 5.15
Civilian Casualties in Iraq and Expectations, Early April 2003

"What about the level of Iraqi civilian casualties in the Iraq war so far? Has it been higher than you expected, lower than you expected, or about what you expected?"	Percent
Higher	18
As expected	45
Lower	27
Don't know	10

SOURCE: *Newsweek*/PSRA poll conducted April 10–11, 2003, N = 1,000.

Table 5.16
Assessment of U.S. Efforts to Minimize Civilian Casualties in Iraq,
April–December 2003

"(Now I'm going to read you some goals that the United States had in the war with Iraq. For each, please tell me whether you think that the United States has been successful in that goal.) Minimizing Iraqi civilian casualties?"	4/12–13/2003 (%)	7/26–28/2003 (%)	12/14/2003 (%)
Successful	82	68	60
Not successful	11	24	28
Not sure	7	8	12

SOURCE: NBC News/*The Wall Street Journal*/Hart and Teeter Research poll conducted April 12–13, 2003, N = 605; July 26–28, 2003, N = 1,007; and December 14, 2003, N = 512.

casualties.[12] In a similar vein, only 39–43 percent told Zogby International that they would support the war if it meant thousands of Iraq civilian casualties (Zogby International polls conducted February 6–8, 2003, N = 1,002, and March 14–15, 2003, N = 1,129).

Table 5.17 reports a question asked by the *Los Angeles Times* that asked respondents whether a war to depose Saddam would still be successful if it involved various hypothesized numbers of civilian casualties.

The data in Table 5.17 suggest that if support depended solely on the question of civilian casualties, majority support for the war might be lost at about 500 Iraqi civilian deaths.[13]

Figure 5.8 plots these data as the percentages that said that they would consider the war a success at each level of hypothesized civilian casualties. The figure suggests that the relationship between judgments

---

[12] The question was, "Suppose U.S. military action in Iraq would result in substantial Iraqi civilian casualties; then would you favor or oppose the United States taking military action against Iraq?" and was asked September 2–5, 2002, N = 937; October 3–5, 2002, N = 668; October 27–31, 2002, N = 1,018; February 10–12, 2003, N = 747; and March 7–9, 2003, N = 1,010. The percentage saying they would still favor military action ranged from 46 to 50 percent.

[13] That is, the 14 percent who were willing to accept an unlimited number of civilian deaths, plus the 10 percent who said more than 5,000, plus the 6 percent who said up to 5,000, plus the 8 percent who said up to 1,000, plus the 13 percent who said up to 500.

Table 5.17
War in Iraq Successful if Civilian Casualties Result? Early April 2003

"Would you say the war in Iraq was successful if it removed Saddam Hussein from power and fewer than 100 Iraqi civilians were killed in battle, or would you not say it was successful in that case? (If Yes, ask:) Would you still say it was successful if up to 500 Iraqi civilians were killed in battle? (If Yes, ask:) Up to 1,000? (If Yes, ask:) Up to 5,000? (If Yes, ask:) Would you say that the military action against Iraq has been successful if Saddam Hussein was removed from power, no matter what it costs in Iraqi civilian casualties?"	Percent
Not successful	18
Up to 100	18
Up to 500	13
Up to 1,000	8
Up to 5,000	6
More than 5,000 but not unlimited	10
Unlimited	14
Don't know	13

SOURCE: *Los Angeles Times* poll conducted April 2–3, 2003, N = 745.

about success and civilian casualties is an entirely sensible demandlike function: The percentage saying the war would be successful declines as the hypothesized number of civilian casualties increases. This phenomenon also has been observed in many past public opinion questions that have asked about prospective support for U.S. military operations contingent upon various hypothesized numbers of U.S. military casualties (Larson, 1996a; Larson and Savych, 2005a).

Nevertheless, there also is some evidence that most Americans did not have a particularly good idea of how many Iraqi civilians might have died, and that beliefs about civilian deaths did not in any case affect support for the war.

Polling by the PIPA and Knowledge Networks in March and August 2004 asked respondents to estimate the number of Iraqi civilian casualties. On average, the median estimate of civilian deaths estimated in March 2003 was 800 Iraqi civilians killed, and the median

Figure 5.8
Belief That War Would Be a Success Given Hypothesized Civilian Casualties,
Early April 2003

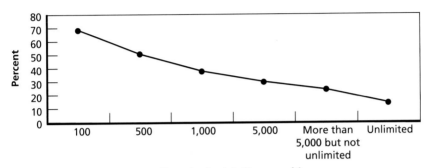

SOURCE: *Los Angeles Times* poll conducted April 2–3, 2003, N = 745.
NOTE: Question read, "Would you say the war in Iraq was successful if it removed
Saddam Hussein from power and fewer than 100 Iraqi civilians were killed in battle, or
would you not say it was successful in that case? (If Yes, ask:) Would you still say it was
successful if up to 500 Iraqi civilians were killed in battle? (If Yes, ask:) Up to 1,000? (If
Yes, ask:) Up to 5,000? (If Yes, ask:) Would you say that the military action against Iraq
has been successful if Saddam Hussein was removed from power, no matter what it
costs in Iraqi civilian casualties?"
RAND *MG441-5.8*

estimate in August 2004 was 2,000, well below the prevailing estimates
of civilian losses during major combat operations that were described
at the beginning of this chapter (PIPA and Knowledge Networks,
2004). Their study also showed that those who estimated higher numbers of civilian fatalities were not significantly less likely to support the
war than those who estimated lower numbers of casualties (PIPA and
Knowledge Networks, 2004).

This suggests both that Americans have had great difficulties estimating Iraqi civilian losses in the war in Iraq and that the relationship between support and beliefs about civilian casualties may depend
on the structure and wording of the question, especially whether the
question cues the respondent with a growing number of hypothetical
casualties.

The result also contrasts starkly with the polling data from the
1991 Gulf War that was presented earlier, in which the public's esti-

mates of Iraqi civilian deaths generally were in line with Iraqi claims and press reporting at the time.[14]

Statistical Results. Some, although not all, of the data presented above suggest that beliefs about civilian casualties played a role in prospective support or opposition to the war.

To better assess the importance of civilian casualties in support for the war, we estimated multivariate statistical models using two respondent-level datasets from polling by ABC News and *The Washington Post*. Our model for the March 20, 2003, ABC News/*The Washington Post* poll correctly predicted support or opposition for 79 percent of the respondents, and our model for the ABC News/*The Washington Post* poll of April 3, 2003, did nearly as well, predicting support or opposition for the war for 78 percent of the respondents.

In the first model, the most important predictors of support were as follows, in declining order of importance (valence of coefficients in parentheses):

- self-identification as a Democrat (–)
- the belief that the United States had vital interests in Iraq (+)
- the belief that the United States should strike in areas where civilians might be killed (+)
- the belief that there would be a significant number of U.S. military casualties (–)
- self-identification as a political Independent (–).

Neither sex nor the belief that the United States had good prospects for a short war attained statistical significance in the model.

For our second model, all the variables attained statistical significance, with the exception of sex. The most important predictors of support or opposition in this model were as follows, in declining order:

- self-identification as a Democrat (–)
- optimism about how well the war was going (+)

---

[14] Just after the Al Firdos bunker bombing, civilian deaths generally were estimated to be in the hundreds to thousands, and 44 percent of those polled thought that hundreds of Iraqi civilians had been killed, and another 37 percent thought that thousands had been killed.

- the belief that the war could be justified even if weapons of mass destruction were not found (+)
- status as a self-identified Independent (–)
- the civilian casualties variable—whether the United States was doing enough to avoid civilian casualties (+).

The least important predictor in the model—although still statistically significant—was respondents' beliefs about the likelihood of a significant number of U.S. military casualties.

This is reasonably strong confirmatory evidence that civilian casualties were a second-order consideration in decisions to support or oppose the war in Iraq; the question that mentioned civilian casualties is a poor one for judging the importance of civilian casualties in support for the war.

Antiwar Demonstrations. As suggested by Figure 5.9, which reports the number of major newspaper and television news reports on antiwar demonstrations, antiwar protest activity grew during the run-up to the war and peaked in the early days after the war began on March 19, 2003.[15]

Early in the war, antiwar protests took place in Washington, D.C., San Francisco, Los Angeles, Boston, St. Louis, and other American cities (Tomsho, 2003; "War with Iraq," 2003; Hernandez and Hymon, 2003; Fernandez, 2003), and at the end of March, an estimated 15,000 took part in an antiwar protest in Boston and about 500 people rallied in San Francisco in a demonstration in support of the war (James, 2003). Protest activity tapered off dramatically in April, and seemed to all but disappear with the conclusion of military operations in early May.

---

[15] Antiwar demonstrations were widely reported in the press at the end of 2002, for example (O'Neill, 2002). Several large demonstrations were held worldwide on February 15 (Horrock, 2003; Garofoli and May, 2003; Marks, Popham, and Gumbel, 2003). Finally, as war approached, large antiwar demonstrations took place worldwide on March 15, and included protest activity in Washington, D.C., and San Francisco (see CNN, 2003). The peak in major television news reporting on protest activity was 28 stories on March 22, nearly twice the 15 stories on antiwar activity on March 21.

Figure 5.9
Reporting on Antiwar Demonstrations in Major U.S. Media,
August 2002–March 2004

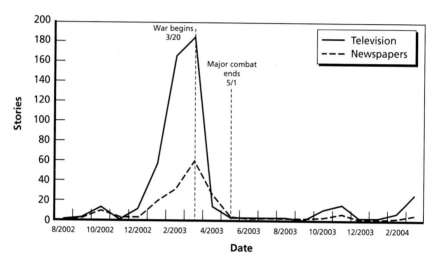

SOURCE: Search for "Iraq" and "antiwar demonstration," "antiwar protest," or "
antiwar rally" in *The Christian Science Monitor, Los Angeles Times, The New York
Times, The Wall Street Journal, The Washington Post,* ABC News, CBS News, CNN, and
NBC News.
RAND *MG441-5.9*

Foreign Media and Public Opinion

Foreign Media. In most respects, foreign media reporting seems
to have behaved much as U.S. reporting did: growing attention to Iraq
as war approached, with a peak in reporting at the time combat operations began. Figures 5.10 and 5.11 present data on the number of stories with Iraq in the title in selected foreign media.[16]

Figure 5.10 shows reporting by AFP and describes a fairly dramatic increase in reporting on Iraq at the time of President Bush's September 2002 speech to the United Nations in which he challenged the
UN to bring Iraq to account for its violations of past UN resolutions.
All three sources in the figure showed increased reporting until their

---

[16] Because searches for "Iraq" in the full text of articles routinely exceeded the 1,000-record
limit for reporting results in LexisNexis, we searched for "Iraq" in the title only.

Figure 5.10
Selected Foreign Media Reporting on Iraq, August 2002–March 2004

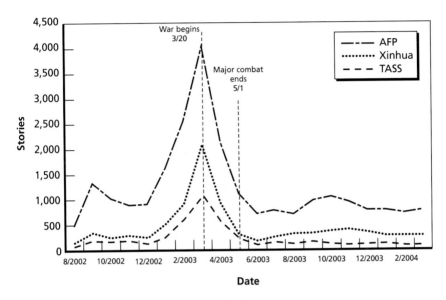

SOURCE: Search for "Iraq" in AFP, TASS, and Xinhua.

RAND *MG441-5.10*

peaks in March 2003 when the war began, and an equally dramatic fall-off thereafter. Figure 5.11, which plots data for three other foreign media outlets, shows a very similar pattern.

To better understand the prevalence of the topic over time, we counted the number of articles that mentioned both Iraq and civilian casualties in AFP, *The Guardian*, Xinhua, and TASS during three periods: the run-up to the war from August 2002 to March 18, 2003; major combat operations, from March 19 to May 1, 2003; and the postcombat stability operations, from May 2, 2003, through March 2004 (Figure 5.12).

Figure 5.12 shows, as expected—and as was the case with the U.S. media reporting—that civilian casualties were most frequently mentioned during the combat phase of operations. The higher levels of media attention to the issue of civilian casualties would have been expected to increase its salience to foreign publics.

Figure 5.11
Selected Foreign Media Reporting on Iraq, August 2002–March 2004

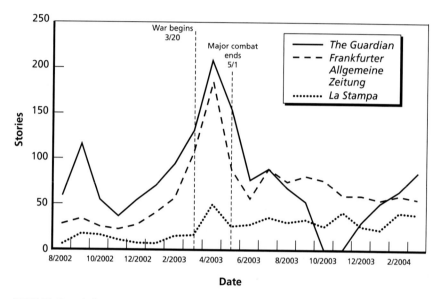

SOURCE: Search for "Iraq" in *The Guardian, Frankfurter Allgemeine Zeitung (Germany),* and *La Stampa* (Italy).

RAND *MG441-5.11*

Foreign Public Opinion. World opinion generally was against any U.S. war in Iraq that lacked UNSC authorization.

The Pew Research Center's Global Attitudes survey of 21 publics in April and May 2003 found that majorities in only three of the publics in the U.S. coalition—the United States (74 percent), the United Kingdom (61 percent), and Australia (59 percent)—thought their nation had made the right decision to use military force against Iraq; a majority (59 percent) of Spanish thought it had been the wrong decision.[17] And where a large majority (83 percent) of Kuwaitis thought that it had been the right decision to make bases available to the U.S. coalition, 63 percent of Turks thought it had been the wrong

---

[17] The Pew Research Center poll asked, "On the subject of Iraq, did (survey country) make the right decision or the wrong decision to use military force against Iraq?" (Pew Research Center for the People and the Press, 2003b).

Figure 5.12
Mentions of Iraq and Civilian Casualties in Selected Foreign Media by Period

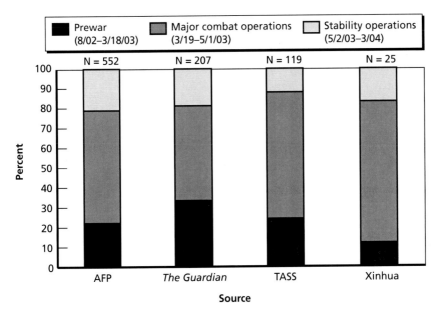

SOURCE: Search for "Iraq" and "civilian casualties," "civilian deaths," or "collateral damage" in AFP, *The Guardian*, TASS, and Xinhua.
RAND *MG441-5.12*

decision.[18] Large majorities in 14 other countries (Canada, Brazil, France, Germany, Italy, Russia, South Korea, Indonesia, Nigeria, Pakistan, Lebanon, Jordan, Morocco, and Israel) thought their countries had made the right decision to stay out of the war.[19]

The relatively high simple correlation ($r = 0.53$) between the total percentages supporting the war in Iraq in 21 countries and the belief that the United States tried very hard to avoid civilian casualties provides some empirical basis for believing that, like Americans', foreign

---

[18] The Pew Research Center poll asked, "On the subject of Iraq, did (survey country) make the right decision or the wrong decision to allow the U.S. and its allies to use bases for military action in Iraq?"

[19] Some discussion of the role of the war in Iraq on South Korean sentiment toward the United States can be found in Larson et al. (2004).

publics' support for and opposition to the war also was related to beliefs about the efforts the U.S. coalition was making to avoid civilian casualties; it would be useful to test this relationship at the respondent level.[20]

Antiwar Demonstrations. Anecdotally, antiwar demonstrations abroad seem to have peaked in the first days of the war, again in late March several days after the marketplace incident, and then again in mid-April.[21]

In the first two weeks of the war, demonstrations took place in Canada, Germany, France, Spain, Italy, Greece, the Netherlands, Ireland, Poland, Hungary, Bulgaria, Russia, South Korea, China, Japan, Malaysia, Chile, Venezuela, Egypt, Jordan, Pakistan, India, Indonesia, Cyprus, and other locations (Renfrew, 2003; Vidal and Branigan, 2003; Ford, 2003; Bernstein, 2003; Moulson, 2003; Linton, 2003; Cran, 2003). Boycotts of American goods also were organized. Another round of protests took place on April 12 in more than 40 countries, including New Zealand, Japan, South Korea, Italy, Greece, France, Germany, Iran, India, and Bangladesh (Simon O'Hagan, 2003). Protests in the United Kingdom reportedly declined in size following the rally in British support for the war once it was under way, and the numbers attending Australian demonstrations reportedly also had fallen by mid-April.[22]

With this overview of media reporting, public opinion, and antiwar demonstrations related to Iraq concluded, we now turn to the March 26, 2003, marketplace incident in Baghdad.

---

[20] At the time this research was being completed, the Pew Research Center had not as yet released the dataset for its May 2003 poll. Although it is not clear the extent to which civilian casualties might have contributed to the decline, the belief that NATO was essential to their country's security fell 11 points between July 2002 and April 2003 in France, three points in Germany, seven points in Italy, and 13 points in the United Kingdom (Eichenberg, 2003b, pp. 651–654).

[21] The question asked was, "On the subject of Iraq, did (survey country) make the right decision or the wrong decision to not use military force against Iraq?" A "wrong decision" response was an indication of support for the war.

[22] Images of British soldiers who had been executed apparently played a role in the Britons' rally. Australian demonstrations are described in Deutsche Presse-Agentur (2003).

The Marketplace Incident

Background on the Incident

On March 26, 2003, Iraq claimed that a coalition missile fell on a Baghdad marketplace, killing 14 and injuring more than 30 civilians.[23] By March 28, Iraqi officials were claiming that at least 35 people, and possibly as many as 58, had been killed in the incident ("At Least 35 Died in Marketplace Blast," 2003).

Table 5.18 summarizes the postincident media reporting and official statements in the immediate aftermath of the incident.

Table 5.18
Postincident Timeline for March 26, 2003, Marketplace Incident

Media Reporting Highlights	Official Handling Highlights
3/26 0300–0330: Incident occurs 0500: *CNN Daybreak* airs; Nippon Hoso Kyokai (NHK) breaking news from Reuters 0523: Deutsche Presse-Agentur reporting 0700: CBS airs *Early Show*; ABC airs *Good Morning America* 0800: Al-Jazeera and NBC News reporting 1700: CNN airs *Wolf Blitzer Reports* 1830: *CBS Evening News* and *NBC Nightly News* air 2100: CBS airs *60 Minutes II* and CNN airs *Larry King Live* 2200: CNN airs *Newsnight with Aaron Brown*	3/26 0936: UN Secretary-General Annan calls on "all belligerents" to protect civilians and prisoners of war 0805: CENTCOM daily press briefing takes questions 1300: CENTCOM says civilian damage possible from strikes on surface-to-air missiles (SAMs) 1500: Arab League and 115 nonaligned countries call for emergency session of UNSC 1531: DoD holds news briefing; UK Foreign Secretary Geoffrey Hoon is questioned in Parliament
	3/27 0706: CENTCOM daily press briefing takes questions
	3/28 0707: CENTCOM daily press briefing takes questions

NOTE: All times are Eastern.

---

[23] See Goldenberg (2003). Goldenberg's story claims that two U.S. bombs were reported to have fallen.

As suggested by the media reporting timeline, news of the incident spread to U.S. and foreign media fairly quickly and occasioned a great deal of high-level official attention to the incident by the United States and others.

For the purposes of the U.S. coalition, the matter seems to have been laid to rest on March 27, when MG Stanley A. McChrystal, vice director for Operations, J-3, Joint Staff, denied that U.S. bombs or missiles had been dropped or fired in the area of the Sha'ab district (see Figure 5.13):

> There are recent press reports that coalition forces bombed a marketplace in Baghdad. Coalition forces did not target a marketplace, nor were any bombs or missiles dropped or fired in the district outlined in blue on this image. And that's called the Sha'ab district. The [innermost] circle in the center for reference contains the presidential palace. Gives you a feel where we are. We'll continue to look and see if we missed anything, but another explanation could be the triple-A fire or surface-to-air missile that missed its target, fell back into the marketplace area. (DoD, 2003)

In retrospect, the cause of the deaths in the marketplace appears to have been Iraqi antiaircraft munitions that fell back to earth.[24]

U.S. Media and Public Opinion Responses

U.S. Media. As measured by major U.S. television and newspaper stories, reporting on civilian casualties actually had risen in the days preceding the incident and dropped off within a day or two of the incident (Figure 5.14). The conclusion we draw is that, while the March 26 marketplace incident may have helped to sustain civilian casualties as a topic of U.S. media news reporting, reporting does not appear to have increased as a result of the incident.

U.S. Public Opinion. As described, several key attitudes—including the belief, held by more than eight in ten, that the U.S.

---

[24] This was the conclusion of a number of participants at a November 8–9, 2004, Harvard University Carr Center for Human Rights conference in Washington, D.C., titled "Measuring the Humanitarian Impact of War" (Carr Center for Human Rights Policy, 2004).

Figure 5.13
High-Altitude Diagram Used by MG McChrystal

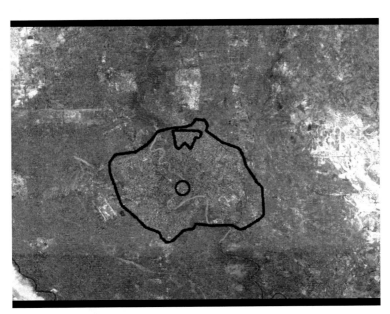

SOURCE: DoD (2003).

RAND *MG441-5.13*

military was doing its best to avoid civilian casualties—remained favorable throughout the war and showed no change in the immediate aftermath of the March 26 incident. Nor did the marketplace incident occasion any change in support or the moral justification for the war in Iraq.

Table 5.19 suggests that support for the war and the belief that the war was morally justified actually may have *increased* after the attack, although the increases in support were not statistically significant, and the questions on the moral justification for the war were asked by different polling organizations using different wording.

We also compared responses to a number of questions that were asked about war fatigue and the sorts of emotions that respondents were having about the war, asked in the Pew Research Center's March 20–27 polling (Table 5.20).

Figure 5.14
Reporting on Civilian Casualties, Marketplace Incident

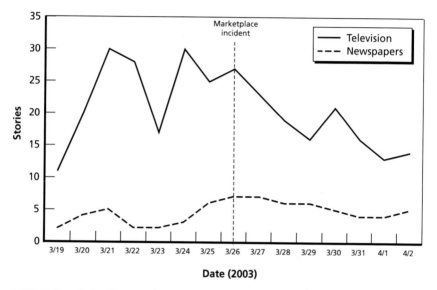

SOURCE: Search for "Iraq" and "civilian casualties," "civilian deaths," or "collateral damage" in *The Christian Science Monitor, Los Angeles Times, The New York Times, The Wall Street Journal, The Washington Post*, ABC News, CBS News, CNN, and NBC News.

RAND *MG441-5.14*

As shown, some of the responses suggest that war fatigue may have grown after the incident, although this fatigue could just as easily have been the result of reporting on the tough fighting that was going on at the time (Pew Research Center for the People and the Press, 2003a); as described previously, however, even if fatigue was setting in, there were no apparent effects on support for the war.

We also compared confidence in the U.S. military and press before and after the incident (Table 5.21), and found that confidence in the military may have grown, while confidence in the press may have declined; whether the marketplace incident played any role in these changes cannot be determined.

Table 5.19
Approval Before and After March 26 Marketplace Incident

Survey	Before	After	Change
Approve Military Action			
"Do you approve or disapprove of the United States taking military action against Iraq to try to remove Saddam Hussein from power?" (CBS News/*The New York Times*)	N = 427 3/24/2003 75%	N = 868 3/26–27/2003 77%	+2%
"Do you support or oppose the United States taking military action to disarm Iraq and remove Iraqi President Saddam Hussein? (If Support/Oppose, ask:) Is that strongly support/oppose or only somewhat support/oppose?" (Fox News/Opinion Dynamics)	N = 900 3/25–26/2003 78%	N = 900 4/8–9/2003 81%	+3%
War Morally Justified			
"Regardless of whether you think the U.S. (United States) should or should not use ground troops to remove Saddam Hussein from power, do you think the United States would be morally justified or morally unjustified if it sends troops into Iraq to remove Hussein from power?" (*Time*/CNN/Harris poll conducted January 15–16, 2003, N = 1,010)	66%		
"Do you think the United States action in Iraq is morally justified, or not?" (Gallup/CNN/*USA Today* poll conducted March 29–30, 2003, N = 1,012)	73%		

Antiwar Demonstrations. To understand the prevalence of antiwar demonstrations before and after the March 26 marketplace incident, we simply counted the number of major newspaper and television news reports on antiwar demonstrations in the week before and after the incident. The results—major newspaper reporting on antiwar demonstrations grew from 17 to 19 stories, while television news reporting fell from 14 to five stories—do not suggest that the incident increased antiwar activity.[25]

---

[25] The number of news reports on antiwar demonstrations in major newspapers (*The New York Times, The Washington Post, Los Angeles Times, The Wall Street Journal,* and *The Chris-*

Table 5.20
Fatigue Before and After March 26 Marketplace Incident

Survey	Before (%)	After (%)	Change (%)
"Have you felt yourself depressed by the war in Iraq?"			
Yes, depressed	33	41	+8
"I'd like to ask you a few questions about how you feel when you are watching coverage of the war on TV. For each statement that I read tell me if you strongly agree, agree, disagree or strongly disagree. [ROTATE. READ STATEMENT] [% strongly agreeing]"			
I can't stop watching the news	11	8	−3
I feel sad when watching	17	21	+4
It's frightening to watch	13	13	—
It tires me out to watch	7	10	+3
The war doesn't seem real	7	7	—

SOURCES: Pew Research Center poll conducted March 20–25, 2003, N = 1,600, and March 28–April 1, 2003, N = 674.

Table 5.21
Confidence in U.S. Military and Press Before and After March 26 Marketplace Incident

Survey	Before (%)	After (%)	Change (%)
"How much confidence do you have that the U.S. military is giving the public an accurate picture of how the war is going?"			
Great deal/fair amount	83	86	+3
"How much confidence do you have that the press is giving the public an accurate picture of how the war is going?"			
Great deal/fair amount	85	79	−6

SOURCES: Pew Research Center poll conducted March 20–24, 2003, N = 1,495; March 25–27, 2003, N = 539.

---

tian Science Monitor) increased from 17 the week before the incident to 19 the week after the incident, while the number of news reports in major television news (ABC, CBS, CNN, and NBC) fell from 14 reports in the week preceding the incident to five stories in the week after the incident.

Foreign Media and Public Opinion Responses

We now turn to the foreign media and public reactions to the incidents.

Foreign Media. Following the marketplace incident, the extremely critical reporting on the war in Iraq that had characterized most foreign media reporting simply continued;[26] the data suggest that there was a fairly dramatic increase in reporting on civilian casualties in Iraq in AFP, while TASS and Xinhua continued to report on the subject at approximately the same levels that preceded the incident (Figure 5.15). Anecdotally, commentary in the Arabic press was particularly critical (Harman, 2003; Murphy, 2003; Shadid, 2003; Trofimov, 2003; Wax, 2003; Wax and Morello, 2003).

Unfavorable reporting seems to have dominated the Chinese and Russian press, for example, and in Germany and much of the Arab world, the press played to the public's general opposition to the war by playing up civilian casualties, fiercer than expected Iraqi resistance, and apparent U.S. military setbacks.[27] Criticism of the war in Turkish media reporting, and across much of the Arab world, was withering even before the incident (Bernstein, 2003), and, according to some

---

[26] See, for example, Jaulmes (2003). FBIS cited an Iraqi interview with Peter Arnett, an NBC correspondent in Baghdad that was described as follows:

> Arnette [sic] appreciates the "courtesy" of the Iraqi people and the cooperation of the Iraqi Ministry of Information over the past 12 years. He notes that there is domestic opposition to the war in the United States. He describes Baghdad as a city of "discipline." He adds that the increasing civilian casualties pose a challenge to the "American policy." He contends that the "American Administration misjudged the resolve of the Iraqi forces." That is why a new war plan is being prepared, Arnette [sic] says. (FBIS, 2003a)

Egyptian media were said not to focus much on Iraqi civilian casualties (FBIS, 2003b). An editorial in the *Tehran Times* claimed that Iraqi civilians were the main victims in the war (see "Perspective: Civilians Main Victims of War in Iraq," 2003).

[27] European media reporting was not uniformly negative, however: The conservative German daily *Die Welt* and the Italian dailies *Il Foglio* and *La Stampa*, for example, criticized the antiwar protesters (Bernstein, 2003).

Figure 5.15
Daily Foreign Reporting on Civilian Casualties in Iraq, Marketplace Incident,
March 19–April 2

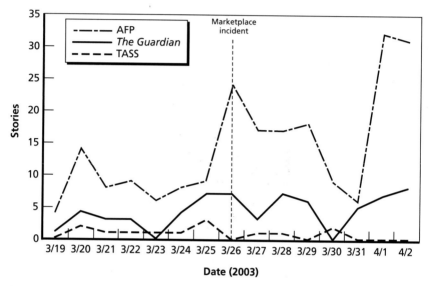

SOURCE: Search for "Iraq" and "civilian casualties," "civilian deaths," or "collateral damage" in AFP, *The Guardian*, and TASS.
RAND *MG441-5.15*

reports, the Arab media "exploded in anger" in the aftermath of the incident.[28]

Foreign Public Opinion. Two separate polls asked U.S. and foreign publics questions about the United States' efforts to avoid civilian casualties, and the result in each case was quite striking: Whereas Americans overwhelmingly believed that the United States tried very hard to avoid civilian casualties, many foreign publics generally did not (Figures 5.16 and 5.17).

---

[28] The headline in Saudi Arabia's *Al Riyadh*, for example, was "Yet another massacre by the coalition of invaders" (see Michael Dobbs and Allen, 2003). See also Trofimov (2003). A search of *Al Ahram, Al Bawaba, Arab News*, and Al-Jazeera with the LexisNexis online retrieval service did not suggest that there was dramatic increase in reporting on civilian deaths in Iraq following the incident.

Figure 5.16
Belief in 20 Countries That United States Tried Very Hard to Avoid Civilian Casualties in Iraq, April–May 2003

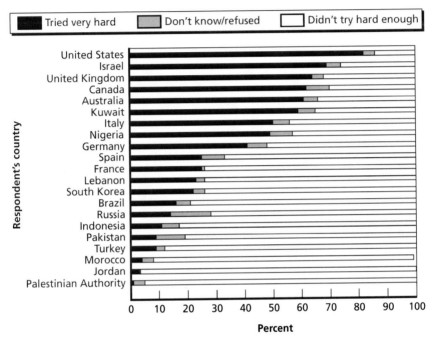

SOURCE: Pew Research Center for People and the Press (2005).
NOTE: Question read, "Did the U.S. and its allies try very hard to avoid civilian casualties in Iraq or didn't they try hard enough?"
RAND MG441-5.16

The Pew Research Center's Global Attitudes survey in April and May 2003 (Figure 5.16) found that of the 20 nations it surveyed, majorities in only seven countries—the United States, Israel, the United Kingdom, Canada, Australia, Kuwait, and Italy—thought that the United States and its allies had tried very hard to avoid civilian casualties in Iraq; in the same vein, the BBC's What the World Thinks of America survey of 11 nations in May and June 2003 (Figure 5.17) found that majorities in 10 of the 11 nations thought that the United States could do more to avoid civilian casualties: Only there did a majority of the respondents say they believed that the United States did enough to avoid civilian casualties.

Figure 5.17
Does the United States Do Enough to Avoid (Civilian) Casualties?
Results from 11 Countries

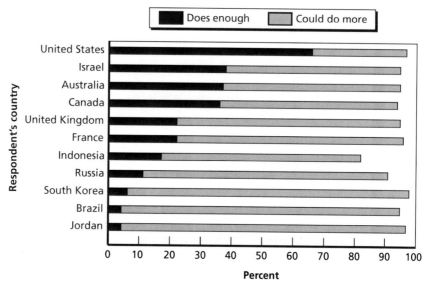

SOURCE: ICM Research (2003).
NOTE: Question read, "In military conflicts, do you think the USA does enough to avoid civilian casualties?"
RAND MG441-5.17

The belief that the United States was not doing enough to avoid deaths of innocent Iraqis also was prevalent in Iraq itself (Figure 5.18). Only 11 percent of Iraqis polled in March and April 2004 felt that the United States often tried to keep ordinary Iraqis from being killed or wounded during exchanges of gunfire, although the generally pro-U.S. Kurds seemed far more predisposed to believe that the U.S. coalition was trying avoid civilian casualties than most other Iraqis.

As was the case with the U.S. public opinion data, moreover, Iraqis' attitudes on the question of whether the United States was doing enough to avoid civilian deaths appeared to be a fairly good predictor of support and opposition.

Chi-squared tests of cross-tabulated data of this question with various measures of support for the coalition presence demonstrated a statistically significant association between beliefs about U.S. efforts to

Figure 5.18
Iraqi Beliefs About How Hard the United States Is Trying to Avoid
Casualties, Spring 2004

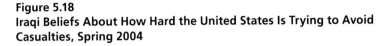

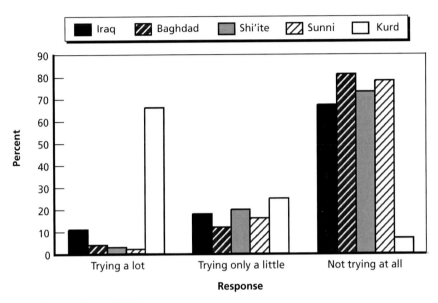

SOURCE: *USA Today* (2005).
NOTE: Question read, "For each of the following, does it happen a lot, a little or not at all? Trying to keep ordinary Iraqis from being killed or wounded during exchanges in gunfire?"
RAND *MG441-5.18*

avoid Iraqi casualties and the belief that the U.S. military action in Iraq was morally justified,[29] that attacks against U.S. forces in Iraq were morally justified,[30] and judgments regarding when U.S. forces should

---

[29] Gallup asked, "There are many actions some people as individuals or as groups or states do. I will read out to you a number of these acts/events and I would like you to indicate to which extent you can personally justify them morally. The U.S.-British military action in Iraq." Eric Nielsen of The Gallup Organization provided all cross-tabulations. As we did not have the respondent-level data, we were not able to assess the relative importance of these variables in a multivariate statistical model as we were able to do with the U.S. public opinion data.

[30] Gallup asked, "There are many actions some people as individuals or as groups or states do. I will read out to you a number of these acts/events and I would like you to indicate to

leave Iraq.[31] In all three cases, the statistical significance level was less than 0.001.

Antiwar Demonstrations. Although the theme of Iraqi civilian deaths appears to have been a prominent one in animating demonstrators' opposition to the war, as demonstrations already were under way before the March 26 marketplace incident, it is not clear what if any impact the incident may have had on these demonstrations.[32] Quantitatively, foreign news reporting mentioning antiwar demonstrations was much higher in the week before the March 26 marketplace incident than the week after, suggesting little or no impact in terms of the prevalence of protest activity worldwide.[33]

Key Lessons

There are a number of interesting lessons to be gleaned from our analysis of the 2003 war in Iraq and the March 26, 2003, marketplace incident.

First, regarding the United States' Iraqi adversary, the heavy focus on a ground offensive largely outside of Baghdad and the relatively rapid collapse of the Baghdad regime probably limited Iraq's ability to either accurately assess the magnitude of Iraqi civilian deaths during the war or to exploit the issue by engaging in the sort of media manage-

---

which extent you can personally justify them morally. Current attacks against U.S. forces in Iraq."

[31] Gallup asked, "In your opinion which would you prefer U.S. and British forces to leave: Immediately, say in the next few months; They should stay in Iraq for a longer period of time; Do not know."

[32] On March 30, four days after the marketplace incident, FBIS covered Iraqi reporting on huge antiwar protests in Manama, Bahrain, and similar protests in Iran and Pakistan (FBIS, 2003a). On April 6, another Iraqi report accented antiwar protests in Jordan, Mauritania, and Egypt (FBIS, 2003b).

[33] According to data from LexisNexis, the number of European media reports fell from 729 to 389, Asian reports fell from 633 to 477, and Middle East/Africa media reports fell from 662 to 519.

ment and propagandizing on civilian casualties and collateral damage that was observed in the 1991 Gulf War.

With respect to the media, U.S. major newspaper and television news reporting on civilian casualties was growing even before the March 26 marketplace incident. Although the incident was reported prominently, there is little evidence that it dramatically affected subsequent coverage of the issue, however. And of the three foreign news reporting sources we examined, only one (AFP) showed a dramatic increase in reporting on civilian casualties after the incident.

From a public opinion perspective, for a number of reasons, the evidence suggests much greater American sensitivity to civilian casualties in Operation Iraqi Freedom than in Operation Desert Storm 12 years earlier. Americans seem to have been acutely aware both of the prevalence of opposition to the war outside the "coalition of the willing," and the burdens and responsibilities inherent in conducting a war without a UNSC resolution providing explicit authorization for the war. That said, for most Americans, concern about civilian deaths appears to have been of secondary importance in judgments regarding whether or not to support the war, and a majority of Americans expressed the belief that the U.S. military was doing everything that it could to minimize civilian casualties. Foreign publics outside the so-called "coalition of the willing" generally appear to have opposed the war in principle, and appear to have judged harshly the United States' efforts to minimize Iraqi civilian casualties. Notably, these harsh judgments included the Iraqis themselves.

For U.S. military leaders and policymakers, the efforts to acquaint the public and press with the procedures that were being used to avoid civilian casualties, and the general tenor in which claims of civilian casualties were handled—disputing claims that seemed to lack foundation, while expressing regret for those that might have merit—appears to have resonated well with the American public, but failed to do so with foreign publics. Why this should be so is addressed in the next, and final, chapter.

CHAPTER SIX

Implications and Conclusions

As described in the case studies, concern about and sensitivity to civilian casualties has varied somewhat across past U.S. military operations: Of those we examined, sensitivity appears to have been highest in the war in Kosovo after the Chinese embassy incident, lowest in the 1991 Gulf War and 2001 war in Afghanistan, and somewhere in between in the 2003 war in Iraq.

Subject to the limiting condition that there may be significant differences in the sensitivity to civilian casualties that hinge on beliefs about the specific merits of each military operation, there also is some evidence that concern about civilian casualties may be growing at home and abroad (Figure 6.1).

Figure 6.1 reports the annual frequency with which civilian casualties have been mentioned in official briefings, news conferences, and other official U.S. government activities, as well as the Congressional Record. The figure shows that civilian casualties have increasingly been a topic of official Washington, especially during wartime.

One reason for the growing attention to civilian casualties in the press and the public may be the role that NGOs have played in bringing attention to the issue: Since 1990, NGOs increasingly have been mentioned in news reporting on wars and military operations (see Figure 6.2).

Figure 6.1
Annual Mentions by Opinion Leaders of Civilian Casualties, 1990–2003

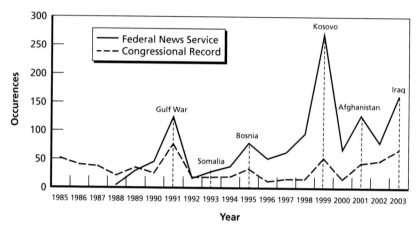

SOURCE: Search for "civilian casualties," "civilian deaths," or "civilian damage" in
Congressional Record and Federal News Service.
RAND MG441-6.1

Figure 6.2
Major U.S. Media Reporting on War and Selected NGOs, 1990–2003

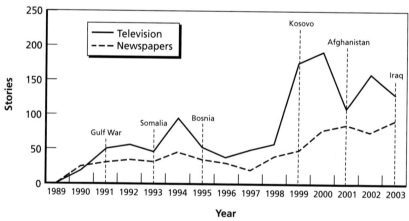

SOURCE: Search for "human rights watch," "Amnesty International," "Medicins sans
Frontieres," or "Doctors Without Borders," and "war" or "military" in *The Christian
Science Monitor, Los Angeles Times, The New York Times, The Wall Street Journal,
The Washington Post,* ABC News, CBS News, CNN, and NBC News.
RAND MG441-6.2

Figure 6.2 shows that official commentary on civilian casualties was much higher in the 1999 war in Kosovo than in the 1991 Gulf War, which comports with the general impression that one would reach in comparing those two case studies. The frequency with which NGOs have been mentioned in connection with war or military issues has, moreover, been increasing over the long term, punctuated by spikes in several years: The 1994 peak in television reporting probably is accountable to he genocide in Rwanda and Russian activities in Chechnya, that in 1999–2000 largely accountable to NATO action in Kosovo, and that in 2002 to U.S. action in Afghanistan and possible action in Iraq.

Figure 6.3 suggests that U.S. media reporting on antiwar demonstrations has peaked during periods when the United States was conducting major wars or military operations—the 1991 Gulf War, the 1999 war in Kosovo, and the 2003 war in Iraq—also shown, the high point in the series was Operation Iraqi Freedom in 2003.

Figure 6.3
Annual Mentions of Antiwar Demonstrations in U.S. Major Media Reporting, 1990–2003

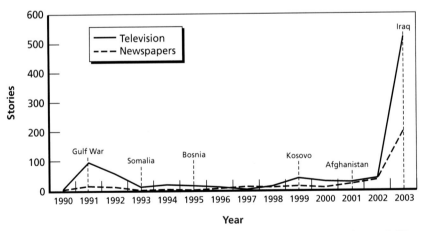

SOURCE: Search for "antiwar demonstration," "antiwar protest," or "antiwar rally" in *The Christian Science Monitor, Los Angeles Times, The New York Times, The Wall Street Journal, The Washington Post,* ABC News, CBS News, CNN, and NBC News.

RAND *MG441-6.3*

We also found that there was a moderately high correlation between the annual number of stories mentioning civilian casualties and those mentioning antiwar demonstrations in U.S. major newspapers and major television news reporting, no doubt due to the fact that they each had a common cause: a U.S. war or military operation.[1] Put another way, war generates media reporting on both civilian casualties and antiwar protest activity.

As shown in Chapter One, the pattern of U.S. and foreign press reporting on civilian casualties also suggests increased concern about civilian casualties over the years. Taken together, these various trends suggest not only that concern about civilian casualties in wartime is likely to continue but that it also may be growing in importance, especially outside the United States, as evidenced both by the more dramatic growth in foreign news reporting on civilian casualties (Figures 1.1 and 1.2), which would be expected to increase the salience of the issue, and by the far less prevalent belief within foreign publics that the United States actually makes enough of an effort to avoid civilian casualties during its military operations.

The Military: A Highly Credible Institution

As described in this monograph, Americans and others believe that it is important to minimize civilian casualties in U.S. military operations, and fully expect the U.S. military to make efforts to do so.

---

[1] The correlation between the number of annual stories mentioning civilian casualties and those mentioning antiwar demonstrations in the major U.S. newspapers was 0.68; the correlation for major U.S. television news reporting was a 0.56. Nevertheless, a search for stories containing references both to civilian casualties and to antiwar demonstrations turned up few such stories. Only in 2003 were there a reasonably large number of stories mentioning both antiwar demonstrations and civilian casualties: We found 42 co-occurrences in TV news reporting in 2003, which constituted only about 8 percent of the TV news stories on antiwar demonstrations and suggests that civilian casualties were not a terribly prominent theme in the demonstrations, or at least the reporting on them was not. All told, we found only five major TV news stories in 1991 that mentioned civilian casualties and antiwar demonstrations (the year of the Gulf War), another five in 1999 (the year of the war in Kosovo), one story in 2002 (the second year of operations in Afghanistan), and 42 stories in 2003 (the year that Operation Iraqi Freedom began).

In fact, the results reported in the preceding chapters suggest that the principal connection between support for U.S. military operations and civilian casualties is the belief that the United States is making serious efforts to avoid civilian casualties: Those who hold this belief are more likely to support U.S. military operations than those who do not, and this result holds both in the American public and foreign publics. Moreover, in the one case we examined in which a civilian casualty incident may have reduced support—the Chinese embassy bombing in the air war in Kosovo—both the belief that the U.S. military was being careful enough and support for the war appear to have declined together.

Substantial majorities of Americans have consistently expressed the belief that the U.S. military and its coalition partners were making all necessary efforts to avoid civilian casualties and that the casualties that resulted, while regrettable, ultimately were unavoidable consequences of war. By comparison, only a small minority of Americans usually has held the view that the U.S. military was making inadequate efforts to avoid civilian deaths. *This finding suggests that the argument that the American public has unreasonably high expectations for zero-casualty warfare is exactly wrong: In fact, most Americans appear to have a fairly realistic view of the possibilities for eliminating civilian casualties entirely from modern warfare.*

Compared to U.S. audiences, the view that the United States is making sufficient efforts to avoid civilian casualties has been far less prevalent within foreign publics, though it is not clear whether skepticism abroad about U.S. efforts to avoid civilian casualties leads to opposition to U.S. military operations or whether the causal arrow is the other way around. As was described here, there is much that we still do not know about foreign attitudes toward U.S. military operations and what factors go into their decisions to support or oppose U.S. operations.

Stepping back from the civilian casualties issue, it seems reasonable to conclude that the high level of trust Americans have that the U.S. military is trying to avoid civilian deaths may in part be accountable to the high levels of confidence that most Americans express in the

U.S. military and its leadership and the high level of credibility that serving military officers have with the U.S. public.

Figure 6.4 presents data from Gallup on the percentage who have said they have a great deal or a lot of confidence in the U.S. military as an institution in American society, and data from Harris on the percentage who said they had a great deal of confidence in military leaders.

Figure 6.4 shows that there has been a mild upward trend in the regard for the military and its leaders since the Vietnam War, but also some variation: notably, an ephemeral peak during the 1991 Gulf War, followed by a flattening out and some turbulence during the peace operations of the 1990s and then a return to the overall upward trend in recent years. In the most recent period, the military has been said to enjoy the highest levels of confidence among the American public since

Figure 6.4
Percent Saying They Have a "Great Deal" or "Quite a Lot" of Confidence in Military, 1971–2005

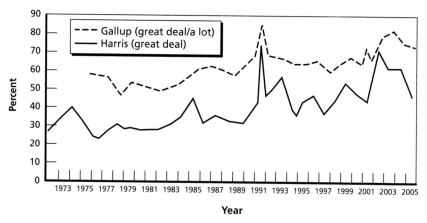

NOTE: Questions read, "I am going to read you a list of institutions in American society. Please tell me how much confidence you, yourself, have in each one—a great deal, quite a lot, some, or very little...the military (Gallup)
As far as people in charge of running...are concerned, would you say you have a great deal of confidence, only some confidence, or hardly any confidence in them?...the military (Harris)."
RAND MG441-6.4

the early Vietnam War era.[2] Nevertheless, a decline of eight points between June 2003 and May 2004 is evident in Gallup's polling, and there has been a decline of 15 points between December 2002 and February 2005 in Harris' polling.[3]

As suggested by the data on confidence in the military presented in Figure 6.4, however, the regard in which the military are held, while growing over the last dozen or so years, also has been subject to disturbances, with peaks occurring at the time of popular and successful military operations and downturns occurring during unpopular and unsuccessful operations and military scandals.[4]

By comparison, Figure 6.5 shows that most other U.S. institutions do not fare nearly as well as the military, which, for a great many years has been the top-rated institution in American society.[5]

Indeed, the percentage of Americans who said they had a great deal of confidence in the military in May 2004 was half again that for the presidency, nearly twice that for organized religion, and 2.5 times the percentage for television news, newspapers, and Congress.

Although military officers are judged to tell the truth no more often than average men and women, as might be expected, when it comes to the use of force, the American public find senior military

---

[2] There do not appear to be many studies of the factors that have been associated with Americans' changing level of confidence in the military (Paul, 2002).

[3] Although it is difficult to say with certainty, this is possibly due to allegations that U.S. military personnel were abusing Iraqi inmates at the Abu Ghraib prison that emerged in early May 2004, and allegations about prisoner treatment at Guantanamo (Saad, 2004). Sixty-three percent of those polled by ABC News in late May 2004 said that torture was not an acceptable policy, while 51 percent said that the U.S. government, as a matter of policy, was doing it anyway (ABC News, 2004).

[4] Gallup's analysis of its 1997 polling on confidence in U.S. institutions attributed the 1997 downturn in the public's confidence rating for the military to sex scandals involving serving military officers and enlisted personnel. The 2004 analysis attributed the sharp downturn in regard for churches and organized religion in 2002 to the sexual abuse scandals plaguing the Catholic church at that time (Newport, 1997; Saad 2004).

[5] See, for example, Chambers (2000), McAneny (1999), Newport (2001, 2002, 2003).

Figure 6.5
Americans' Confidence in Institutions, June 2003

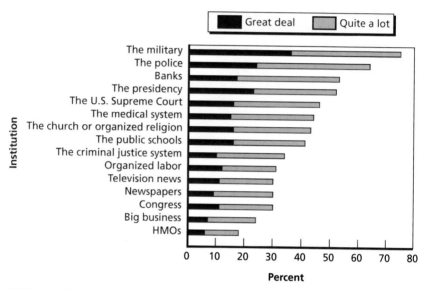

SOURCE: Gallup poll conducted May 21–23, 2004, N = 1,002.
NOTE: Question read, "I am going to read you a list of institutions in American society. Please tell me how much confidence you, yourself, have in each one—a great deal, quite a lot, some, or very little."
RAND *MG441-6.5*

officials and civilian officials in national security positions to be highly credible (Table 6.1).[6]

Table 6.1 reports that the average credibility score (out of 100) on the use of force for high-level military officers was around 80, higher

---

[6] Polling by Harris in November 2002 found 65 percent who said that they would generally trust military officers to tell the truth. In comparison, the percentages who said they would generally trust members of other groups were as follows: teachers (80 percent); doctors (77 percent); professors (75 percent); police officers (69 percent); scientists (68 percent); the president, judges, civil servants, and ordinary men and women (65 percent each); clergy members or priests (64 percent); accountants (55 percent); bankers (51 percent); television newscasters (46 percent); pollsters (44 percent); journalists (39 percent); members of Congress (35 percent); trade union leaders (30 percent); lawyers (24 percent); and stockbrokers (23 percent) (Harris poll conducted November 14–18, 2002, N = 1,010). It is worth noting that many or even most of the highest-ranked individuals in Table 6.1, military experts, are former military officers.

Table 6.1
Credibility Scores of Various Sources from National Credibility Index

Rank	Information Source	Mean Rating
1	Military affairs expert	81.2
2	Secretary of Defense	80.4
3	Chairman, Joint Chiefs of Staff	80.4
4	Foreign policy expert	79.0
5	High-ranking military officer	77.7
6	National Security Advisor	75.5
7	Secretary of State	74.4
8	U.S. United Nations Ambassador	74.4
9	Member of the armed forces	72.5
10	Representative of national veterans group	71.4
11	U.S. President	69.6
12	U.S. Vice President	69.3
13	Member of U.S. Senate	67.1
14	Member of U.S. House of Representatives	66.3
15	Representative of a human rights organization	57.0
16	National religious leader	55.5
17	Major newspaper/magazine reporter	53.2
18	National civil rights leader	52.6
19	National syndicated columnist	52.2
20	Local religious leader	51.9
21	Ordinary citizen	51.4
22	TV network anchor	51.0
23	Student activist	36.9
24	TV/radio talk show host	35.6
25	Famous entertainer	27.6

SOURCE: Public Relations Society of America (undated).

than that of most other groups. By comparison, the credibility of those who might criticize the military on the moral conduct of a military operation—including reporters, members of human rights organizations, religious leaders, student activists, and entertainers—are judged as having much lower levels of credibility on issues related to the use of force.

Taken together, one should expect that in public debates regarding the conduct of a military operation—including in the aftermath of civilian casualty incidents—the competence and expertise that senior military and civilian leaders bring to issues related to the use of force are likely to confer a higher level of credibility than many of their critics will have.

There also are data available that suggest that European publics also hold their militaries in high regard relative to potential wartime critics. A Eurobarometer poll of 15 European publics conducted in November and December 2000 found that 71 percent of Europeans said they "tended to trust" the military, although the percentage trusting ranged from a low of 65 percent (in Spain) to a high of 91 percent (in Finland) (Manigart, 2001). By comparison, 55 percent of Europeans polled said they tended to trust radio news reports, 54 percent said they trusted television news reports, and 38 percent said that they trusted the written press (Manigart, 2001). Gallup International's July–September 2002 Voice of the People survey of 47 countries found a similar result: Respondents judged their armed forces as most likely to operate in society's best interests (World Economic Forum, 2002).

This suggests that the most effective strategy for reaching coalition partners' publics (and possibly many others) following possible civilian casualty incidents may be for their own senior military officers to brief their national press organizations. Of course, when coalition partners are few, the opportunities to reach foreign audiences will be correspondingly diminished.

Recommendations

Given the evident importance that Americans ascribe to minimizing civilian harm and the importance in support for U.S. military operations of beliefs that the U.S. military is making efforts to avoid casualties, the obvious implication is that the military must continue to demonstrate its commitment to minimizing civilian casualties, both through its words and its deeds. The question is how best to accomplish this.

Incidents of civilian deaths are, by definition, tragedies, and there are no "silver bullets" that can diminish the media attention and public emotions—ranging from hopelessness and sorrow to anger—they can generate. There are, however, some things that the USAF and DoD profitably may be able to do in this area:

- Public affairs personnel can prepare for the eventuality of possible incidents even before they actually happen.[7] For example, public affairs officers can brief the press and public on measures that are being taken to minimize casualties to better sensitize these audiences to the importance the military assigns to avoiding civilian casualties, and the sophisticated—if by no means foolproof—processes and procedures that have been developed to minimize their likelihood; they also can develop overall guidance and procedures for dealing with incidents. In a similar vein, even before missions are flown, Judge Advocate General (JAG) personnel can document their judgments about the legal justification for the highest-risk missions, thereby better positioning commanders to respond in an informed and timely manner if an incident should occur.
- Until timely and accurate combat assessment capabilities are available, the ability to counter an adversary's claims of civilian damage incidents will be quite limited. More timely and accurate

---

[7] As described previously, prior to Operation Iraqi Freedom, DoD did in fact prebrief the press on (1) U.S. efforts to minimize civilian deaths and collateral damage, and (2) enemy efforts to cause these sorts of incidents through violations of the laws of war, and to fabricate evidence of such incidents.

combat assessment capabilities could improve commanders' ability to reconstruct more quickly and reliably the facts surrounding civilian casualty incidents and to enable more timely and accurate explanations of these incidents to be communicated to the media and public. Such improvements also would have the salutary benefits of reducing the likelihood of constantly changing (or even contradictory) explanations that can erode credibility, and opening the possibility of putting these incidents to rest much more quickly, rather than drawing out speculation over days, or even weeks, while the necessary facts are being collected.

- Public affairs guidance that is used to explain specific civilian casualty incidents should be sure to touch upon all the issues likely to be of concern to key audiences. The provisions of Article 57(2) of Protocol I to the Geneva Conventions provide a very useful framework for discussing incidents in such terms as military value, military necessity, discrimination, and other constructs that are likely to be of greatest concern to, and resonate with, various audiences.

- Finally, over the longer term, by emphasizing the efforts that are being made to reduce civilian casualties (e.g., increased precision, smaller blast effects, improved target verification, and so on), the Air Force and DoD can help to ensure that the U.S. Congress and public have continued reason to trust that the U.S. military is seeking new ways to reduce the prospects for civilian deaths in future military operations. A demonstrated commitment to a philosophy of continuous improvement may be what is needed to ensure this trust in the future, and, in the case of foreign audiences, to build trust in the first place.

While efforts to further reduce the likelihood of these incidents and their impacts are laudable, policymakers and military leaders should be very careful to avoid giving the impression that civilian deaths ultimately can be eliminated from warfare; such a belief is unwarranted. Indeed, there is good reason to believe that future U.S. adversaries increasingly will rely upon human shields and other techniques to increase the possibilities of innocent deaths at U.S. hands.

Multivariate Statistical Modeling Results

Multivariate Probit Regression

To understand the influence of civilian casualty concerns on support for U.S. military operations when also simultaneously controlling for other variables that have been shown to be reliable predictors, we used multivariate statistical modeling techniques.

For our purposes, questions that asked about support for U.S. military operations (our principal outcome variable) typically were dichotomous (1 if favoring the military operation, 0 if otherwise) or sought to capture the strength of support and opposition (e.g., 0 if very unfavorable, 1 if somewhat unfavorable, 2 if somewhat favorable, 3 if very favorable). The nature of the data—where the outcome variable is discrete and binary (0,1)—suggested using probit regression as the main approach to modeling individual responses.[1]

Whereas ordinary least square (OLS) regression models assume linear relationships between variables and use the method of least squares estimation (LSE) to minimize the sum of the squared errors, by comparison, probit regression techniques allow for nonlinear relationships between dependent and independent variables and use maximum likelihood estimation (MLE) to estimate parameters so as to maximize

---

[1] Discrete variables are those that have a discrete number of mutually exclusive, and collectively exhaustive, values. Outcomes also may be inherently ordered, where the outcome associated with a higher value of the outcome variable is ranked higher than the outcome associated with a lower value of the variable, i.e., where the dependent variable is ordinal and stronger outcomes are associated with higher values of the variable, but where the numbers have no cardinal significance (Borooah, 2002, pp. 1–5).

the probability or likelihood of having obtained the observed sample for the outcome variable (Aldrich and Nelson, 1984, p. 51); the estimated parameters thus maximize the likelihood of observing the distribution of the sample amongst the outcome categories.

Explanation of Table Coefficients

Due to the nature of the data and modeling technique, the coefficients in the tables of results are the change in probability at the mean values of the independent variables when holding all other variables constant. For example, a coefficient of 0.33 would indicate that the probability of being in favor of a military operation would increase by 0.33 for each unit increase in the independent variable, holding all other variables constant.

Goodness of Fit

Goodness of fit of the probit regression can be determined using the Wald Chi-square test, which compares the prediction with a "naïve" model that predicts all cases to be in the modal category of the dependent variable, and allows estimate of the percentage reduction in error in moving from the naïve to the full model. Goodness of fit for the probit regression also can be assessed by calculating the percentage of correct predictions from the data and comparing these prediction levels to some baseline proportion we would expect by randomly assigning observations into the categories of the outcome variable (e.g., 50 percent). Finally, goodness of fit can be assessed by reporting the maximized value of the log-likelihood function.

Diagnostics to Demonstrate No Violations of Technical Assumptions

Multicollinearity arises when some of the independent variables are highly correlated with each other, and can produce unstable and biased estimates of the regression coefficients. There always is some correlation between right-side variables, but the question here is of degree: whether this correlation is big enough to distort our estimates. Accordingly, as with any statistical analysis, we first checked the correlation between independent variables.

We examined the possibility of multicollinearity in several steps. First, we looked at the correlation coefficients between variables. Although the correlations between variables we used in the regressions were not particularly high, they often were statistically significant, suggesting that there was a modest but real relationship between independent variables.

Next we used a more elaborate technique called variance inflation factors (VIFs) to determine whether multicollinearity was an issue in our analysis. Variance inflation factors are a measure of the multicollinearity in a regression design matrix and take into account higher-order collinearity than a simple correlation matrix. In all our cases, VIF was not large enough to suggest that multicollinearity was an issue.

Establishing Causality

It is important to note that we cannot really make causal arguments from our data or models. In order to make causal arguments with observational data, we would need to demonstrate several things. First, we would need to demonstrate that we have randomly chosen our sample of respondents. This is not entirely true, however, because we rarely have a 100-percent response rate. The most important reason for noncompletion is refusal or midinterview termination. Second, we would need to include all other factors that theoretically could determine the relationship in our regression so that we could avoid a misspecification in our model, which would constitute a potential source of bias; as a practical matter, however, we considered ourselves lucky to find data sets that allowed us to populate full models for each military operation (i.e., models in which all the variables of theoretical importance were included in the regression model). While we also tested models that included some other variables, we cannot say that we eliminated the possibility that other variables also might have affected outcomes. However, we can say that the robustness of the general model across a wide range of military operations over a long span of time strongly implies that our models have not left out any important variables.

Although we cannot address the first problem, we can address the second one. We do this through the structure of the analysis: We first ran regressions of the dependent variable on the main independent variables (we call this the reduced model). We then added all possible demographic factors that might influence the results (this is called the full model). Although some of the covariates might not be significant in one case, they might become significant in the other case.

Variables that are included in the model can potentially explain additional variation. For example, it is necessary to include respondents' self-identification as to party because members of one party (e.g., the President's party) are likely to have more favorable views of a U.S. military operation than are members of other parties. This reasoning can be applied to other variables as well. Moreover, by adding covariates to the regression, we can see whether or not the coefficients for the main variables change; if so, that would suggest that our initial estimation was somewhat biased. If not, however, that would suggest that our reduced-form models are relatively robust.

Thus, although we cannot make causal arguments using our models, we confirmed the robustness of these models across a wide range of military operations over time, which suggests that we can use these models to diagnose the relative importance of various factors in support for different military operations, and also for making contingent predictions about possible public opinion responses to various developments.

Operation Desert Storm (Iraq and Kuwait, 1991)

To ascertain the importance of civilian casualties in judgments about approval and disapproval of the war, we estimated several multivariate probit regression models that included variables for civilian casualties along with variables that past work has suggested are the key predictors of support or opposition for military operations.

The civilian casualties variables were from questions that asked respondents whether they thought that the United States was doing all it could to keep down the number of civilian casualties and asked respondents to estimate the number of civilian deaths. The other variables that were included in our multivariate model were variables that have been identified in past work as reasonably reliable predictors of support or opposition in past U.S. military operations: Respondents' beliefs about whether vital national interests were at stake, whether U.S. actions were morally justified, how well the war was proceeding, how many U.S. casualties had been sustained, membership in the President's party, and race and gender.[2]

Table A.1 presents the results of the reduced-form model that predicts support or opposition to the Gulf War just after the February 13, 1991, Al Firdos bunker incident,[3] Table A.2 presents the results of models that predict the belief that the war had been worth the U.S. military and civilian casualties, and Table A.3 reports the question wording for the variables used in the various models.

Table A.1 shows that the model correctly predicted support or opposition for 86 percent of the respondents to the survey. Given that neither belief about civilian casualties—whether the United States was making enough effort to avoid civilian casualties or how many civilian casualties the respondent thought might have been incurred to that time—actually attained statistical significance in the model, the results suggest that civilian casualties were not a particularly important predictor of support and opposition.

Table A.2 presents the results of two other models: The first predicted the belief that what the United States had accomplished in the war to date had been worth the number of U.S. military deaths and injuries and correctly predicted 78 percent of the responses; the second asked whether it had been worth the civilian deaths and injuries, and correctly predicted 71 percent of the responses.

---

[2] Probit regression is appropriate when the dependent variable is binary, e.g., approve or disapprove. Very briefly, the probability of approval would be expected to be higher for those with beliefs that vital interests were involved, that U.S. actions were morally justified, that the war was proceeding well, and that only a small number of U.S. casualties had been sustained, as well as those who were members of the president's party, not black, or male (Larson and Savych, 2005a).

[3] The reduced-form model dropped several other demographic factors that failed to make a statistically significant contribution to the prediction.

Table A.1

Reduced-Form Coefficients from Probit Estimates of Approval of Gulf War, February 15–17, 1991

Variable	Change in Probability at Mean Values	Robust Standard Error
National interest (Q22)	0.033	0.011***
Moral reasons (Q43)	0.136	0.019***
Prospects (Q27)	−0.002	0.022
Military casualties (Q42)	−0.016	0.006**
Civilian casualties (Q31)	−0.019	0.019
Civilian casualties (Q33)	−0.023	0.018
Party 1 if Democrat[a]	−0.128	0.049***
Party 1 if Independent[a]	−0.117	0.044***
Race 1 if black[a]	−0.187	0.091**
Gender 1 if female[a]	−0.034	0.024
Observations	1,314	
Wald Chi-square	188.04	
Log likelihood	−352.46	
Percent correctly specified	86%	

SOURCE: *Los Angeles Times* poll conducted February 15–17, 1991. Question wording given in Table A.3.

NOTES: Approval estimated using question 10 in Table A.1. Significance level: ** = significant at 5 percent; *** = significant at 1 percent. Robust standard error in parentheses.

[a] dF/dx is for discrete change of dummy variable from 0 to 1.

As shown, the most important predictor of the belief that the war had been worth the civilian casualties was the belief that the war was morally justified; next most important were status as a woman or Democrat, both of which reduced the likelihood of saying that the war had been worth the civilian casualties, and beliefs as to whether the argument that "the United States did not have a vital interest" was a good or bad reason for opposing the war.

**Table A.2
Coefficients from the Probit Estimates (Reduced Form) for Beliefs About
the Worth of the Campaign in Iraq, February 1991**

Variable	Worth Military Casualties (Q29)	Worth Civilian Casualties (Q30)
National interest (Q22)	0.084 (0.023)***	0.104 (0.025)***
Moral reasons (Q43)	0.240 (0.031)***	0.238 (0.030)***
Prospects (Q27)	0.073 (0.037)**	0.075 (0.036)**
Military casualties (Q42)	−0.027 (0.013)**	−0.015 (0.013)
Civilian casualties (Q31)	−0.121 (0.055)**	−0.103 (0.050)**
Civilian casualties (Q33)	0.030 (0.033)	−0.006 (0.034)
Party 1 if Democrat[a]	−0.110 (0.065)*	−0.116 (0.064)*
Party 1 if Independent[a]	−0.172 (0.058)***	−0.102 (0.058)*
Race 1 if black[a]	−0.004 (0.087)	−0.018 (0.081)
Gender 1 if female[a]	−0.147 (0.046)***	−0.139 (0.046)***
Observations	1,328	1,326
Wald Chi-square	156.72	190.20
Percent correctly specified	78%	71%

SOURCE: *Los Angeles Times* poll conducted February 15–17, 1991. Question wording given in Table A.3.

NOTES: Change in Probability at mean values (Robust Standard Error). Significance level: * = significant at 10 percent; ** = significant at 5 percent; *** = significant at 1 percent. Robust standard error in parentheses.

[a] dF/dx is for discrete change of dummy variable from 0 to 1.

Importantly, the belief that the United States was doing all it could to minimize civilian casualties was a statistically significant predictor of beliefs about whether the war was worth the civilian deaths that had been incurred, roughly as important as beliefs regarding U.S. vital interests in Iraq and status as a self-identified political Independent, but not so important as beliefs that the war was morally justified, or gender or Democratic party identification.

Table A.3
Wording of Questions in Tables A.1 and A.2

Variable	Question Wording
Approval	10. Overall, do you approve or disapprove of the United States carrying on the war against Iraq? (IF APPROVE OR DISAPPROVE) Is that (approve/ disapprove) strongly or (approve/disapprove) somewhat?
Worth military casualties	29. Do you feel what the U.S. has accomplished in the war against Iraq so far has been worth the number of deaths and injuries suffered by American forces, or not?
Worth civilian casualties	30. Do you feel what the U.S. has accomplished in the war against Iraq so far has been worth the number of deaths and injuries suffered by civilians in the war zone, or not?
National interest	22. "America's vital interests are not at stake." Do you think that's an excellent, good, not so good or poor argument for opposing the U.S. decision to go to war?
Moral reasons	43. Do you think the U.S. action in the Mideast is morally justified, or not?
Prospects	27. So far, is the U.S. war against Iraq going better than you expected it would, or going worse than you expected it would, or is the war against Iraq going about the way you expected?
Military casualties	42. Overall, how many U. S. soldiers do you expect will be killed in the war against Iraq: close to 100, close to 500, close to 1,000, close to 2,500, close to 5,000, close to 10,000, close to 20,000 or more than 20,000?
Civilian casualties	31. Do you think the U.S. military is doing all it can to keep down the number of civilian casualties in the war against Iraq, or not?
Civilian casualties	33. To the best of your knowledge, do you think Iraqi civilian deaths as a result of the war so far are in the dozens, in the hundreds, in the thousands or in the tens of thousands?

SOURCE: *Los Angeles Times* poll conducted February 15–17, 1991.

Our interpretation of the modeling results is that, at least in comparison to other factors that have been shown to be important in predicting support or opposition, civilian casualties simply were not terribly important in individuals' decisions about whether to support or oppose the Gulf War, a result that echoes some of the other findings presented earlier in this appendix.

Operation Allied Force (Kosovo, 1999)

To understand the importance of civilian casualties and collateral damage in support for Kosovo when controlling for other factors that are predictors of support and opposition for U.S. military operations, we analyzed a respondent-level data set from polling in May 1999 conducted by PSRA for the Pew Research Center that included these variables, as well as variables for civilian casualties (Table A.4).

The poll that we analyzed had questions that could be used to populate a full model that predicted respondents' support or opposition from beliefs about the stakes, prospects, U.S. casualties, party, race,

Table A.4
Coefficients from Probit Estimates for Approval (Q13) of Kosovo Campaign, May 1999

Variable	Change in Probability at Mean Values	Robust Standard Error
Moral reasons (Q16b)	0.211	0.045***
Prospects (Q17c)	0.209	0.038***
Military casualties (Q17a)	0.183	0.082**
Civilian deaths (Q17e)	−0.046	0.037
Party, 1 if Republican[a]	−0.157	0.069**
Party, 1 if Independent[a]	−0.138	0.065**
Race, 1 if black[a]	−0.134	0.083
Gender, 1 if female[a]	−0.045	0.053
Observations	497	
Wald Chi-square	69.7	
Correctly specified	70%	

SOURCE: Pew Research Center/PSRA poll conducted May 12–16, 1999. Question wording given in Table A.5.

NOTES: Significance level: ** = significant at 5 percent; *** = significant at 1 percent. Robust standard error in parentheses.

[a] dF/dx is for discrete change of dummy variable from 0 to 1.

and gender, as well as questions about civilian deaths, which enabled us to estimate the importance of collateral damage while controlling for these other influences.

Based upon our aggregate-level analyses, reported above, we expected that consideration of civilian casualties might have been an important factor in the May poll, which was conducted after the Chinese embassy incident, during a time when elite commentary and media reporting seems to have turned against the operation. As a result, we expected that concern about civilian casualties would be relatively salient. Our statistical modeling did not confirm these expectations.

Using probit regression modeling, we were able to correctly predict approval or disapproval for the war for 70 percent of the respondents based on beliefs about the stakes, prospects for success, military casualties, party, and several other individual-level characteristics. The results from the reduced-form model are reported in Table A.4, and the wording of the questions is in Table A.5.[4]

As shown in Table A.5, the coefficients for our civilian casualties variables were much smaller than those for several other factors, most notably, beliefs that the war was morally justified and judgments about whether the coalition's air war alone would be successful in forcing Milosevic's capitulation. Moreover, the civilian casualty variable failed to attain statistical significance in the model, suggesting that it made no independent contribution to explaining support and opposition when controlling for other influences.

Thus, both on the basis of the small coefficient values and the failure to attain statistical significance in the multivariate model, we judge that concern about civilian casualties did not influence support for and opposition to the war. On the other hand, it suggests that beliefs about the moral stakes and prospects for the campaign were the most important predictors of approval for the campaign.

---

[4] The full model includes education and income variables, whereas the reduced-form model leaves out these variables because they have not been theoretically and empirically justified as being important predictors of support and opposition to past U.S. wars and military operations.

Table A.5
Wording of Questions in Table A.4

Variable	Question Wording
Approval	13. Do you approve or disapprove of NATO forces, including the United States, conducting air strikes against Serbia to force the Serbs to agree to the terms of the peace agreement and end the fighting in Kosovo?
Moral reasons	16b. Here are some reasons being given for using U.S. troops to help secure peace in Kosovo, Serbia. For each one, please tell me whether, in your opinion, it is a very important reason, a somewhat important reason, a not too important reason, or not at all important reason for the use of U.S. troops to prevent the killing of citizens in Kosovo.
Prospects	17c. How worried are you that U.S. troops could be involved in Kosovo for a long time—very worried, somewhat worried, not too worried, or not at all worried?
Military casualties	17a. How worried are you that U.S. troops in Kosovo might suffer casualties—very worried, somewhat worried, not too worried, or not at all worried?
Financial costs	17b. How worried are you about the financial cost of sending U.S. troops to Kosovo—very worried, somewhat worried, not too worried, or not at all worried?
Civilian casualties	17e. How worried are you that innocent people are being hurt or killed by U.S. and NATO airstrikes—very worried, somewhat worried, not too worried, or not at all worried?

Put another way, our modeling results suggest that beliefs about civilian casualties a week after the bombing of the Chinese embassy were not an important predictor of support for or opposition to the military campaign, when one would have expected the issues of collateral damage and civilian casualties to be highly salient.

Given that our multivariate statistical modeling for the 1991 Gulf War failed to demonstrate the importance of concerns about civilian casualties in decisions to support or oppose the war, it is not terribly surprising that the civilian casualties variable failed to achieve statistical significance in the multivariate probit model.

Operation Enduring Freedom (Afghanistan, 2001–)

We were unable to find a data set that would enable us to estimate a multivariate model that included a civilian casualties variable along with variables indicating respondents' views on factors that have in the past been shown to be excellent predictors of support and opposition: the perceived importance of the stakes, prospects for success, U.S. military casualties, and party orientation.

However, as described in Table A.6 (question wordings in Table A.7), our multivariate probit model correctly predicted approval or disapproval for about 84 percent of the respondents in the poll based solely upon their beliefs about whether the United States' security interests demanded a leading role for the United States in taking action against al Qaeda, the prospects for success, and U.S. military casualties.[5] As shown, Americans generally were united in their beliefs: Neither party, race, nor gender turned out to be statistically significant discriminators in predicting support for U.S. military action in Afghanistan.

Again, beliefs that are hypothesized to be the key predictors of support and opposition contributed the most to predicting respondents' support or opposition: In declining order of importance, these were the prospects for success, the importance of the stakes, and expected U.S. military casualties.[6] It may be that, because eight in ten or more had favorable beliefs and approved of the war, there was not much variation left to be accounted for. Although membership in the President's party was in the predicted direction, it was not statistically significant.[7]

---

[5]   The President also may have benefited from his still-preternaturally high approval rating: ABC News/*The Washington Post* found 80 percent approved of the President's job handling in the poll we used for our statistical modeling (ABC News/*The Washington Post* poll conducted November 27, 2001, N = 759).

[6]   The generally small size of the coefficients raises questions about their substantive significance as discriminators; it may be that their effects washed out somewhat as a result of the preternaturally high support for military action among Americans following 9/11.

[7]   We also estimated a number of other models using two other data sets that had differently worded questions; these correctly predicted approval or disapproval in 79–85 percent of the cases.

Table A.6
Marginal Probability from the Probit Estimates of Approval of Operations in Afghanistan (Q2)

Variable	Change in Probability at Mean Values	Robust Standard Error
Stakes (Q8d)	0.012	0.007*
Prospects (Q5)	0.023	0.007***
Casualties (Q7)	−0.009	0.005*
Party 1 if Democrat[a]	−0.003	0.012
Party 1 if Independent[a]	−0.014	0.012
Race 1 if black[a]	−0.051	0.034
Gender 1 if female[a]	0.007	0.008
Wald Chi-square (Prod>Chi2)	54.76 (0.000)	
Log likelihood	−85.75	
Observations	711	
% correctly specified	84%	

SOURCE: ABC News/*The Washington Post* poll conducted November 27, 2001.
NOTES: Significance level: * = significant at 10 percent; *** = significant at 1 percent.
[a] dF/dx is for discrete change of dummy variable from 0 to 1.

Table A.7
Wording of Questions in Table A.6

Variable	Question Wording
Support	2. Do you support or oppose the U.S. military action in Afghanistan? Do you support/oppose this strongly or somewhat?
Security interests	8d. When it comes to (READ ITEM) do you think the United States should take the leading role, a large role but not the lead, a lesser role or no role at all? Taking military action against terrorist groups that try to re-establish themselves in Afghanistan
Prospects	5. Do you think the U.S. military action in Afghanistan is going very well, fairly well, not too well or not well at all?
Costs	7. How likely do you think it is that there will be a large number of U.S. military casualties in Afghanistan—very likely, somewhat likely, somewhat unlikely or very unlikely?

Operation Iraqi Freedom (Iraq, 2003–)

Some, although not all, of the data presented above suggest that beliefs about civilian casualties played a role in prospective support or opposition to the war.

To better assess the importance of civilian casualties in support for the war, we estimated a number of multivariate statistical models using two different respondent-level data sets from polling by ABC News and *The Washington Post*. As shown in Table A.8, our model for the March 20, 2003, ABC News/*The Washington Post* poll correctly predicted support or opposition for 79 percent of the respondents (question wordings are given in Table A.9).

Table A.8
Coefficients from the Probit Estimates for Approval (Q3) of the Military Campaign in Iraq, March 2003

Variable	Change in Probability at Mean Values	Robust Standard Error
Vital interests (Q11)	0.323	0.057***
Prospects (Q13)	0.027	0.022
Military casualties (Q14)	−0.117	0.052**
Civilian casualties (Q7)	0.225	0.046***
Party 1 if Democrat[a]	−0.371	0.069***
Party 1 if Independent[a]	−0.146	0.068**
Gender, 1 if female[a]	−0.072	0.047
Wald Chi-square (Pr>Chi-sq)	90.41 (0.000)	
Observations	377	
% Correctly specified	78.5	

SOURCE: ABC News/*The Washington Post* poll conducted March 20, 2003. Question wordings are given in Table A.9.

NOTE: Significance level: ** = significant at 5 percent; *** = significant at 1 percent. Robust standard error in parentheses.

[a] dF/dx is for discrete change of dummy variable from 0 to 1.

The most important predictors of support were Democratic party affiliation (which reduced the probability of supporting the war) and the belief that the United States had vital interests in Iraq (which increased support). The civilian casualties variable—which asked whether the respondent thought that the United States should strike in areas where civilians might be killed—attained statistical significance and also turned out to be the third-most important predictor of support and opposition.

The civilian casualties variable is a somewhat odd one: Not terribly surprisingly, those who expressed the belief that the United States should strike in areas where civilians might be killed also were more likely to support the war. On the other hand, the belief that there would be a significant number of military casualties, or self-identification as a political Independent, both reduced support somewhat. Neither the belief that the United States had good prospects for a short war, nor gender, attained statistical significance in the model.

Our second model used an ABC News/*The Washington Post* poll conducted in early April 2003, and also correctly predicted support

Table A.9
Wording of Questions in Table A.8

Variable	Wording of Question
Support	3. As you may know, the United States went to war with Iraq last night. Do you support or oppose the United States having gone to war with Iraq?
Vital interests	11. Do you think America's vital interests are at stake in the situation involving Iraq, or not?
Prospects	13. Just your best guess, how long do you think the war with Iraq will last—days, weeks, months, about a year, or longer than that?
Military casualties	14. Do you think there will or will not be a significant number of U.S. military casualties in the war with Iraq?
Civilian casualties	Q7. Do you think the United States should (strike Iraqi military targets even if they are located in areas where civilians might be killed), or should the United States (avoid striking Iraqi military targets located in civilian areas)?

NOTE: Data set also includes party affiliation and gender.

or opposition for 79 percent of the respondents (Table A.10; question wordings are in Table A.11).

In this case, all the variables attained statistical significance, with the exception of gender. The most important predictor of support or opposition in this model was once again status as a self-identified Democrat, followed by the respondent's optimism about how well the war was going, a belief that the war could be justified even if weapons of mass destruction were not found, status as a self-identified Independent, and the civilian casualties variable—whether the United States was doing enough to avoid civilian casualties. The least important predictor in the model—although still statistically significant—was respondents' beliefs about the likelihood of a significant number of U.S. military casualties.

Table A.10
Coefficients from Probit Estimates for Support of the Military Campaign in Iraq, April 2003

Variable	Change in Probability at Mean Values	Robust Standard Error
Vital interests (Q11)	0.158	0.046***
Prospects (Q3)	0.168	0.031***
Military casualties (Q7)	−0.106	0.038***
Avoiding civilian casualties (Q8)	−0.134	0.039***
Party 1 if Democrat	−0.314	0.072***
Party 1 if Independent	−0.146	0.060**
Gender, 1 if female	−0.020	0.038
Wald Chi-square (Pr>Chi-sq)	101.95 (0.000)	
Observations	436	
% Correctly specified	78.2	

SOURCE: ABC News/*The Washington Post* poll conducted April 3, 2003.
NOTE: Significance level: ** = significant at 5 percent; *** = significant at 1 percent. Robust standard error in parentheses.

Table A.11
Wording of Questions in Table A.10

Variable	Question Wording
Support	2. Do you support or oppose the United States having gone to war with Iraq? Do you support/oppose it strongly or only somewhat?
Vital interests	11. Do you think the United States will be able to justify this war ONLY if it finds weapons of mass destruction, such as chemical or biological weapons, in Iraq; or do you think the United States will be able to justify this war for other reasons, even if it does NOT find weapons of mass destruction in Iraq?
Prospects	3. How would you say the war is going for the United States and its allies: very well, fairly well, not too well or not well at all?
Military casualties	7. Do you think there will or will not be a significant number of additional U.S. military casualties in the war with Iraq?
Avoiding civilian casualties	Q8. In its efforts to try to avoid civilian casualties in Iraq, do you think the United states is doing too much, too little, or about right amount?

NOTE: Data set also includes party affiliation and gender.

This is reasonably strong confirmatory evidence that civilian casualties were a second-order consideration in decisions to support or oppose the war in Iraq; the question that mentioned civilian casualties is a poor one for judging the importance of civilian casualties in support for the war.

Bibliography

ABC News, *ABC Evening News*, April 14, 1999a.

———, *Nightlight*, April 14, 1999b.

———, "Most Americans Reject Torture, but Back Some Coercive Practices," ABC News/*The Washington Post* Poll press release, May 27, 2004. Poll conducted by telephone May 20–23, 2004, among random national sample of 1,005 adults. As of December 2, 2005:
http://abcnews.go.com/images/pdf/955a3Torture.pdf

"Additional to the Geneva Conventions of 12 August 1949, and Relating to the Protection of Victims of International Armed Conflicts, 8 June 1977," *Reference Guide to the Geneva Conventions*, 1977, with preface and author note updated in 2000. As of November 17, 2005:
http://www.genevaconventions.org

"Afghanistan's Civilian Casualties," *The New York Times*, February 13, 2002, p. A30.

AFP—*see* Agence France Presse.

Agence France Presse, "France Bans Serb Demonstrations in Paris 26 Mar," March 26, 1999a.

———, "URGENT at Least 20 Killed in Kosovo Bombing: Witnesses," April 14, 1999b.

———, "Refugee Convoy Bombing Tape Broadcast by Serbs Was Doctored, Says NATO," April 19, 1999c.

———, "NATO Admits to Seventh Bombing Error in Yugoslavia," May 7, 1999d.

———, "Pro-Kosovo Demonstration in Tirana," May 12, 1999e.

Aitkenhead, Decca, "We Want to Do Battle, Yet Don't Like the Killing. But Isn't That What War Is?" *The Guardian* (London), April 2, 1999.

Aldrich, John Herbert, and Forrest D. Nelson, *Linear Probability, Logit, and Probit Models*, Beverly Hills, Calif.: Sage Publications, 1984.

American Bar Association, and American Association for the Advancement of Science, *Political Killings in Kosova/Kosovo, March–June 1999*, Washington, D.C.: American Bar Association Central and East European Law Initiative, 2000.

Angus Reid Group, "Five Country (US, UK, France, Italy, Germany) Rapid Turnaround Poll," April 26, 1999.

AP—*see* Associated Press.

Apple, R. W., "Iraqi Lifts Estimate of Civilian Loss to Thousands," *The New York Times*, February 12, 1991, p. A13.

Arian, Asher, and Carol Gordon, "The Political and Psychological Impact of the Gulf War on the Israeli Public," in Stanley Allen Renshon, ed., *The Political Psychology of the Gulf War: Leaders, Publics, and the Process of Conflict*, Pittsburgh, Pa.: University of Pittsburgh Press, 1993, pp. 227–250.

Arkin, William M., "Baghdad: The Urban Sanctuary in Desert Storm?" *Aerospace Power Journal*, 1997, pp. 4–21.

Associated Press, "Peace Activists Demonstrate in London," January 7, 1991a.

———, "Anti-War Marches Continue After Deadline Expires," January 16, 1991b.

———, "More Arrests as Demonstrators Protest Gulf," January 16, 1991c.

———, "Day-by-Day Chronology of the Gulf War," February 8, 1991d.

———, "Demonstrators Block NATO Supply Convoy," April 15, 1999.

———, "A Breakdown of AP's Count of Iraqi Civilian Deaths," June 11, 2003.

Associated Press Online, "UN Critical of US Action in Afghanistan," March 6, 2002.

Associated Press Worldstream, "Urgent Serb Police: Refugee Convoy Bombed, 64 Said Dead," April 14, 1999a.

———, "Greece Says NATO Missed Political Target in Kosovo," April 16, 1999b.

———, "Greek Protests Mount Against NATO Airstrikes," April 18, 1999c.

———, "Events in U.S. Bombing Campaign in Afghanistan by the Associated Press," February 11, 2002.

"At Least 35 Died in Marketplace Blast, Iraq Says: Survivors, Relatives Blame Attack in Suburban Baghdad on Britain, U.S.," *Milwaukee Journal Sentinel*, March 28, 2003. As of December 2, 2005:
http://www.jsonline.com/news/gen/mar03/129451.asp

Atkinson, Rick, and Ann Devoy, "Soviet Proposal 'Falls Well Short,' Bush Says; Primakov: 'The Slaughter Must Be Stopped,'" *The Washington Post*, February 20, 1991, p. A1.

Ball, Patrick, Wendy Betts, Fritz Scheuren, Jana Dudukovich, and Jana Asher, *Killings and Refugee Flow in Kosovo, March–June 1999: A Report to the International Criminal Tribunal for the Former Yugoslavia*, Washington, D.C.: American Association for the Advancement of Science, 2002. As of November 18, 2005: http://shr.aaas.org/kosovo/icty_report.pdf

BBC News, "Iraqi Deputy Prime Minister's News Conference in Amman," February 10, 1991.

———, "Serb Media: NATO Lies Over Rapes," April 10, 1999a. As of November 18, 2005:
http://news.bbc.co.uk/1/hi/world/monitoring/316147.stm

———, "Air Strikes 'Kill Refugees,'" April 15, 1999b. As of November 26, 2005:
http://news.bbc.co.uk/1/hi/world/europe/319539.stm

Bearak, Barry, "A Nation Challenged: Casualties; Uncertain Toll in the Fog of War: Civilian Deaths in Afghanistan," *The New York Times*, February 10, 2002, p. A1.

Beelman, Maud S., "Thousands Turn Out for Gulf Protests," Associated Press, January 13, 1991a.

———, "Anti-War Demonstrations Held Worldwide," Associated Press, January 14, 1991b.

Beeston, Richard, "Stage-Managed Crowds Chant Support for Saddam's War," *The Times* (London), January 16, 1991.

Belgrade BETA, "BETA Reports on Attacks, Casualties 11 May," May 11, 1999.

Belgrade Radio B92, "Radio B92: NATO Aircraft Bomb Passenger Car Convoy," April 14, 1999.

Belgrade Radio Beograd Network, "Serbian Radio: NATO Hits Chinese Embassy in Belgrade," May 7, 1999a.

———, "FYI—Belgrade Radio, TV Off Air 8 May," May 7, 1999b.

———, "Milosevic Calls NATO Strikes 'Crime Against Humanity,'" May 8, 1999c.

Belgrade Tanjug, "FYI—Tanjug Reports on NATO Raids 1 May," May 1, 1999a.

————, "Tanjug Reports Further on NATO Raids 1 May," May 1, 1999b.

————, "Tanjug: NATO Strategy Is to Kill Civilians," May 31, 1999c.

Bercovitch, Jacob, and Richard Jackson, *International Conflict: A Chronological Encyclopedia of Conflicts and Their Management 1945–1995*, Washington, D.C.: Congressional Quarterly, 1997.

Berger, Sandy, "Special White House Briefing on President Clinton's Address on Kosovo to the American Society of Newspaper Editors," April 15, 1999.

Bernstein, Richard, "A Nation at War: The Mood Overseas; Press and Public Abroad Seem to Grow Ever Angrier About the U.S.," *The New York Times*, March 27, 2003, p. B2.

Bone, James, "UN Holds Secret Talks," *The Times* (London), February 16, 1991.

Borooah, Vani K., *Logit and Probit: Ordered and Multinomial Models*, Thousand Oaks, Calif.: Sage Publications, 2002.

Boston, William, "Antiwar Protesters in Europe Plan Action," *The Wall Street Journal*, October 12, 2001, p. A13.

Boustany, Nora, "Iraq Charges High Civilian Toll in Air Raids," *The Washington Post*, February 7, 1991, p. A1.

Brauchli, Marcus W., "Chinese Critics of Embassy Attack Jar Foreigners as Beijing Demands NATO Apology and Probe," *The Wall Street Journal*, May 11, 1999, p. A12.

Brody, Richard A., *Assessing the President: The Media, Elite Opinion, and Public Support*, Stanford, Calif.: Stanford University Press, 1991.

Bulloch, John, "Crisis in the Gulf—Life in Iraq and Its 19th Province: Allied Onslaught Shifts Arab Opinion Towards Iraq; The Ferocity of the Air Assault on Saddam Hussein Is Opening Cracks in the Coalition Which He Faces," *The Independent* (London), February 10, 1991, p. 14.

Byman, Daniel, Matthew C. Waxman, and Eric V. Larson, *Air Power as a Coercive Instrument*, Santa Monica, Calif.: RAND Corporation, MR-1061-AF, 1999. As of November 17, 2005:
http://www.rand.org/publications/MR/MR1061

"Calculating Casualties," *Pittsburgh Post-Gazette*, February 16, 2003. As of November 17, 2005:
http://www.post-gazette.com/nation/20030216casualtiesbox0216P9.asp

Cameron, Alison, and Joe Quinn, "Thousands Join Anti-War Marches," Press Association, January 13, 1991.

Campbell, Murray, "Thousands of Afghans Likely Killed in Bombings," *The Globe and Mail* (Toronto), January 3, 2002, p. A1.

Çani, H., "People Demonstrate in Support of Kosovars," Albanian Telegraphic Agency, March 30, 1999. As of November 29, 2005: http://www.telpress.it/ata/1999/mars_99/hdarch30.htm

Carr Center for Human Rights Policy, *Measuring the Humanitarian Impact of War Workshop*, Washington, D.C.: John F. Kennedy School of Government, Harvard University, November 8–9, 2004. As of December 2, 2005: http://www.ksg.harvard.edu/cchrp/Nov04Agenda.shtml

Castle, Stephen, "The Convoy Massacre: NATO Offers Its Evidence," *The Independent* (London), April 20, 1999.

CBS News, *CBS Evening News*, April 14, 1999.

CENTCOM—*see* U.S. Central Command.

Center for Media and Public Affairs, "Crisis in Kosovo: TV News Coverage of the NATO Strikes on Yugoslavia," *Media Monitor*, Vol. 13, No. 2, May–June 1999. As of July 27, 2006: http://www.cmpa.com/mediaMonitor/MediaMonitorArchive.htm

———, "1999 Year in Review: TV's Leading News Topics, Reporters, and Political Jokes," *Media Monitor*, Vol. 14, No. 1, January–February 2000. As of November 29, 2005: http://www.cmpa.com/MediaMonitor/documents/janfeb00.pdf

———, "The Media Go to War: TV News Coverage of the War in Iraq," *Media Monitor*, Vol. 17, No. 2, July–August 2003a. As of December 2, 2005: http://www.cmpa.com/mediaMonitor/documents/julaug03.pdf

———, "George Bush's Postwar Blues: TV News Coverage of President Bush Since the Iraq War," *Media Monitor*, Vol. 17, No. 4, November–December 2003b. As of December 2, 2005: http://www.cmpa.com/mediaMonitor/documents/novdec03.pdf

Central Intelligence Agency, *Putting Noncombatants at Risk: Saddam's Use of "Human Shields,"* Washington, D.C.: Central Intelligence Agency, 2003. As of November 17, 2005: http://purl.access.gpo.gov/GPO/LPS27932

Central News Agency–Taiwan, "Taiwan Activists Stage Demonstration at AIT," May 10, 1999.

Centre for Peace in the Balkans, "Photo—Novi Sad," undated online photo gallery. As of November 18, 2005: http://www.balkanpeace.org/library/gallery/novisad/index.html

Chafetz, Josh, "Body Count: Inside the Voodoo Science of Calculating Civilian Casualties," *The Weekly Standard*, April 16, 2003. As of November 30, 2005: http://www.weeklystandard.com/Content/Public/Articles/000/000/002/554awdqo.asp

Chambers, Chris, "Military Number One in Public Confidence, HMOs Last: Religion and Police Also Receive High Ratings," The Gallup Poll, July 10, 2000.

Chen, Edwin, "Bush Issues Call to Action; Policy: The President, Speaking at West Point's Graduation, Says the Nation Must Preempt Terrorist Threats and Stand Up to Evil-Doers Anywhere in the World," Los Angeles Times, June 2, 2002, p. A1.

Cheney, Richard, "Remarks by Secretary of Defense Dick Cheney to the U.S. Chamber of Commerce," Washington, D.C., February 13, 1991.

Chicago Council on Foreign Relations, Worldviews 2002: Comparing American and European Public Opinion on Foreign Policy—Transatlantic Key Findings Topline Data, Full Release, Chicago, Ill.: Chicago Council on Foreign Relations, 2002.

"China Puts Gas on the Fire," Los Angeles Times, May 11, 1999, p. 6.

Cirera, Daniel, "Lost Illusions, Europe's Peace Movement," in Phyllis Bennis and Michel Moushabeck, Beyond the Storm: A Gulf Crisis Reader, Brooklyn, N.Y.: Olive Branch Press, 1991, pp. 280–291.

Clarke, Michael, "Majority of UK Public Says NATO Strikes Should Go On," London Press Association, April 19, 1999.

Clinton, Bill, "Remarks and a Question-and-Answer Session with the American Society of Newspaper Editors in San Francisco, California," April 15, 1999.

Clodfelter, Michael, Warfare and Armed Conflicts: A Statistical Reference to Casualty and Other Figures, 1500–2000, 2nd ed., Jefferson, N.C.: McFarland, 2002.

CMPA—see Center for Media and Public Affairs.

CNN, CNN Evening News, April 14, 1999a.

———, CNN News Day, April 14, 1999b.

———, CNN Sunday, April 18, 1999c.

———, "NATO and the Media Fight a Battle Over Facts; The Press and the Tragedy: Have Journalists Learned Lessons from the Past?" CNN Reliable Resources, April 24, 1999d.

———, "NATO Says 'Human Shields' Account for Bombing Deaths," May 18, 1999e. As of November 18, 2005:
http://www.cnn.com/WORLD/europe/9905/17/kosovo.03/index.html

———, "Mass Protests in Nation's Capital," segment on CNN Saturday Night, April 20, 2002a.

———, "Second Day of Protests Getting Underway in Washington," CNN Sunday Morning, April 21, 2002b.

————, "Antiwar Rallies Across the World," March 15, 2003. As of November 18, 2005:
http://www.cnn.com/2003/WORLD/europe/03/15/sprj.irq.protests/index.html

Cohen, Eliot A., *Gulf War Air Power Survey*, Washington, D.C.: Office of the Secretary of the Air Force, 1993.

Commission of the European Communities, *Eurobarometer 34*, Brussels, 1990.

Conetta, Carl, *The Wages of War: Iraqi Combatant and Noncombatant Fatalities in the 2003 Conflict*, Cambridge Mass.: Project on Defense Alternatives, Research Monograph No. 8, 2003. As of November 30, 2005:
http://www.comw.org/pda/fulltext/0310rm8.pdf

Cooper, Alice Holmes, "Media Framing and Social Movement Mobilization: German Peace Protest Against INF Missiles, the Gulf War, and NATO Peace Enforcement in Bosnia," *European Journal of Political Research*, Vol. 41, 2002, pp. 37–80.

Cormier, William, "Peace Protesters Rally Worldwide with World at Edge of War," Associated Press, January 16, 1991.

Cran, Christina, "Anger Escalates as Hundreds of Thousands Protest Around World," *The Scotsman*, March 31, 2003, p. 7.

Cullen, Kevin, "NATO Seeks to Better Its Press Office; Crisis in Kosovo/Public Information," *The Boston Globe*, April 20, 1999, p. A17.

Cummins, Chip, "Pentagon Widens Probe of Its Deadly Raid," *The Wall Street Journal*, February 12, 2002, p. A4.

Curtius, Mary, and John Aloysius Farrell, "US Moves to Limit Diplomatic Damage; War in the Middle East," *The Boston Globe*, February 14, 1991, p. 1.

Daley, Suzanne, "A Nation Challenged: The Continent; Europeans Pledge Troops, if Necessary," *The New York Times*, October 9, 2001, p. B8.

"Demonstrator Arrested Outside U.S. Consulate," *The Toronto Star*, January 9, 1991, p. A2.

Deutsche Presse-Agentur, "Serbs Accuse NATO of Bombing Kosovo Refugees," April 14, 1999a.

————, "China's Embassy, Ambassador's Home in Belgrade Hit by Air Attack," May 7, 1999b.

————, "1st Lead: At Least 40 Killed in U.S. Attack in Afghanistan," July 1, 2002a.

————, "Urgent: At Least 40 Killed in U.S. Attack on Wedding Party in Afghanistan, Kabul," July 1, 2002b.

————, "Numbers Down at Australian Peace Marches," April 13, 2003.

DeYoung, Karen, "More Bombing Casualties Alleged; U.N. Aide 'Concerned'; Rumsfeld Defends Airstrike Targeting," *The Washington Post*, January 4, 2002, p. A18.

Diebel, Linda, "Bush Aide Fears Iraq Winning PR Battle," *Toronto Star*, February 12, 1991, p. A10.

Dionne, E. J., Jr., "This Time, Anti-War Movement Gets Administration's Respect," *The Washington Post*, January 29, 1991, p. A16.

Dobbs, Lou, *Lou Dobbs Moneyline*, CNN, September 21, 2001.

Dobbs, Michael, and Mike Allen, "Images of Destruction Inflict Setback for U.S. Propaganda War," *The Washington Post*, March 30, 2003, p. A26.

Dobbs, Michael, and Karl Vick, "Scores of Refugees Killed on Road; NATO Says Jets Aimed at Military," *The Washington Post*, April 15, 1999, p. A01.

DoD—*see* U.S. Department of Defense.

Dovkants, Keith, "NATO Bombed Two Convoys; Admission Over Refugee Deaths but Serbs Accused of Using Civilian Shields," *The Evening Standard* (London), April 19, 1999.

Drozdiak, William, "The Reaction in Europe; Bombing Breeds Allied Misgivings," *The Washington Post*, May 11, 1999, p. A16.

Dunham, Will, "Allies Not Detered [sic] by Iraqis Use of Civilians as Shields," United Press International, February 14, 1991.

Dupin, Eric, "The International Opinion Wonders About the Intervention of NATO," Ipsos, April 23, 1999. As of November 23, 2005: http://www.ipsos.fr/CanalIpsos/articles/388.asp?rubid=388

Dwan, Renata, and Micaela Gustavsson, "Major Armed Conflicts," *SIPRI Yearbook 2004: Armaments, Disarmament, and International Security*, Oxford: Oxford University Press, 2004. As of November 17, 2005: http://editors.sipri.se/pubs/yb04/ch03.html

Eckholm, Erik, "Crisis in the Balkans: News Analysis; China's Leaders Stoke Anger at U.S. at Their Peril," *The New York Times*, May 10, 1999a, p. A8.

———, "Crisis in the Balkans: China; China Raises Then Lowers Tone in Anti-U.S. Protests at Embassy," *The New York Times*, May 11, 1999b, p. A1.

Eichenberg, Richard C., "Gender Differences in Public Attitudes Toward the Use of Force by the United States, 1990–2003," *International Security*, Vol. 28, No. 1, June 2003a, pp. 110–141.

———, "Having It Both Ways: European Defense Integration and the Commitment to NATO," *Public Opinion Quarterly*, Vol. 67, No. 4, Winter 2003b, pp. 627–659.

————, "Victory Has Many Friends: U.S. Public Opinion and the Use of Military Force, 1981–2005," *International Security*, Vol. 30, No. 1, Summer 2005, pp. 140–177.

————, *Defense in Democracies: Public Opinion on National Security and Why It Matters*, forthcoming.

Elbaum, Max, "The Storm at Home: The U.S. Anti-War Movement," in Phyllis Bennis and Michel Moushabeck, eds., *Beyond the Storm: A Gulf Crisis Reader*, Brooklyn, N.Y.: Olive Branch Press, 1991, pp. 142–159.

Erlanger, Steven, "Crisis in the Balkans: A Serbian Account: Special NATO Pilot Was Ordered to Bomb Convoy, Belgrade Says," *The New York Times*, April 20, 1999, p. A12.

European Commission, *Flash Eurobarometer 114: International Crisis*, Brussels: European Commission, 2001. As of November 30, 2005: http://europa.eu.int/comm/public_opinion/flash/fl114_en.pdf

European Community, *Eurobarometer 35.0*, Basic English Questionnaire, INRA (Europe), Luxembourg: Office for Official Publications of the European Communities, March 1991. As of July 27, 2006: http://ec.europea.ed/public_opinion/archives/eb/eb35/eb35_en.htm

Evans, Michael, "Briefing Reveals the Secrets of Modern Warfare," *The Times* (London), April 20, 1999.

Farooq, Sabya, Isabelle Guitard, David McCoy, and Jack Piachaud, *Continuing Collateral Damage: The Health and Environmental Costs of War on Iraq 2003*, London: Medact, 2003. As of January 22, 2007: http://www.medact.org/article_publications.php?articleID=573

FBIS—*see* Foreign Broadcast Information Service.

Feaver, Peter D., and Christopher Gelpi, "A Look at . . . Casualty Aversion; How Many Deaths Are Acceptable? A Surprising Answer," *The Washington Post*, November 7, 1999, p. B3.

————, *Choosing Your Battles: American Civil-Military Relations and the Use of Force*, Princeton, N.J.: Princeton University Press, 2004.

Federal Ministry of Foreign Affairs, *NATO Crimes in Yugoslavia: Documentary Evidence*, Belgrade: Federal Ministry of Foreign Affairs, 1999.

Federal News Service, "Defense Department Special Briefing Re: Effects Based Operations; Briefer: Colonel Gary L. Crowder, Chief of Strategy, Concepts and Doctrine, Air Combat Command; Location: Pentagon Briefing Room, Arlington, Virginia," March 19, 2003a.

————, "Press Conference with British Foreign Secretary Jack Straw; Location: London," March 20, 2003b.

————, "The White House Regular Briefing; Briefer: Ari Fleischer, White House Spokesman; Location: White House Briefing Room, Washington, D.C.," March 20, 2003c.

————, "U.K. Ministry of Defense Briefing with Geoff Hoon, Minister of Defense and Admiral Michael Boyce, Chief of Staff; Location: Ministry of Defense, London, England," March 22, 2003d.

————, "United States Central Command Briefing with CENTCOM Chief General Tommy Franks; Subject: Military Operations in Iraq; Location: Doha, Qatar," March 22, 2003e.

————, "State Department Regular Briefing; Briefer: Richard Boucher, Department Spokesman; Location: State Department Briefing Room, Washington, D.C.," March 24, 2003f.

————, "Press Conference with Iraqi Trade Minister Mohammed Mahdi Saleh; Location: Baghdad, Iraq," March 25, 2003g.

————, "Press Conference with Iraqi Information Minister Mohammed Saeed Sahaf, Baghdad, Iraq, Approx. 4:10 AM EST, March 28, 2003," March 28, 2003h.

————, "United States Central Command Daily Briefing; Briefer: Brigadier General Vincent Brooks, Deputy Director of Operations," March 28, 2003i.

————, "Defense Department Operational Update Briefing; Briefers: Victoria Clarke, Assistant Secretary of Defense for Public Affairs; Major General Stanley McChrystal, U.S. Army; Location: Pentagon Briefing Room, Arlington, Virginia," March 31, 2003j.

————, "Media Stakeout with Secretary of Defense Donald Rumsfeld; General Richard Myers, Chairman, Joint Chiefs of Staff; Senator John Warner (R-VA); Representative Duncan Hunter (R-CA); Location: The Capitol, Washington, D.C.," April 1, 2003k.

————, "Foreign Press Center Briefing with Major General Stanley McChrystal; Subject: Special Targeting Procedures; Location: State Department's Foreign Press Center, Washington, D.C.," April 3, 2003l.

Fernandez, Manny, "D.C. Braces for Weekend of Rallies," *The Washington Post*, April 11, 2003, p. B1.

Fialka, John J., and Andy Pasztor, "Grim Calculus: If Mideast War Erupts, Air Power Will Hold Key to U.S. Casualties," *The Wall Street Journal*, November 15, 1990, p. A1.

Finkelstein, Norman, "Reflections on Palestinian Attitudes During the Gulf War," *Journal of Palestinian Studies*, Vol. 21, No. 3, 1992, pp. 54–70.

Ford, Peter, "Iraq Invasion Triggers Anger from Bahrain to Barcelona," *The Christian Science Monitor*, March 24, 2003, p. 10.

Foreign Broadcast Information Service, "FYI—Iraqi Media Behavior 0800–1000 GMT 30 Mar 03 (128)," March 30, 2003a.

————, "FYI—Iraq Media Behavior 0800–1000 GMT 06 Apr 03 (212)," April 6, 2003b.

————, "FYI—Egyptian Media Behavior 6 Apr," April 6, 2003c.

"French People's Warlike Spirit Flagging in Third Month of War," *Paris Match*, June 10, 1999, p. 79.

Gamson, William A., "Reflections on 'The Strategy of Social Protest,'" *Sociological Forum*, Vol. 4, No. 3, September 1989, pp. 455–467.

————, *The Strategy of Social Protest*, 2nd ed., Belmont, Calif.: Wadsworth Pub., 1990.

Gannett Foundation Media Center, *The Media at War: The Press and the Persian Gulf Conflict: A Report of the Gannett Foundation*, New York: Gannett Foundation Media Center, 1991.

Garofoli, Joe, and Meredith May, "Organizers of Peace Rallies Expect 10 Million Worldwide," *The San Francisco Chronicle*, February 15, 2003, p. A19.

Gartner, Scott Sigmund, and Gary M. Segura, "War, Casualties, and Public Opinion," *The Journal of Conflict Resolution*, Vol. 42, No. 3, June 1998, pp. 278–300.

————, "Race, Casualties, and Opinion in the Vietnam War," *The Journal of Politics*, Vol. 62, No. 1, February 2000, pp. 115–146.

Gartner, Scott Sigmund, Gary M. Segura, and Michael Wilkening, "All Politics Are Local: Local Losses and Individual Attitudes Toward the Vietnam War," *The Journal of Conflict Resolution*, Vol. 41, No. 5, October 1997, pp. 669–694.

Gelpi, Christopher, Peter D. Feaver, and Jason Reifler, "Casualty Sensitivity and the War in Iraq," draft manuscript, 2005. As of November 17, 2005: http://www.duke.edu/~gelpi/iraq.casualties.pdf

George, Alexander L., and Richard Smoke, *Deterrence in American Foreign Policy: Theory and Practice*, New York: Columbia University Press, 1974.

Gillespie, Mark, "Support Grows for Kosovo Mission, but Public Still Divided: Latest Poll Shows U.S. Public Accepts Moral Obligation as Justification for Launching Bombing Raids," The Gallup Poll, March 26, 1999a.

————, "Support for Mission Holds Steady, but Skepticism Grows," The Gallup Poll, April 2, 1999b.

————, "Support for NATO Air Strikes Holds Steady in Wake of Embassy Attack: Almost Half of Americans Favor Cease-Fire to Clear Way for Peace Talks," The Gallup Poll, May 11, 1999c.

GMA Network, "Chinese-Filipinos to Stage Protest at U.S. Embassy 13 May," May 10, 1999.

Goldenberg, Suzanne, "War in the Gulf: Wayward Bombs Bring Marketplace Carnage," *The Guardian* (London), March 27, 2003, p. 1. As of December 2, 2005:
http://www.guardian.co.uk/Iraq/Story/0,2763,922755,00.html

Goodman, Walter, "Critic's Notebook: CNN in Baghdad: Danger of Propaganda vs. Virtue of Reporting," *The New York Times*, January 29, 1991, p. C11.

Gordon, Michael R., "Crisis in the Balkans: Death in Kosovo; Civilians Are Slain in Military Attack on a Kosovo Road," *The New York Times*, April 15, 1999, p. A1.

Gordon, Michael R., and Bernard E. Trainor, *The Generals' War: The Inside Story of the Conflict in the Gulf*, Boston: Little, Brown, 1995.

Graham, Bradley, "Official Explanations Marked by Confusion," *The Washington Post*, April 15, 1999, p. A26.

Graham, Victoria, "Bombing in Baghdad Condemned as U.N. Council Prepares to Debate Gulf," Associated Press, February 13, 1991.

"Gulf War Casualties Continue," *Green Left Weekly Online*, undated. As of November 17, 2005:
http://www.greenleft.org.au/back/1991/25/25p14b.htm

Gurr, Ted Robert, *Why Men Rebel*, Princeton, N.J.: Princeton University Press, 1970.

Hamre, John J., *Testimony of John J. Hamre, Deputy Secretary of Defense, Before the House Select Committee on Intelligence Inadvertent Bombing of the Chinese Embassy in Belgrade, Yugoslavia*, May 7, 1999.

Harman, Danna, "World and America Watching Different Wars," *The Christian Science Monitor*, March 25, 2003, p. 1.

Harmon, Amy, "A Nation Challenged: The Dissenters; Demonstrators Find That the Web Is a Powerful Tool," *The New York Times*, November 21, 2001, p. B8.

Harris, Scott, "Protesters Reach a Lull in Their Battle to End the War Dissent: Groups Say They Expect More Support When a Ground Offensive Starts and the Casualty Count Increases; in the Meantime, They Are Trying to Broaden the Appeal of Their Message," *Los Angeles Times*, February 9, 1991, p. 7.

Havemann, Joel, "Crisis in Yugoslavia: Convoy Deaths May Undermine Moral Authority," *Los Angeles Times*, April 15, 1999, p. 1.

Hernandez, Daniel, and Steve Hymon, "Los Angeles: Antiwar Protest Is Peaceful but Raucous," *Los Angeles Times*, March 31, 2003, p. B3.

Hiltermann, Joost, "Calculating 'Collateral Damage,'" *Middle East Report*, No. 169, 1991, p. 3.

Hong Kong Agence France Press, "AFP: PRC Moves to Cool Nationalist Fury on Bombing," May 11, 1999.

Horrock, Nicholas M., "Protesters Block N.Y. Streets," United Press International, February 15, 2003.

Human Rights Watch, *Needless Deaths in the Gulf War: Civilian Casualties During the Air Campaign and Violations of the Laws of War*, New York: Human Rights Watch, 1991. As of November 18, 2005:
http://www.hrw.org/reports/1991/gulfwar/

————, *Civilian Deaths in the NATO Air Campaign*, Vol. 12, No. 1(d), 2000. As of November 18, 2005:
http://www.hrw.org/reports/2000/nato

————, *Under Orders: War Crimes in Kosovo*, New York, 2001. As of November 18, 2005:
http://www.hrw.org/reports/2001/kosovo

Hunt, Terence, "Civilian Carnage Puts Pressure on Allies, Ground War Timetable," Associated Press, February 13, 1991.

Hyde, Charles K., "Casualty Aversion: Implications for Policy Makers and Senior Military Officers," *Aerospace Power Journal*, Vol. 14, No. 2, Summer 2000, pp. 17–27. As of November 17, 2005:
http://www.airpower.maxwell.af.mil/airchronicles/apj/apj00/sum00/hyde.pdf

ICM Research, "*The Guardian* European Barometer, May 1999," poll of 9,436 respondents in 12 countries between May 6 and May 22, 1999. As of November 29, 2005:
http://www.icmreserach.co.uk/reviews/1999/european-barometer-99.htm

————, *What the World Thinks of America: Prepared by ICM Research for the BBC*, June 2003. As of July 27, 2006:
http://www.cbc.ca/news/america/finaldata.pdf

Independent International Commission on Kosovo, *The Kosovo Report: Conflict, International Response, Lessons Learned*, Oxford and New York: Oxford University Press, 2000.

International Tribunal for the Former Yugoslavia, *Eighth Annual Report of the International Tribunal for the Prosecution of Persons Responsible for Serious Violations of International Humanitarian Law Committed in the Territory of the Former Yugoslavia Since 1991*, New York: United Nations, 2001. As of November 18, 2005:
http://www.un.org/icty/rappannu-e/2001/AR01e.pdf

Ipsos/Sofres, "European Elections: The European Feeling Gains Ground," April 6, 1999.

"Iraq's al-Sahhaf Briefs Press on War Activities, Says 50 Enemy Dead at Airport," *Doha Al-Jazirah Satellite Channel Television in Arabic*, April 6, 2003.

James, Sara, "Anti-War and Pro-War Rallies in United States," *NBC News Transcripts, Sunday Today*, March 30, 2003.

Jaulmes, Adrian, "The Coalition's First Blunder in Baghdad: 14 Dead, 30 Injured," *Le Figaro*, March 27, 2003.

Jentleson, Bruce W., "The Pretty Prudent Public: Post Post-Vietnam American Opinion on the Use of Military Force," *International Studies Quarterly*, Vol. 36, No. 1, March 1992, pp. 49–73.

Jentleson, Bruce W., and Rebecca L. Britton, "Still Pretty Prudent: Post–Cold War American Public Opinion on the Use of Military Force," *The Journal of Conflict Resolution*, Vol. 42, No. 4, August 1998, pp. 395–417.

Jingen, Jiang, "Poll: PRC Majority Against Air Strikes in Yugoslavia," *Beijing China Daily (Internet Version)*, April 1, 1999.

Joya, Alonso Soto, "Iraq: Civilian Death Count Remains Unclear," *The Missourian*, March 19, 2004, p. 1A.

Kellner, Douglas, *The Persian Gulf TV War*, Boulder Colo.: Westview Press, 1992.

Kelly, Jack, "Estimates of Deaths in First War Still in Dispute," *Pittsburgh Post-Gazette*, February 16, 2003. As of November 17, 2005:
http://www.post-gazette.com/nation/2003021casualty0216p5.asp

Kenney, George, "The Bosnian Calculation," *The New York Times Magazine*, April 23, 1995.

Kilborn, Robert, and Lance Carden, "USA," *The Christian Science Monitor*, May 11, 1999, p. 20.

King, Laura, "AP Review of Afghan Civilian Casualties Suggests Toll in Hundreds; Taliban Inflated Count," Associated Press Worldstream, February 11, 2002a.

———, "Review: Afghan Civilian Deaths Lower," Associated Press Online, February 11, 2002b.

————, "The World: Baghdad's Death Toll Assessed: A Times Hospital Survey Finds That at Least 1,700 Civilians Were Killed and More Than 8,000 Injured in Iraq's Capital During the War and Aftermath," *Los Angeles Times*, May 18, 2003, p. A1.

Klarevas, Louis J., *American Public Opinion on Peace Operations: The Cases of Somalia, Rwanda, and Haiti*, Washington, D.C.: American University, doctoral dissertation, 1999.

Komarow, Steven, "Kosovo's Plight Exaggerated: Numbers Were Best Available, Pentagon Says," *USA Today*, July 1, 1999, p. 1A.

Kostroski, Warren Lee, "'War, Presidents, and Public Opinion' by John E. Mueller," *American Political Science Review*, Vol. 71, No. 1, 1977, pp. 363–365.

Kurtz, Howard, "War Coverage Takes a Negative Turn; Civilian Deaths, Military Errors Become Focus as Reporters Revisit Bombing Sites," *The Washington Post*, February 17, 2002, p. A14.

LaMay, Craig, "By the Numbers I: The Bibliometrics of War," in Everette E. Dennis, ed., *The Media at War: The Press and the Persian Gulf Conflict: A Report of the Gannett Foundation*, New York City: Gannett Foundation Media Center, 1991, pp. 41–44.

Lambeth, Benjamin S., *NATO's Air War for Kosovo: A Strategic and Operational Assessment*, Santa Monica, Calif.: RAND Corporation, MR-1365-AF, 2001. As of November 18, 2005:
http://www.rand.org/publications/MR/MR1365

Landsberg, Michele, "Let's Join Rally to Speak Out Against War," *The Toronto Star*, January 11, 1991, p. B1.

Larson, Eric V., *Casualties and Consensus: The Historical Role of Casualties in Domestic Support for U.S. Military Operations*, Santa Monica, Calif.: RAND Corporation, MR-726-RC, 1996a. As of November 27, 2005:
http://www.rand.org/publications/MR/MR726

————, *Ends and Means in the Democratic Conversation: Understanding the Role of Casualties in Support for U.S. Military Operations*, Santa Monica, Calif.: RAND Corporation, RGSD-124, 1996b. As of January 17, 2007:
http://www.rand.org/pubs/rgs_dissertations/RGSD124/

————, "Putting Theory to Work: Diagnosing Public Opinion on the U.S. Intervention in Bosnia," in Miroslav Nincic and Joseph Lepgold, eds., *Being Useful: Policy Relevance and International Relations Theory*, Ann Arbor, Mich.: University of Michigan Press, 2000, pp. 174–233.

Larson, Eric V., Norman D. Levin, Seonhae Baik, and Bogdan Savych, *Ambivalent Allies? A Study of South Korean Attitudes Toward the U.S.*, Santa Monica, Calif.: RAND Corporation, TR-141-SRF, 2004. As of November 17, 2005:
http://www.rand.org/publications/TR/TR141

Larson, Eric V., and Bogdan Savych, *American Public Support for U.S. Military Operations from Mogadishu to Baghdad*, Santa Monica, Calif.: RAND Corporation, MG-231-A, 2005a. As of November 17, 2005: http://www.rand.org/publications/MG/MG231

———, *American Public Support for U.S. MIlitary Operations from Mogadishu to Baghdad: Technical Appendixes*, Santa Monica, Calif.: RAND Corporation, TR-167-A, 2005b. As of November 17, 2005: http://www.rand.org/publications/TR/TR167

Lawrence, Jill, "Vocal Anti-War Protest Disrupts Senate Debate," Associated Press, January 11, 1991.

Linton, Leyla, "Iraq Conflict: Opposition—Unconvinced and Unhappy: Thousands Take to the Streets in Anti-War Protests," *The Independent* (London), March 31, 2003, p. 10.

Little, Alison, "UK Poll: Backing for NATO Strike Grows," London Press Association, April 1, 1999.

Lobe, Jim, "Politics: U.S. Cluster Bombs Still Claim Lives in Afghanistan," IPS-Inter Press Service, December 18, 2002.

Los Angeles Times, "Los Angeles Times Poll: War Against Iraq—One Month Anniversary, 15–17 February, 1991," Roper Center for Public Opinion Research, 1991.

Maier, Timothy W., "War Criminals Face Prosecution in U.S.: President Bush Wants War Criminals, Including Those from the 1991 Gulf War, Judged Severely, but Where They Will Be Tried and by Whom Remains a Subject of Debate," *Insight on the News*, April 29, 2003. As of November 17, 2005: http://www.findarticles.com/p/articles/mi_m1571/is_10_19/ai_100962878

Manigart, Philippe, *Public Opinion and European Defense*, paper presented at the International Symposium on Public Opinion and European Defense, Brussels, April 3–4, 2001, translation dated July 2001. As of December 2, 2005: http://europa.eu.int/comm/public_opinion/archives/ebs/ebs_146_en.pdf

Marks, Alexandra, "A Minority of Americans Calls Out—Loudly—for Peace," *The Christian Science Monitor*, October 10, 2001, p. 5.

Marks, Kathy, Peter Popham, and Andrew Gumbel, "The Threat of War: All Across the World, the Peace Demonstrations Begin; Protests," *The Independent* (London), February 15, 2003, p. 9.

McAneny, Leslie, "Military on Top, HMOs Last in Public Confidence Poll: Religion and Police Also Receive High Ratings," The Gallup Poll, July 14, 1999.

McNeill, John H., Deputy General Counsel (International Affairs and Intelligence), "Report on Iraqi War Crimes (Desert Shield/Desert Storm)," Memorandum for the Judge Advocate General, U.S. Department of the Army, November 19, 1992. As of November 17, 2005: http://www.gwu.edu/~nsarchiv/news/20030320/iraqicrimes.pdf

Mehren, Elizabeth, "On Campus and Off, Antiwar Movements See New Vigor; Reaction: Opposition to Military Action Builds with a More Polite, Thoughtful Approach Than in Days of Vietnam," *Los Angeles Times*, October 28, 2001.

Miller, Alan C., "The Nation: Turnout Gives Lift to Activist; Dissent: A Self-Styled 'Old Lefty from the '60s' Finds Kindred Spirits at the Antiwar Rally," *Los Angeles Times*, April 21, 2002, p. A14.

Miller, Charles, "Allies to Change Bombing Strategy After Bunker Deaths," Press Association, February 14, 1991.

Milstein, Jeffrey S., *Dynamics of the Vietnam War: A Quantitative Analysis and Predictive Computer Simulation*, Columbus, Ohio: Ohio State University Press, 1974.

Mitchell, Brian, "How Many Really Died in Kosovo? Body Count So Far Doesn't Support Charges of 'Genocide,'" *Investor's Business Daily*, November 17, 1999, p. A1.

Moulson, Geir, "From Seoul to Santiago, Protesters Turn Out for New Rallies Against Iraq War," Associated Press, March 29, 2003.

"Mounting Tally of Blunders," *The Guardian* (London), May 10, 1999, p. 3.

Mueller, John E., "Trends in Popular Support for the Wars in Korea and Vietnam," *American Political Science Review*, Vol. 65, No. 2, 1971, pp. 358–375.

———, *War, Presidents, and Public Opinion*, New York: Wiley, 1973.

———, *Policy and Opinion in the Gulf War*, Chicago, Ill.: University of Chicago Press, 1994.

Mufson, Steven, "'Strategic Partnership' Takes a Hit; Historically Uneasy Relations Dealt Major Blow by Bombing," *The Washington Post*, May 11, 1999, p. A17.

Muravchik, Joshua, "The Prof Who Can't Count Straight and the Journalists Who Cite Him," *The Weekly Standard*, Vol. 7, No. 47, August 26, 2002. As of January 22, 2007: http://www.weeklystandard.com/Content/Public/Articles/000/000/001/565otmps.asp

Murphy, Kim, "War with Iraq/Arab Anger: Ladies' Tea Boils Over as Saudis Rail at U.S.," *Los Angeles Times*, March 27, 2003, p. A1.

Myers, Steven Lee, "The World; All in Favor of This Target, Say Yes, Si, Oui, Ja," *The New York Times*, April 25, 1999, Section 4, p. 4.

Nasrawi, Salah, "Iraq Says Thousands of Civilian Casualties, Calls Up 17-Year-Olds," Associated Press, February 11, 1991.

National Public Radio, "Rumsfeld Says U.S. Military Mistakes in Afghanistan Rare," February 12, 2002.

NATO—*see* North Atlantic Treaty Organization.

NATO Crimes in Yugoslavia: Documentary Evidence, 24 March–24 April 1999, I, Belgrade: Federal Republic of Yugoslavia, Federal Ministry of Foreign Affairs, 1999a.

NATO Crimes in Yugoslavia: Documentary Evidence, 25 April–10 June 1999, II, Belgrade: Federal Republic of Yugoslavia, Federal Ministry of Foreign Affairs, 1999b.

NBC News, *NBC Evening News*, April 14, 1999.

Neuman, Johanna, "The World: Military Action May Get Peace Movement Rolling: Activism: It's Unlikely That Democrats, Not Wanting to Look Soft on Terrorism, Will Buck the White House's War; So, Grass-Roots Groups Are Starting to Organize," *Los Angeles Times*, September 2, 2002, p. A8.

Newport, Frank, "Small Business and Military Generate Most Confidence in Americans: But Confidence in Military Has Eroded Over Last Year," The Gallup Poll, August 15, 1997.

————, "Despite Skepticism, Support Increases for U.S. Involvement in Kosovo Crisis," The Gallup Organization, April 8, 1999a.

————, "Gradual Increase in American Support for Kosovo Involvement Continues," The Gallup Organization, April 16, 1999b.

————, "Public Support for U.S. Involvement in Kosovo Diminishing: Less Than Half Back Call-Up of Military Reservists," The Gallup Organization, April 29, 1999c.

————, "Support for U.S. Kosovo Involvement Drops: Americans Strongly Favor Cease-Fire in Order to Negotiate Peace; Clinton Approval Drops to Lowest Level in Three Years," The Gallup Organization, May 26, 1999d.

————, "Americans Endorse Idea of Peace Plan, but Remain Skeptical of Serb Compliance: Forty-Three Percent of Americans Think U.S. Involvement Has Been a Mistake," The Gallup Organization, June 7, 1999e.

————, "New Poll on Kosovo Finds an Underwhelmed Public: Agreement Is Favored, but Public Split on Issue of Whether or Not Situation Was Worth Military Action," The Gallup Organization, June 11, 1999f.

————, "Americans Hesitant to Give Clinton Credit for Kosovo Peace: Most Are Doubtful That Peace Will Reign as Long as Milosevic Is in Power," The Gallup Organization, June 15, 1999g.

————, "Military Retains Top Position in Americans' Confidence Ratings," The Gallup Organization, June 25, 2001.

————, "Americans' Confidence in Military, Presidency Up; Big Business, Organized Religion Drop: Confidence in Military Is 20 Percentage Points Higher Than Confidence in Any Other Institution," The Gallup Organization, June 28, 2002.

————, "Military, Police Top Gallup's Annual Confidence in Institutions Poll: Little Change in Confidence in Newspapers; Church Enjoys Modest Rebound in Confidence," The Gallup Organization, June 19, 2003.

Niebuhr, Gustav, "A Nation Challenged: Peace Activists; Groups Plan Vigils and Rallies to Urge Alternatives to War," The New York Times, October 5, 2001, p. B3.

Nincic, Miroslav, and Donna J. Nincic, "Race, Gender, and War," Journal of Peace Research, Vol. 39, No. 5, September 2002, pp. 547–568.

North Atlantic Treaty Organization, "Morning Briefing," March 30, 1999a.

————, "Morning Briefing," April 14, 1999b.

————, "NATO Briefing Regarding Military Action in Yugoslavia," April 14, 1999c.

————, "NATO Briefing Regarding Military Action in Yugoslavia," April 15, 1999d.

————, "Press Conference by Jamie Shea and Brigadier General Giuseppe Marani," April 15, 1999e. As of November 26, 2005: http://www.nato.int/kosovo/press/p990415a.htm

————, "NATO Briefing Regarding the Situation in Kosovo," April 19, 1999f.

————, "Press Conference by Brigadier General Daniel P. Leaf," Brussels: NATO Headquarters, April 19, 1999g. As of November 18, 2005: http://www.nato.int/kosovo/press/p990419b.htm

————, "Special NATO Briefing Regarding Civilian Casualties in Convoy Bombing," April 19, 1999h.

————, "Morning Briefing by Mr Jamie Shea," April 30, 1999i. As of November 18, 2005: http://www.nato.int/kosovo/press/b990430b.htm

————, "Press Conference Given by NATO Secretary General, Javier Solana, NATO Spokesman, Jamie Shea and SHAPE Spokesman, Major General Walter Jertz," Brussels: NATO Headquarters, May 8, 1999j.

"Not by Bombs Alone," *The Economist*, April 10, 1999.

O'Donnell, Peter, "NATO Offers Details on Targeted Convoys," United Press International, April 19, 1999.

O'Hagan, Maureen, "Shot Just Misses Antiwar Demonstrator," *The Washington Post*, December 4, 2001, p. B3.

O'Hagan, Simon, "War on Iraq: Controversy: Peace Campaigners Grieve for Iraqis—and Blame Blair; Protest March," *Independent on Sunday* (London), April 13, 2003, p. 9.

O'Neill, Brendan, "What Kind of Antiwar Movement Is This?" *The Christian Science Monitor*, December 13, 2002, p. 11.

Olson, Mancur, *The Logic of Collective Action: Public Goods and the Theory of Groups*, Cambridge, Mass.: Harvard University Press, 1965.

Organization for Security and Cooperation in Europe, *Kosovo/Kosova as Seen, as Told: An Analysis of the Human Rights Findings of the OSCE Kosovo Verification Mission October 1998 to June 1999*, Warsaw: OSCE Office for Democratic Institutions and Human Rights, 1999. As of June 9, 2006: http://www.osce.org/publications/odihr/1999/11/17755_506_en.pdf

Paul, Pamela, "Attitudes Toward the Military," *American Demographics*, Vol. 24, No. 2, 2002, pp. 22–23.

Perlez, Jane, "Crisis in the Balkans: Diplomacy; Embassy Bombing May Badly Impede Kosovo Diplomacy," *The New York Times*, May 11, 1999, p. A1.

"Perspectives: Civilians Main Victims of War in Iraq," *Tehran Times*, April 6, 2003.

Pew Research Center for the People and the Press, "Americans Disengaging from Kosovo," May 18, 1999. As of November 23, 2005: http://people-press.org/reports/display.php3?ReportID=62

————, *2002 Global Attitudes Survey Final Topline*, December 2002. As of July 27, 2006: http://pewglobal.org/reports/display.php?ReportID=165

————, "TV Combat Fatigue on the Rise: But 'Embeds' Viewed Favorably," March 28, 2003a. As of November 23, 2005: http://people-press.org/reports/displayphp3?ReportID=178

————, "Views of a Changing World 2003: War with Iraq Further Divides Global Publics," June 3, 2003b. As of November 23, 2005: http://people-press.org/reports/display.php3?ReportID=185

———, *American Character Gets Mixed Reviews: U.S. Image Up Slightly, but Still Negative*, June 23, 2005. As of July 27, 2006:
http://pewglobal.org/reports/display.php?ReportID=247

Pincus, Walter, "Spy Suspect Fired at Los Alamos Lab," *The Washington Post*, March 9, 1999, p. A1.

PIPA—*see* Program on International Policy Attitudes.

Platt, Kevin, "A Protest China's Leaders Can Use," *The Christian Science Monitor*, May 10, 1999, p. 6.

Pollack, Jonathan D., "Commentary: Perspective on the China Crisis: More Than Bombing Roils the Waters of U.S.-Sino Relations; Beijing's Sanctioning of Demonstrations Is Disquieting, but We Are Not Yet at the Point of No Retreat," *Los Angeles Times*, May 11, 1999, p. 7.

Price, Niko, "AP Tallies 3,240 Civilian Deaths in Iraq," Associated Press Online, June 11, 2003.

Program on International Policy Attitudes, and Knowledge Networks, *US Public Beliefs on Iraq and the Presidential Election*, April 22, 2004. As of January 22, 2007:
http://www.pipa.org/OnlineReports/Iraq/IraqBeliefs_Apr04/IraqBeliefs%20Apr04%20rpt.pdf

"Protests in Nation's Capital Remain Peaceful," *CNN Saturday*, April 20, 2002. As of November 30, 2005:
http://transcripts.cnn.com/TRANSCRIPTS/0204/20/cst.09.html

Public Relations Society of America, *National Credibility Index: Making Personal Investment Decisions*, undated.

Radio-Televizija Srbije, "FRY Government Condemns 'Deliberate' PRC Embassy Bombing," May 8, 1999.

Randal, Jonathan, "The Gulf War; Allied Bombs 'Kill 3,000 Civilians' in Kurdish Area," *The Guardian* (London), February 12, 1991.

Rather, Dan, "NATO Bomb Possibly Hit Belgrade Chinese Embassy," *CBS Evening News*, May 7, 1999.

Reif, Karlheinz, and Anna Melich, *Euro-Barometer 35.0: Foreign Relations, the Common Agricultural Policy, and Environmental Concerns, Spring 1991*, Ann Arbor, Mich.: Inter-University Consortium for Political and Social Research, 1994. As of November 17, 2005:
http://webapp.icpsr.umich.edu/cocoon/ICPSR-STUDY/09697.xml

Renfrew, Barry, "Anti-War Protesters Across the World Refuse to Give Up," The Associated Press, March 22, 2003.

Richter, Paul, "News Analysis: Support for War Seen Despite Baghdad Deaths; Public Opinion: Heavy Civilian Casualties in Earlier Wars Saddened Americans but Did Not Greatly Change Their View of Those Conflicts," *Los Angeles Times*, February 15, 1991, p. 5.

Riddell, Peter, "The Gulf War; Baghdad Bunker Bombing Fails to Alter US Citizens' Support for War," *Financial Times* (London), February 15, 1991, p. 12.

Risen, James, "U.S. Fires Scientist Suspected of Giving China Bomb Data," *The New York Times*, March 9, 1999, p. A1.

Robbins, Carla Anne, "NATO, Serbs Trade Blame for Refugee Killings," *The Wa Street Journal*, April 15, 1999, p. A14.

Rosenthal, Andrew, "War in the Gulf: Bush Quandary; Civilian Toll in Iraq Could Strain Alliance and Bring Pressure to Speed a Ground War," *The New York Times*, February 14, 1991, p. A1.

Rosenthal, Elisabeth, "Crisis in the Balkans: The Ambassador; Envoy Says Stonin Will End, Ties Won't," *The New York Times*, May 11, 1999, p. A11.

"RSA Serbian Demonstrators in Johannesburg Burn U.S. Flag," Johannesburg SABC 3 Television Network, March 28, 1999.

RTS—*see* Radio-Televizija Srbije.

Rubin, Alissa J., "The Conflict in Iraq: 40 Killed in U.S. Attack on Iraqi Border Village," *Los Angeles Times*, May 20, 2004, p. A1.

Saad, Lydia, "Americans Hesitant, as Usual, About U.S. Military Action in the Balkans," The Gallup Poll, March 24, 1999.

———, "Military Still Americans' Top-Rated Institution: Police Still a Clear Second," The Gallup Poll, June 1, 2004.

Salvage, Jane, June Crown, Richard Garfield, Douglas Holdstock, Victor W. Side and John Yudkin, *Collateral Damage: The Health and Environmental Costs of War on Iraq*, London: Medact, 2002. As of January 22, 2007: http://www.medact.org/article_publications.php?articleID=572

Sanchez, Rene, "Radical Change in Berkeley: Peacemongers Tolerate a Little Bombing," *The Washington Post*, November 10, 2001, p. C1.

Sanger, David E., "Crisis in the Balkans: Trade; Aides Fear Clinton's China Deal Has Become Collateral Damage," *The New York Times*, May 11, 1999, p. A11.

Savva, N., "500 Die in 'Sacrifice': U.S. Defends Hit on War Bunker," *Herald Sun*, February 14, 1991.

Scarborough, Rowan, "As Strikes Mount, So Do Errors; NATO Cites Overall Accuracy, but Gaffes Undercut Moral Stance," *The Washington Times*, May 11, 1999, p. A1.

Scheffer, David J., "The Case for Justice in Iraq," remarks delivered to a Middle East Institute and Iraq Foundation Forum at the National Press Club, Washington, D.C., September 18, 2000. As of November 17, 2005: http://www.fas.org/news/iraq/2000/09/iraq-000918.htm

Schrodr, Philip A., Shannon G. Davis, and Judith L. Weddle, "Political Science: KEDS—A Program for the Machine Coding of Event Data," *Social Science Computer Review*, Vol. 12, No. 3, 1994, pp. 561–588.

Schwarzkopf, H. Norman, and Peter Petre, *It Doesn't Take a Hero: General H. Norman Schwarzkopf, the Autobiography*, New York: Bantam Books, 1992.

"Second Day of Protests Getting Underway in Washington," *CNN Sunday Morning*, April 21, 2002. As of November 30, 2005: http://transcripts.cnn.com/TRANSCRIPTS/0204/21/sm.07.html

Seybolt, Taylor B., "Major Armed Conflicts," in *SIPRI Yearbook 2000: Armaments, Disarmament, and International Security*, Oxford: Oxford University Press, 2000, pp. 15–49.

———, "Major Armed Conflicts," in *SIPRI Yearbook 2002: Armaments, Disarmament, and International Security*, Oxford: Oxford University Press, 2002, pp. 21–62.

Shadid, Anthony, "'The Whole World Cries'; Crowded Market Turns into Scene of Carnage," *The Washington Post*, March 29, 2003, p. A1.

"Shots Fired as Protestors Storm US Embassy in Phnom Penh," *Hong Kong AFP in English*, May 13, 1999.

Simmons, Michael, "The Gulf War: Iraq Raises Death Toll," *The Guardian* (London), February 12, 1991.

Sivard, Ruth Leger, *World Military and Social Expenditures 1996*, 16th ed., Leesburg, Va.: WMSE Publications, 1996.

Sloboda, John, "100 Names of Civilians Killed: and Only 2% of a Vital Task Completed," *Iraq Body Count*, May 27, 2003. As of November 30, 2005: http://www.iraqbodycount.net/editorial_may2703.htm

Sloboda, John, and Hamit Dardagan, "Counting the Human Cost: A Survey of Projects Counting Civilians Killed by the War in Iraq," *Iraq Body Count*, June 12, 2003. As of November 30, 2005: http://www.iraqbodycount.net/editorial_june1203.htm

Smith, R. Jeffrey, "U.S. Military Is Pressed About Civilian Casualties; TV Scenes of Damage Raise Concerns in Arab World," *The Washington Post*, February 3, 1991, p. A23.

Steele, Jonathan, "Body Counts," *The Guardian* (London), May 28, 2003. As of July 27, 2006: http://www.guardian.co.uk/analysis/story/0,,965385,00.html

Stein, Rob, "Experts Say War Backing Can Endure Rising Toll," *The Washington Post*, March 24, 2003, p. A24.

Stockholm International Peace Research Institute, *SIPRI Yearbook 2000: Armaments, Disarmaments, and International Security*, Oxford: Oxford University Press, 2000.

Suarez, Ray, "Civilian Casualties in Iraq," *The NewsHour with Jim Lehrer*, April 26, 2004. As of November 30, 2005:
http://www.pbs.org/newshour/bb/middle_east/jan-june04/civilians_04-26.html

Surovtseva, Yelena, "Russian Poll Shows 91 Percent Sympathize with Serbs," *Moscow Krasnaya Zvezda*, March 30, 1999, p. 3.

Telhami, Shibley, "Arab Public Opinion and the Gulf War," *Political Science Quarterly*, Vol. 108, No. 3, Autumn 1993, pp. 437–452.

Tomsho, Robert, "The Assault on Iraq: Antiwar Protests Intensify in U.S., Abroad," *The Wall Street Journal*, March 21, 2003, p. A6.

Travis, Alan, "Huge Swing in Support for Ground Troops," *The Guardian* (London), April 2, 1999.

Trejos, Nancy, "Antiwar Activists Plan to Stay the Course; Women Settling in for Four-Month Vigil," *The Washington Post*, November 18, 2002, p. B5.

Trofimov, Yaroslav, "Al-Jazeera Effect: On Arab Street, Iraqi Resistance Strikes a Chord," *The Wall Street Journal*, March 26, 2003, p. A1.

UK Ministry of Defence, "Briefing by the Defence Secretary, Mr. George Robertson, the International Development Secretary, Ms. Clare Short, and the Deputy Chief of the Defence Staff (Commitments), Air Marshal Sir John Day," April 14, 1999. As of November 23, 2005:
http://www.kosovo.mod.uk/brief140499.htm

United Nations, "Briefing by War Crimes Tribunal Prosecutors," press briefing, New York: United Nations, November 10, 1999. As of November 18, 2005:
http://www.un.org/News/briefings/docs/1999/19991110.delponte/brf.doc.html

United Press International, "UPI Focus: Serbs Protest NATO Strikes in NYC," March 24, 1999a.

————, "NYC Protest Kosovo Airstrikes," March 27, 1999b.

U.S. Central Command, "Unclassified Executive Summary: Investigation of Civilian Casualties, Oruzgan Province, Operation Full Throttle, 30 June 2002," June 30, 2002. As of November 30, 2005:
http://www.centcom.mil/CENTCOMNews/Reports/Investigation_Oruzgan_Province.htm

U.S. Department of Defense, "DoD News Briefing," April 14, 1999a. As of July 27, 2005:
http://www.defenselink.mil/transcripts/1999/t04141999_t0414asd.html

———, "DoD News Briefing," April 16, 1999b. As of July 27, 2006:
http://www.defenselink.mil/transcripts/1999/t04161999asd.html

———, "DoD News Briefing," April 17, 1999c. As of July 27, 2006:
http://www.defenselink.mil/transcripts/1999/t04171999_t0417asd.html

———, "DoD News Briefing," April 19, 1999d. As of November 26, 2005:
http://www.pentagon.mil/transcripts/1999/t04191999_t0419asd.html

———, "Special Defense Department Briefing on NATO Operation Allied Force," April 22, 1999e.

———, "Joint Statement by Secretary of Defense William S. Cohen and CIA Director George J. Tenet," May 8, 1999f. As of November 28, 2005:
http://www.defenselink.mil/releases/1999/b05101999_bt225-99.html

———, "DoD News Briefing," May 10, 1999g. As of November 28, 2005:
http://www.pentagon.mil/transcripts/1999/t05101999_t51099sd.html

———, "DoD News Briefing," May 12, 1999h. As of November 28, 2005:
http://www.pentagon.mil/transcripts/1999/t05121999_t512cohn.html

———, "DoD News Briefing," May 14, 1999i. As of November 28, 2005:
http://www.pentagon.mil/transcripts/1999/t05141999_0514asd.html

———, "DoD News Briefing, Monday, May 17, 1999—1:35 p.m.," Washington, D.C.: U.S. Department of Defense, 1999j. As of November 18, 2005:
http://www.defenselink.mil/transcripts/1999/t05171999_t0517asd.html

———, *Department of Defense Dictionary of Military and Associated Terms*, Washington, D.C.: U.S. Department of State, Joint Publication 1-02, April 12, 2001, as amended through August 31, 2005. As of November 17, 2005:
http://www.dtic.mil/doctrine/jel/new_pubs/jpl_02.pdf

———, "DoD News Briefing: ASD PA Clarke and Maj. Gen. McChrystal," March 26, 2003. As of December 2, 2005:
http://www.pentagon.mil/transcripts/2003/t0327202_t0326asd.html

U.S. Department of State, *Bosnia and Herzegovina Country Report on Human Rights Practices for 1996*, January 30, 1997. As of November 18, 2005:
http://www.state.gov/www/global/human_rights/1996_hrp_report/bosniahe.html

———, *Ethnic Cleansing in Kosovo: An Accounting*, Washington, D.C.: U.S. Department of State, 1999.

U.S. House of Representatives, House Select Committee on Intelligence, *Testimony of John J. Hamre, Deputy Secretary of Defense, Before the House Select Committee on Intelligence, Inadvertent Bombing of the Chinese Embassy in Belgrade, Yugoslavia*, May 7, 1999.

U.S. Senate, Armed Services Committee, *Hearing of the Senate Armed Services Committee*, April 15, 1999.

U.S. Senate, Senate Appropriations Committee, *Hearing of the Defense Subcommittee of the Senate Appropriations Committee, FY 2000 Defense Department Wrap-Up*, May 11, 1999.

USA Today, "Key Findings: Nationwide Survey of 3,500 Iraqis," May 20, 2005. As of July 27, 2006:
http://www.usatoday.com/news/world/iraq/2004-04-28-gallup-iraq-findings.htm

Vidal, John, and Tania Branigan, "War in the Gulf: UK Sees Biggest Wartime Protest: Organiser Claims World Outcry Is Saving Iraqi Lives," *The Guardian* (London), March 24, 2003, p. 13.

Vogel, Steve, and Vernon Loeb, "U.S. Frees 27 Afghans Held in Raid; Families of 18 Killed Get CIA Cash Compensation," *The Washington Post*, February 7, 2002, p. A1.

Walker, Martin, and Richard Norton-Taylor, "Vital Query Remains Over RAF Warning," *The Guardian* (London), April 20, 1999, p. 3.

"War in the Gulf; Backers of Gulf War Turn Out for a Capital Demonstration," *The New York Times*, February 4, 1991, p. A10.

"War with Iraq: Reaction: U.S. Antiwar Protests Go Coast to Coast," *Los Angeles Times*, March 29, 2003, p. A18.

Ward, Olivia, "War Threatens 'Millions of Civilians,' U.N. Chief Says," *Toronto Star*, February 11, 1991a, p. A13.

———, "Ceasefire Call Sparks Anger at U.N.," *Toronto Star*, February 16, 1991b, p. A12.

Watson, Paul, "Jordanians' Greif [sic] at Bomb Carnage Flames into Rage," *The Toronto Star*, February 14, 1991, p. A14.

———, "Crisis in Yugoslavia; Dispatch from Kosovo; Cluster Bombs May Be What Killed Refugees," *Los Angeles Times*, April 17, 1999, p. 1.

Wax, Emily, "Arab World Is Seeing War Far Differently; Media, Mistrust of U.S. Help Shape Perspective," *The Washington Post*, March 28, 2003, p. A33.

Wax, Emily, and Carol Morello, "Arabs Protest War with Prayers and Boycotts; Government Pressure Convinces Demonstrators, Clerics to Show Restraint," *The Washington Post*, March 29, 2003, p. A31.

White, Matthew, "Secondary Wars and Atrocities of the Twentieth Century," 2004. As of December 3, 2005:
http://users.erols.com/mwhite28/warstat3.htm

————, "Death Tolls for the Major Wars and Atrocities of the Twentieth Century," 2005a. As of December 3, 2005:
http://users.erols.com/mwhite28/warstat2.htm

————, "Deaths by Mass Unpleasantness: Estimated Totals for the Entire 20th Century," 2005b. As of December 3, 2005:
http://users.erols.com/mwhite28/warstat8.htm

————, "The Lesser Unpleasantries of the Twentieth Century," 2005c. As of December 3, 2005:
http://users.erols.com/mwhite28/warstat5.htm

————, "Mid-Range Wars and Atrocities of the Twentieth Century," 2005d. As of December 3, 2005:
http://users.erols.com/mwhite28/warstat4.htm

————, "Minor Atrocities of the Twentieth Century," 2005e. As of December 3, 2005:
http://users.erols.com/mwhite28/warstat6.htm

————, "Minor Atrocities of the Twentieth Century," 2005f. As of December 3, 2005:
http://users.erols.com/mwhite28/warstat7.htm

————, "Source List and Detailed Death Tolls for the Man-Made Megadeaths of the Twentieth Century," 2005g. As of December 3, 2005:
http://users.erols.com/mwhite28/warstats.htm

————, "Soutce List and Detailed Death Tolls for the Twentieth Century Hemoclysm," 2005h. As of December 3, 2005:
http://users.erols.com/mwhite28/warstat1.htm

————, "Statistics of Wars, Oppressions, and Atrocities of the Twenty-First Century," 2005i. As of December 3, 2005:
http://users/erols.com/mwhite28/wars21c.htm

White House, "Statement by White House Spokesman Marlin Fitzwater," February 13, 1991a.

————, White House briefing, February 13, 1991b.

————, White House briefing, April 14, 1999a.

————, "Remarks by President Bill Clinton to the American Society of Newspaper Editors Regarding the Situation in Kosovo; the Fairmont Hotel, San Francisco, California," April 15, 1999b.

————, "Remarks by the President to the Pool," Tinker Air Force Base, Okla.: White House, May 8, 1999c. As of November 18, 2005:
http://clinton6.nara.gov/1999/05/1999-05-08-remarks-by-the-president-on-china-to-travel-pool.html

————, "Press Briefing by Joe Lockhart," Washington, D.C.: The White House, May 10, 1999d.

————, "Remarks by the President upon Departure for Littleton, Colorado," Washington, D.C.: The White House, May 20, 1999e. As of November 18, 2005:
http://clinton4.nara.gov/WH/New/html/19990520.html

Wilgoren, Jodi, "Campuses Split Over Afghanistan," *The New York Times*, October 15, 2001, p. A17.

Williams, Daniel, "NATO, Pentagon Struggle to Explain Errant Airstrike," *The Washington Post*, April 16, 1999, p. A24.

Winestock, Geoff, "EU Leaders Pledge Support of US Despite Pressures," *The Wall Street Journal*, October 22, 2001, p. A16.

Winnefeld, James A., Preston Niblack, and Dana J. Johnson, *A League of Airmen: U.S. Air Power in the Gulf War*, Santa Monica, Calif.: RAND Corporation, MR-343-AF, 1994. As of December 3, 2005:
http://www.rand.org/publications/MR/MR343

Wittstock, Melinda, "Press Group Complains of 'Moulded' Information," *The Times* (London), February 20, 1991.

Woehrel, Steven J., *Kosovo and U.S. Policy*, Washington, D.C.: Congressional Research Service, RL31053, updated December 4, 2001.

World Economic Forum, "Trust Will be the Challenge of 2003: Poll Reveals a Lack of Trust in All Institutions, Including Democratic Institutions, Large Companies, NGOs, and Media Across the World," press release, November 8, 2002.

Xinhua General News Service, "Over 200 Protesters Rally Against NATO Outside White House," April 17, 1999a.

————, "Further on Diplomats, Generals Condemning NATO Bombing," May 8, 1999b.

————, "PRC Generals, Diplomats Denounce NATO Bombing," May 8, 1999c.

————, "London Demonstrators Condemn NATO Bombing of Embassy," May 9, 1999d.

————, "China Students Hold Anti-NATO Demonostrations in Germany," May 11, 1999e.

————, "Chinese Students in Japan Condemn NATO 'Atrocity,'" May 11, 1999f.

———, "Jiang Zemin Meets Chernomyrdin on NATO Bombing," May 11, 1999g.

———, "Military Strategists Say NATO Attack Not Accidental," May 11, 1999h.

———, "Overseas Chinese in Canada Protest Against NATO's Attacks," May 11, 1999i.

Yugoslav Army Supreme Command Headquarters, "Banned Weaponry Used on Civilian Targets," May 2, 1999a.

———, Information Service, Daily Review 58, "NATO Raids on Manufacturing and Civilian Facilities on May 30th and in the Night Between May 30th and 31st, 1999," Press Center, May 31, 1999b.